ROOKIE WARDEN

Fearless, principled, and naïvely navigating a man's world...

Kim Camery Millick

Rookie Warden

ISBN: 978-1-63381-165-2

Designed and produced by:
Maine Authors Publishing
12 High Street, Thomaston, Maine
www.maineauthorspublishing.com

Printed in the United States of America

For Miles J. Camery, US Fish and Wildlife Agent and dad who offered a shoulder, advice, or a kick in the butt when needed.

TABLE OF CONTENTS

1

ROOKIE WARDEN

The package is thin but heavy. I shake it but it doesn't rattle. Its weight is unbalanced to one side. My kitchen knife barely severs the thick tape. I unfold the box top and peer inside, wondering. Newspaper is stuffed into the corners. More newsprint binds the contents as I remove and lay them on my table.

Whatever it is, is hard and heavy and tightly wrapped. The tape snaps away quickly and I flinch. I unwind the paper that hides the object, transforming it from something innocuous to something ominous.

I pull the green metal sheath off to expose a seven-inch hardened steel blade, pointed and sharp on one side, angry serrations at its top. The handle is a steel shank covered by thick straps of leather. Steel for strength, leather for grip. The bands of leather are shaped and smooth and sweat-stained. The blade is polished to a sheen.

I can't help but take a piece of the paper and try to slice it, like I've seen in the movies. Yep, it slices nice and fine. I grip the handle. My fingers wrap around the bands of leather comfortably. I turn the knife in my hand with the tip pointing down. I lunge and bring the knife down on my make-believe aggressor and nearly plunge the blade into my thigh. Better re-sheath this thing before I hurt myself. Then I bury it deep within the clothes in my suitcase.

The drive to my new place will take a couple of hours. I'm nervous and excited at the same time. I have new work, in a town I've only passed through before. I make a call to the package's sender, Big Mike.

"I understand you won't carry a gun yet," says the deep voice on the other end of the line.

"That's true, but what am I gonna do with a knife like this? Do you think I'll even use it?"

"Oh, you'll use it," he says. "Do you even own a knife of your own?"

"Sure. How do you think I got through the packaging? There's also that Swiss army knife I got for graduation. I just gotta find it."

Big Mike is an army veteran and has been a game warden for years. He's now a federal agent in DC, stuck in some desk job.

"Catherine, trust me…"

"Ohhh, here we go, Dad," I reply, then pause. "Thank you for thinking of me."

"Catherine, the sheath is made to wear on your belt. You never know when you'll need it."

"Yes, Dad. I'm putting it on my belt right now. Listen…hear this? I'm putting the sheath on my belt as we talk."

"Good. I'm worried about how they've got you set up without a gun. You know you'll be at a disadvantage if things go down with the violators."

"What makes you think they'll go down?"

"Cat, this is no kid's game. You will be stopping people who don't want to be stopped, and it's adversarial. A citation will cost them money and could land them in jail. You've only been trained in the classroom. This job is the real deal. Promise me you'll use your head out there."

"Yes, sir. I will."

"I feel better now, and I know your mother will feel better, too. Please call her later, after you're settled in. She worries about you."

"I will, Dad. Love you."

"I love you, too, Catherine."

I crest the hill coming into the town of Eagle Shores, and there in front of me lies Eagle Lake, dominating my view. The lake extends beyond the horizon, with a few islands dotting its vast blueness. With the dark greens of the wooded hillsides against the blues of the water, my eyes could explore forever and not be tired.

After a few turns, I'm through the downtown, which doesn't take long. It comprises a few streets of shops and offices interspersed with churches, schools, and the Elks Lodge next to the senior center. I turn onto a gravel road that will lead me to my new home.

My little Toyota rattles more now that I'm on dirt with potholes scattered about. The car has a bazillion miles on it, and well-worn tires. It used to be turquoise, but the paint is faded and is now highlighted with

Bondo-gray and rust. Thank heaven it runs better than it looks. I think I got my new job as a game warden because I was one of the few student candidates to own a car.

The woods open to reveal Eagle Lake Sporting Camps and Lodge located on a point of land jutting out into the lake. It'll be convenient to town and headquarters but quiet, as the lane ends at the lake. I park, get out, and drink in the beauty of this spot before I move toward the lodge and look for my new landlady, Bessie MaCoeur.

The steps leading up to the porch are made of dense timber, worn smooth with years of use. Stained dark time after time, the wood is almost black. A sign near the door welcomes "friends." I grab the knocker centered above my head, hoping to notify someone I'm here. While I wait for a response, I wonder, *What would happen to non-friends?* Hearing no one in the house, I walk off the porch and around to the rear. "Hello?"

"I'm back here!" comes a friendly voice. I see a woman, hoe in hand, mingling with tomato plants. "Hello," she says, finding her way out of the maze of green and stakes to greet me. Her hair is short and silvery with a hint of black strands.

"Hi, I'm Catherine Higloss," I announce as I walk toward her. "Are you Bessie MaCoeur?"

She smiles warmly, walks away from her garden, and reaches out to shake my hand. "I sure am, Catherine. It's nice to finally meet you," she says, laying aside her hoe.

"Please call me Cat."

"Okay, Cat. I'll bet you're anxious to see your new place." She lifts her sunglasses now, letting me see her soft blue eyes that have seen seventy or so years of life.

"Yes, I am, but with this view, I'd be happy to camp out," I reply.

Bessie has a soft chuckle. "You might think so today, but wait till January." She pauses and points. "Let me show you the cabin."

"Great," I say as I follow Bessie across the grounds and take in seven identical cabins nestled under giant pines, each with a front porch overlooking the lake's shoreline. A dock reaches out across from her main house. A small aluminum boat is tied to it. Two brightly colored kayaks lie on shore beside the dock.

Bessie leads me on to cabin number four. The main door has been opened, leaving only the screen door to block the outside critters from getting in. "I thought you'd like the fresh air," she says as she opens the screen and lets me lead her inside.

"Yes, thank you," I say, getting the first view of my new place. Just inside the door is a small living area, a tiny kitchen, and a short hall that leads to what should be a bedroom and bath. "Rustic" is a good description of the décor. Log walls and wood floors are varnished—or *were*, sometime around the 1930s. The fireplace is made of rounded river-washed stones burnished black by years of fires in the hearth. A woodstove sits nearby, almost white from use. An old leather couch and chair have seen better days but look comfortable. Bessie turns on a lamp, which lights the inside to a golden glow. "This is nice, Bessie."

"Thank you, dear. I think you'll be comfortable." She reaches up by the door to unhook a set of keys. "You might prefer to lock your door, but I leave mine open most of the time," she says. "Easier that way." And returns the keys to the hook. "Well, I'll leave you to move in."

"Thank you," I say as I follow her out to retrieve my belongings.

I look around the bedroom as I unpack my suitcase. Tired curtains cover one small window. They were once red plaid. Now faded but clean, they offer little color to this room in my new residence. The freestanding closet isn't nice enough to be called an armoire, but it'll hold what few clothes I have to hang. The bureau is solid oak with drawers that pull hard and rebel with a squeal. Fresh air wafts into the room along with the chipping of nearby squirrels. Otherwise, it's quiet as I empty my suitcase and store it in the only out-of-the-way place I know of—under the bed. The knife goes under my pillow.

It's best to keep Big Mike's gift close by as I get used to my surroundings. The community seems quaint and quiet, but his words of caution come from years of experience. I respect his advice and want to make him proud that I've chosen to follow his career as a game warden. He didn't try to talk me out of this line of work. He said he had confidence in me, and I don't want to let him down.

Walking out to the living area, the old leather couch and chair are accented by two tables with lamps made from antlers. The shades are yellowed with age. The space contains the ghosts of bearded fishermen drinking their warm brandies after a day on the lake. But since I don't drink brandy this early in the day, I settle for making a cup of coffee on the vintage stove and calling Mom.

"Hello-o-o?" Mother sings. "Catherine? How are you, dear?"

"Good, Mom. How are you?"

"Your father said you called. We are just doing great!" she says with cheerleader enthusiasm. "Are you eating well, dear?"

Why is it mothers always wonder about their kids' eating habits?

"I've gained five pounds since you saw me," I lie.

"Oh, good, dear! That's great. It sounds like you're getting along just fine."

"I am, Mom."

"Are you moved in, Catherine?"

"Yeah. There wasn't much to move but clothes," I say, reaching for a slice of bread to pop in the toaster. At the press of the lever, my bread drops in and the cabin goes dark. "Mom, my lights just went out. I gotta go."

"Is everything okay, dear?"

"It's fine. I just blew a fuse, I think."

"No one is following you, are they?"

"No, Mom. No one even knows I'm here. It's just a fuse."

"Please stay in touch. We love to hear from you and want to know all about your new job."

"Love you, too, Mom."

Only the rattle and hum of the ancient refrigerator is heard. I put my phone down to find the fuse box. It has curious round knobs where switches should be, so I go looking for Bessie.

As I walk out of the cabin, the cool, clean air splashes over me. Before turning toward the main house, I hear, "Cat! Are you looking for me?"

It takes a moment to recognize that the voice is coming from the lake. There's Bessie in a lemon-yellow kayak, paddling into shore. She takes a few strokes, waves at me, and then easily lifts herself off the open boat and pulls it up on the grass. She's thick around the middle, but solid. Her skin is golden-brown and leathery from years in the outdoors.

"Cat, how are you making out? Are you all moved in?" she asks with a friendly smile as she walks toward me.

"Unpacking didn't take me long, but it seems I've tripped the electricity off and don't know anything about this kind of fuse box."

"Oh, of course," she replies. "I meant to warn you about that. I've got a bag of fuses up to the house for you." In her bare feet, Bessie walks spryly to the main house and up onto the porch. The wraparound covered deck gives the lodge a homey look. Four Adirondack chairs are huddled together, inviting guests to converse and enjoy the view. It doesn't take a minute before she returns with a bag. "Come on, Catherine. I'll show you."

And she does, by unscrewing a knob and replacing it with a fresh one from her bag. "See? Easy-peasy," she says, handing me the bag of newer knobs.

"How often will I need to change these?" I say, looking down at a dozen fuses.

"It depends on how much light you want with your toast, I guess," she says with another chuckle. "Why don't you come up to the house tonight for burgers on the grill and fresh sweet corn? We can talk more then."

"My mouth is watering already," I say. "What time?"

"How about five-thirty, and we can get to know one another while we're cooking," she says. "Meanwhile I've got some chores to get done."

"I'm heading for the store. Do you need anything?" I ask.

"No, but thanks for asking, dear," she replies.

My little Toyota Corolla carries me without complaint wherever I need to go. I take it through the center of town and notice that most people wave as we pass each other. Near East Cove, the light blinks yellow at the intersection. But it may be a waste of electricity, as only four cars go by before I make my turn. And this is the heavy traffic of the tourist season.

The local supermarket only has four aisles but seems stocked with the necessities. In my case, that's peanut butter, bread, coffee, and milk. Beer for tonight is a special treat.

Returning, I open more windows and the front door of the cabin, allowing gentle breezes to wash through the space as I unpack my groceries and put the beer in the refrigerator.

Later, I head for Bessie's with two bottles. The temperature is comfortable. The sun is lowering in the west while we look east across the lake. We raise our drinks to a good day and sit on Bessie's front porch. The conversation is easy and natural.

"Catherine Higloss is such a beautiful name," Bessie says.

"Yes, it is Bessie," I reply. "But I prefer Cat. It fits me better."

"What do you mean, dear?"

"My parents probably had hopes of fame and elegance at the time they dreamed of their baby girl's future. It just became obvious the package doesn't live up to the hype. I don't like to dress up and actually prefer to dress down; you know—jeans, boots, flannel shirts. My makeup consists of lip gloss and a little mascara, and I usually get them at the grocery store."

"But you're such a pretty girl," she replies.

"Thank you, Bessie," I say, smiling. "But I've always preferred being outdoors, feeling the dirt between my fingers and breathing fresh air rather than sewing and cooking in a stuffy ol' house. My friends were usually boys who were always doing interesting stuff like riding bikes and exploring. Playing house or school was boring."

"I can relate to that," she says. "In my day, girls had three options: teaching, nursing, or staying at home and raising a family. I chose nursing and still work part-time when the hospital needs me."

"You live here all your life?" I ask.

"Pretty much," she says. "I spent the first four years out of school working in Boston. But I missed this too much," she says sweeping her arm out toward the lake, the hillside behind it, with the sunglow highlighting the trees on the opposite shore.

Bessie places thick burgers on the grill while we continue to talk. "I never heard of a female game warden," she says. "Isn't becoming a warden a bit extreme?"

"It doesn't matter that I'll be the first woman," I say. "I grew up with my dad bringing orphan animals to the house, banding birds for wildlife studies, and studying natural resources and biology in college. I just can't think of anything I'd rather do."

"Well, you're gonna have your work cut out for you; long hours and lots of night work."

"I look forward to it."

"And you're working for Basil Kwiatkowsky?"

"Yes, I am. Why?"

"Oh, he's a busy guy. He seems to be in the paper a lot. He works with the county commissioners to get money for more help, and he seems to get a lot of press when he snatches poachers." Then Bessie pauses. "Cat, you don't have a gun in the cabin, do you?" She turns to look at me and gauge my reaction.

"No, I don't own a gun and honestly can't carry one till I qualify in my job training. I'm not sure what it takes to qualify, but I can't carry a loaded firearm until I do."

She looks disappointed. "What are you gonna do if you run into gun-toting bad guys?"

"I dunno, Bessie. Guess I'll learn soon enough. They tell me I'll be teamed up with other wardens till I'm trained. We'll work deer shiners at night, but during the day, we'll check fishermen for licenses and boaters for safety equipment, and issue citations if they don't comply with the law."

The burgers have an unusual flavor, and Bessie tells me they're venison. She tells me about the other year-round resident in a nearby cabin, Harry Blackwolf. "Harry keeps to himself," she says. "He isn't much for small talk, but no trouble either. Living next to the lake is special," Bessie muses as we sit on her front porch after dinner. "It's peaceful, calming…a sanctuary of life," she says.

"It is pretty quiet," I reply.

"But listen; you hear the loons in the distance, the gentle lapping of water on shore, and a few squirrels above us in the canopy. The sun sets with a new kaleidoscope of colors each night, bringing closure to another day."

"It's almost hypnotic when you say it that way," I say.

"I prefer *tranquil*," she says with a smile.

"Well, I've got the great book of hunting laws to read tonight before I get too tranquil. Thank you for dinner," I say, pulling myself off the chair and walking down the lane to my cozy little cabin, number four. I fall asleep reading the list of lakes open only to fly fishing. I don't even know where these lakes are yet.

At three a.m., my little abode is rattling with the sound of a massive engine roaring nearby and shaking me awake. The train whistle sounds like it's next door before the rail cars roll past our road heading north on the tracks: *ta-chin, ta-chin, ta-chin*. So much for tranquility.

By six a.m., I've had my coffee and head to the lake for a swim. The early-morning sun shines on the treetops, reflecting green over the blue of the water. Tiny ripples are highlighted by rays of sunlight. The cool water chills my skin as I dive in from the dock. I surface and stroke toward the opposite shore.

Swimming has always been my sport. As a little girl, I took as many lessons as I could. When I got old enough, there were junior and senior lifesaving classes before you could work at the local pool or beach. I love the feeling of buoyancy and the coolness of the water on warm skin.

It's a good workout by the time I return to the dock. I'm relaxing there when I see Bessie kayak in from my left. She gives a nod and continues her approach to the shore behind me.

"It's a beautiful morning, Cat," she says.

"That it is, Bessie. And quiet…"

"Oh," she chuckles. "You were introduced to our three o'clock visitor."

"How often does it come through?"

"Just once a night."

"Thank God."

"And once a day…" she says with a grin. "It's gotta return somehow," she adds, as she glides into the shore and lifts herself from the boat.

"Guess so. Welcome to tranquil…" I say as I rise from the dock. "I best get ready for my first day."

"Knock 'em dead, Cat," Bessie offers.

2

THE FIRST DAY

I arrive at Basil's home, and office, at eight a.m. on this bright August morning. It's a modest home in town with a front yard that has toys and bikes strewn across it as if the neighborhood kids have been invited to a breakfast of ice cream. I knock on the front screen door, which has a view into the living room. A troop of young boys lie in various positions on the floor and furniture, intently watching *The Three Stooges*, annoyed by the interruption of my knock.

"Grouse, get the door!" hollers someone from another room.

A shirtless little boy with long arms and skinny tan legs comes quickly to the door, pushes it open without a sound, and allows me to enter before reclaiming his space on the floor. Other than a curious look my way, no one seems to notice, or care, that a stranger is among them.

"Thank you," I say, letting the screen door close behind me. "Is Basil here?" I ask of no one in particular.

"Catherine? In here," comes the voice again.

I follow the voice and tiptoe through the tangle of little boys.

Around the corner in the kitchen I spot Basil, bare-chested like the kids, sitting at the head of a table. In front of him lies a tablet of yellow paper beside a cup of coffee. In one hand is a telephone and in the other, a pencil. Basil puts the phone down and extends his hand in greeting. "Morning, Catherine. You made it."

"Yes, sir. No problem," I say, trying to be on my best behavior. "But please call me Cat."

"Okay. Cat it is. Meet my wife, pretty Ms. Janelle." He points to a petite woman with long thick hair standing near the stove.

"Hi, Ms. Janelle," I say with a smile. "You certainly entertain a lot of neighborhood kids for this early in the morning."

Ms. Janelle smiles back with a glance at Basil. "Nice to meet you, Cat. Would you like coffee?"

"That would be great. Yes, ma'am."

Ms. Janelle has a voice that either hasn't cleared early morning cobwebs or suffers from years of a bad habit, but she's friendly and gently sets a mug of coffee in front of me. "You're right," she says, "There are a lot of kids here, but they're all ours."

"Oh..." I've already stuck my foot in my mouth, and I haven't been on the job five minutes. "Thank you for the coffee."

Basil says with pride, "Yep, Ms. Janelle is the mother of those six boys, and just as pretty today as the day I met her." They look at each other with an affection I can feel.

I sip my coffee and nod. "What are we working on today?"

"I've got our list from Dispatch, and we'll see a good part of the county before the day's out. Finish your coffee, grab your gear, and we'll head out."

"Sounds like a plan." I take my cup to the sink, wash it out, and set it on the side board. I turn to see two sets of eyes on me. "What?" I ask.

"None of the other wardens wash their own dishes," Ms. Janelle says.

"Oh..." With a shrug of my shoulders, I say goodbye and help Basil pick up his gear bag.

Basil gives Ms. Janelle a warm kiss and pats her behind before he turns to walk outside.

He hands me a list of locations as we put our gear in the cruiser, including the knife. His blue Chevy has no identifying emblems or markings like other patrol cars. Its lack of whitewalls, pinstripes, and other adornments does make it look different from other cars, but the black spotlight left of the windshield on the driver's side is a clear indicator of law enforcement. Basil calls in to Dispatch that we are 10-8, meaning we're in-service. We head northeast out of town, and I scan the list for the most efficient way to drive to each location.

"What's the list of?" I ask.

"Car kills," he replies without further explanation.

"Oh...I never thought about how they get picked off the roads."

"You have a lot to learn, Rookie, and this is just the beginning," he says with a grin.

And I do. I look at the car's county radio, which is connected to the sheriff's department, then to the state radio that's connected to the state police; both are squawking in the background. There are switches and lights that don't come standard with a car, and Basil is in command of it all. I'm sitting shotgun and observing. It's set up like the cruiser Big Mike sometimes took me in. There are flashlights, different jackets and boots, and other equipment in the backseat, and clipboards of blank citation forms in the console between us.

"We have one state warden in each county," Basil tells me. "But we're lucky the county commissioners support our work and pay for three county wardens, like yourself, to work with me. There's always something going on, so you won't have trouble staying busy."

We drive to the first location and spot a fawn lying motionless on the side of the road. We pull over with hazard lights on and back up to the lifeless body. Basil opens the cruiser's trunk and pulls out a shovel. "Your first official duty, Cat."

I take the shovel and dig a small grave in the ditch nearby. It's not long before the poor creature is buried and we move on to the next spot on our list.

Basil is telling me about the area where we'll be working, and pointing out homes of people he's dealt with. I listen to him describe deer poachers and their favorite spots, good citizens who call in information that can be used, and bad ones you just want to be aware of. "We get tips about violators," Basil says. "Our job is to catch 'em in the act of their violation."

We arrive at the next location from our list but don't see our target. Basil throws on our hazards and creeps along the side of the road. "Roll down your window, Cat." I comply without question while he turns the cruiser around. We cover the opposite ditch line. A whiff of rotting flesh catches both of us. "Guess we found it."

I can hold my breath a lot longer than I thought, and digging shallow graves in record time may be a new skill I'll master. An extra pair of gloves and a clean towel will now be added to my gear bag.

Dispatch calls Basil on the radio. "Three-oh-one, what is your location?"

"Northeast section, about thirty minutes from town."

"Sheriff is asking for assistance. Missing person reported south of town."

"Ten-four, we're on our way," Basil responds as we speed back to a farm south of Eagle Shores. "Better eat your lunch while you can, Cat. If we get involved in a search and rescue, we could be on duty for hours."

But I've lost my appetite after seeing the maggot-infested doe we just buried.

Within a short time, we see a couple of sheriff's cruisers in the dooryard of a small farm. The temperature is climbing into the eighties with haze and humidity creeping in, which makes walking in the sun miserable. Especially when you're dressed in long pants and long-sleeved shirts. We park and join deputies at a table where the sheriff has laid out a map of the area. A man in his late seventies is standing near the sheriff with a worried look on his face. *Probably the spouse.* A younger woman is holding on to him with the same worried expression; *The daughter, I'm guessing.*

"Here's the situation, folks," the sheriff begins. "Maude Polk, age seventy-five, has been missing since about eight this morning. Last seen, she was wearing a white housedress with small blue flower print on it. She has dementia and gets confused. The family has searched the house and barn areas. We need to expand the search to fields, the creek, and nearby woods. With the twelve people we have here, I want to search west of the house first. There's a fence line at the end of that eighty acres that she more than likely would not cross."

I'm assigned a search position between two burly deputies. Merle introduces himself and his partner, Mort. Their uniforms are brown and tan, which blends with the brush, but they are big enough to spot without much trouble.

"This your first search?" Merle asks.

"Does lookin' for my handbag in the mornings count?"

"Nope."

"Then, yep, first search."

"That's okay. Mort and me will take care of you. We try to keep within ten to fifteen feet of each other in thick grass and brush. A person can lie out of sight pretty well, and you can walk right by 'em not even knowing they're there. Get a fix on an object at the far end of the field and walk directly toward it. You walk between us. That way we can keep you in line," Merle says, smiling at his own joke. He looks at Mort to get his reaction. Mort casually nods and smiles.

"That sounds easy enough," I reply.

Once we're organized, we walk cautiously toward the far fence line. The terrain is deceiving. There is a downward slope, but the grass gets taller and thicker as we walk toward the bottom of the hill.

"You work together much?" I ask the two men.

"Yep, we're cousins and brothers-in-law," Merle responds.

"Is that legal?" I ask too quickly. Both stop to look at me. "Sorry; I just never thought about it..." And I grin as I shrug my shoulders.

"As I was saying, we work together a lot," Merle continues. "Our uncle was the sheriff a while back and hired us. You know, people he could trust."

"Got it," I say as I'm thinking, *This is a tight bunch.* I keep looking left and right, and I'm glad they have their hats on in these tall weeds. Talking keeps us close and in alignment. "I'm guessing we might have a few ticks on us tonight."

"Yep, but at least with the tall grass, you won't see the snakes slithering away..."

"Great," I say and start making more noise. Snakes give me the creeps. I don't mind them as long as they stay away from me. Stepping lightly on the ground, I feel the earth as I go and make sure I don't have something slithering underfoot.

We head up an incline and the blessed grass gets shorter. The going is slow and the temperature is rising. High humidity makes breathing harder, and if *I'm* having trouble, I'm especially worried for Maude. Our clothes are already clinging to us.

"I'm sweating like a pig," Merle pipes up.

"Thank you for that information," I say. "It's only one in the afternoon. We'll be a lot warmer by the end of the day."

"The grass is bending and breaking where we walk, so we should notice if another person's been out here," Merle observes.

"That makes sense," I say and point to Mort. "Does he ever talk?"

"Only when he needs to. Less confusing that way."

We reach the fence line with no evidence that Maude has come this way. We move down the fence with the others and walk back toward the farm. The sun is beating on us and the humidity is so thick you can almost swallow it. Our clothes are soaked from skin to badges.

There is water waiting for us at the farm. We wipe our faces with cool wet towels and resume our search in the opposite direction, down toward a creek and brushy area. As we approach the creek, I notice a change in the vegetation. "Stop!" I shout. "Nettles!"

It's too late for Mort. He's bouncing out of there and hollering, "Ow! Son-of-a-sea-biscuit!" He dashes for the creek, drops his gun belt, and splashes into the brook, letting the cool water flow around his body. With only his head above water, he sighs, "Ahh...much better!"

"You move pretty fast for a big feller," I say, laughing.

"Those things are nasty!" Mort complains. "My ankles are stinging. So are my legs...everywhere!"

Other searchers watch from their area and chuckle at the big guy brought low by a plant.

"You're gonna have to learn your plants, Mort," Merle says.

When we quiet down, we can hear a faint moan. We walk toward the sound and see a patch of white at the base of some blackberry briars. It's a lady in a white housedress lying beside the thorny bushes.

"Maude?" Merle and I say in unison.

"Can you hear us, Maude?" Merle asks.

"Help," comes the faint response.

Merle radios the command post of our discovery, and the other searchers come to assist us. I help Maude sit up and give her a sip of water while she gathers some strength. Another searcher checks her pulse while others stand between her and the intense sun. Mort removes his wet hankie, wipes her brow and the nape of her neck. Maude comes around and blinks her eyes a couple of times.

"You found me," she whispers. "I hurt my ankle… But you found me."

The searcher's assessment of her condition shows a swollen ankle, which she probably twisted in her fall. A bowl of blackberries is overturned nearby. We put Maude on a stretcher and carry her across the field. The ambulance is standing by at the farm. Maude appears exhausted and dehydrated but is now in good care. It's gratifying to find the family's loved one for them, especially when we see Maude's smiling daughter and husband. They rush to her side and grab her hand. They are crying and trying to hug her as the EMTs put the gurney on the ground. I feel my own tears well up as I watch.

Plenty of pats on the back and pleasantries are exchanged because we found her before darkness fell. Basil makes his way over to me saying, "Cat, nice job!" He puts his arm around me with a jovial squeeze that feels genuine and good. We're part of a group that has succeeded in saving a woman and bringing her back to her loving family. "It's nice when we find the missing person alive," Basil says. "They don't always work out that way."

The comment isn't wasted on me. It's a positive outcome but only my first day. I wonder how many searches I may be involved in and what other outcomes might look like. I'd rather wallow in the success of today. We recap the events on our way home, laughing at Mort and counting our blessings for Maude and her family.

Arriving at Basil's, I grab my gear from the car.

"Meet me here tomorrow night at six thirty," he says. "I'm teaming you up with Jinot Rideau, who will be your partner in the field."

"Okay."

"It'll be your first time out with night hunters," he warns, "so come prepared."

"Prepared for what?" I ask.

"Working nights. You'll need a flashlight, binoculars, and anything you need to keep yourself comfortable."

"How long will we work?"

"Till we're done," Basil replies matter-of-factly. "You'll find, Cat, we don't work by set hours. If there's a lot of action, we don't stop. Plan to work till after bar time and you won't be caught off guard."

"Okay," I say again, trying to wrap my brain around the idea of working such odd and undefined hours. Not that I have better things to do. New to the area, I haven't made friends yet, I don't cook, and I need some excitement in my life. Yep, this might work just fine. Meanwhile, a dip in the lake this evening will cool me off, another perk to my accommodations.

3

IDA, HEIDI, AND JINOT

Headquarters is located on East Cove with a lovely morning view of Eagle Lake. That's good because the building itself isn't much to look at. Government brown in color, it's a low-budget one-story, built by construction-challenged locals. If it didn't have a big Huey helicopter parked next to it, the building would blend in with the trees next door. That and a bunch of green forestry trucks parked outside marked Department of Natural Resources also give away its identity.

Across from the Huey is an antique steamship now hired to take tourists up the lake. But in yesteryear, these old steamships hauled booms of logs across the lake on the first part of their journey before each piece floated downriver to the sawmills. Logs were hauled out onto the ice during the winter. When the spring thaws melted the ice, boom chains wrapped thousands of floating logs to be hauled down the lake, where men waited to sluice each piece into rivers raging with snowmelt and spring rains.

The bulletin board outside the government building posts all sorts of important information about boating and fire regulations. At least that's what I can see. Sun-washed and riddled with insect poop, the messages are hard to decipher and likely have been faded and stained for quite a while. I walk in the public entrance. A Formica-covered counter greets me. It's meant to separate visitors from staff. However, there are no visitors or staff right now except me. A nameplate says "Heidi Holmes" should be close by. Across the room, six desks are covered with professional magazines, and in-boxes are stacked high with paper. The desks are lined up in rows like a school for adults. Maps paper the walls on all sides of the big room. More maps cover a cabinet in the back. These are not the desks of people who spend a lot of time at them and even less cleaning them off.

A nice-looking young woman enters from a hallway, a bit surprised to find me standing at her counter. In her midthirties, she has light-brown hair pulled back in a ponytail, and her face is clearly sleep-deprived. Her casual pullover is one size too small, and her jeans have a department-store look with their nondescript design and snugness around the butt.

"Good morning," I say. She's holding a cup in both hands, steam escaping. It smells like coffee.

A bit on guard, she says, "Can I help you?"

"Are you Heidi?" I ask as she walks across to the counter.

"Yes..." she says as if I've solved some puzzle. She's more focused on sipping her hot coffee without burning her lips than on my presence.

"I'm Cat, Heidi." I pause to get a reaction. When there is none, I proceed. "I'm Basil's new warden trainee."

"Oh yeah, I heard he has a new girl coming in," she says, still more interested in her drink. "What can I do for you?"

"Well...I just thought I'd come by and introduce myself," I say, getting an icy reception. She seats herself without showing interest in me or anything on her desk.

The door opens behind me with a *whoosh*, and in walks a whirlwind that blows the dust off the countertop.

"Morning, everyone!" says the twenty-something motion-maker. "How's everyone, and how's Heidi-the-Happy this morning?"

"Morning, Ida," says Heidi with considerably less warmth than her coffee. "This is Cat, the new girl."

"Warden," I correct.

"Cat, I've been waiting for you to show up!" Ida pivots and puts a big ol' bear hug on me. I can feel her extra-large boobs press against me as she holds onto me as if she's afraid I'll escape. "You and me will be bosom buddies here, girlfriend."

I'm anxious to retreat as the air is forced out of me. Looking at her drab green uniform and Department of Conservation arm patch, I say, "I take it you're a forester, Ida."

"Yes, of course! Would I wear a uniform in this shade of green otherwise?" she says with a wide smile and sparkling brown eyes. "I'm Ida Dombrosky," she says, holding out her hand for me to shake. "I keep telling folks I'da found a different job if I'da known I had to dress like this." Heidi rolls her eyes as Ida puts her arm around me and steers me to the back hallway. "Let's get acquainted over coffee."

Ida tells me she's only been stationed at Eagle Lake for three months. She takes me out to the garage where shovels, axes, water-can backpacks, and other forestry tools are neatly lined up on shelving. She smiles when I look impressed, and we head back to the office area.

"How do I get maps," I ask, "equipment I need, and uniforms?"

"I've got the maps you'll need," she says as she hands me a spiral notebook containing maps for each township. "Most equipment needs to be ordered. We'll have to ask Happy Heidi for help with that. But a uniform for you may be hard to come by."

"Why?"

"Because most of the wardens are at least fifty pounds heavier and, quite frankly, aren't built like you," she says with a chuckle. "But last time I was at the farm supply store, I noticed they had gray slacks and shirts. The park guys send their summer help there to get their uniforms."

"Thanks for the tip, Ida. I'd better head out and get my gear before I report to work tonight."

"Have you met Jinot yet?" she asks.

"No, I meet him tonight. Why?"

"All I can say is, I'm glad I don't have to work with him because I couldn't concentrate on my job."

"What's the matter with him?"

"What's the matter? Heck, nothing! That's what I mean; there is nothing the matter with that man," she says, looking at me as if I should know more.

"Ida, nice to meet you. But I better go."

"See you around, Cat. Don't work too hard tonight!"

I find gray slacks and shirts at the farm supply store, along with everything needed to fix barns or raise chickens. They have two shirts sized for small men. I find the smallest pants they have and hold them up. A belt will cinch them tight. The boots they have are wide for my feet but I don't have a choice. On my way to check out, I see they also have tires that might fit my car. I'll keep that in mind.

I take my law book down to the dock to do some more reading before it's time to get ready for work. The sun is warm and waves are lapping the shore, soothing enough to lull me into a nap. I have time to take a shower, make a peanut butter sandwich and a pot of coffee to place in my thermos before I have to leave. I'm learning to live without turning my lights on.

I put it all in my gear bag and see my knife at the bottom. Better pull it out and keep it close. I place the knife, in its sheath, on my belt and hold it close to my backside. I turn to look in the mirror. The knife looks like a machete loaded on my hip, but I want to be prepared.

The evening sun is lowering in the west, providing a golden hue to the treetops. The lake water is calm with a boat motor sounding in the distance as I reach my old Toyota. Dropping into the seat, the sheath hits the car seat before my backside does and pushes my belt up to my ribcage. The crotch of my pants is bunched awkwardly, feeling particularly uncomfortable. The top of the knife handle is somewhere near my shoulder bone. This isn't working. I climb out of the car, push my pants back into place and take the knife off my belt and stuff it back in my bag before backing away from the cabin. I wave to Bessie and slow down as I pass by her place.

"I see the porch light on," she says. "You must be working tonight."

"Yep, I get to meet some of my fellow wardens this evening. We're working together, so don't do any night hunting tonight, Bessie," I say with a smile.

"OK. If you've got the county covered, I'll just stay home for once."

Bessie chuckles with her whole body and laugh lines accent her eyes. Her pink cheeks and salt-and-pepper hair complete her grandma look. Her nurse's uniform must reassure her patients at the hospital that they're in good hands. At seventy, she seems wise and full of energy. She's kind to have given me a rent I couldn't refuse, and in return I'll help with some chores.

I wave goodbye and rattle down our dirt lane and turn toward town. Basil's house isn't far. I pull up in front next to a cruiser. Bicycles of all sizes still litter the lawn like a yard sale. I walk past them and make my way to the side door.

Ms. Janelle has a big pot of water on the stove, boiling potatoes. I see Basil's finishing his dinner of venison with gravy. Across from Basil is a tall, strikingly handsome man with dark features. His hair is trimmed tight to his head with just a wisp of length at the forehead combed back. I like the wet look but try not to stare.

"Good evening," I say, as I drop my gear bag on the floor next to the door, come in, and grab a coffee.

"Hey, Cat," Ms. Janelle says. "Sounds like you did OK on your first day, finding Maude Polk and all."

"Yeah, we were lucky. I think ol' Mort's screaming about the nettles woke her out of her stupor, though."

"'Course it woke her. You could hear him clear up at the house!" Basil added. "Cat, this here is Jinot, another county warden."

"Jinot, nice to meet you," I say as I extend my hand.

"Cat. Same," Jinot says as he takes my hand in his.

His hand is large and warm. A sensation, like an electrical current, runs up my arm as I study his face. He has long dark eyelashes that I wish were mine. His blue eyes remind me of Alaska's glacial ice. His cheekbones are angled perfectly above his mouth.

Ida was right; he could be distracting. Basil's saying something to me, but I'm not hearing very much.

"Jinot will be your primary partner. He's very knowledgeable and will be able to teach you a lot when you're with him."

"Sounds good to me," is all I can say while staring at my new partner before the side door opens again.

"Well, if it isn't Ranger Rick LePine," Basil says to the newcomer.

"Hello, Chief. What's going on?"

"Rick, meet Cat. She's the new recruit I've been talking about. We'll team her up with Jinot tonight."

"Hi, Cat. Good to have you with us," says Rick as he extends his hand.

"Hi, Rick," I reply as we shake.

Rick is weathered, nice-looking...but *definitely* older...and when I shake his hand, there's no sensation.

"Rick is a park ranger from the county Parks Department," Basil adds. The conversation is light while he finishes his meal.

"OK, crew, tonight we're heading northeast of town. We got a report of shots up near Fox Pond and the hills," the chief says. "Let's stay within a mile or two of each other, try to triangulate the shots and corner them."

"Sounds good, Chief," Jinot and Rick reply in unison before we head out the door.

"Grab your gear, Cat, and put it in my car," Jinot tells me.

"I hope I've got everything I'll need tonight," I say as I throw my clattering gear bag in the back.

"What the heck have you got in there that drops with a heavy sound like that?"

I pick up my bag and withdraw the knife and sheath, slowly revealing its length.

"Holy smokes, where'd you get a knife like that?" Basil asks from behind.

"That's some knife, Cat," Jinot says.

"I thought I could ride around like Crocodile Dundee and pull it out when we get into trouble."

"Funny," Jinot says with a smile. "Actually, it's a Ka-Bar, the Marine Corps' fighting knife developed during World War Two."

"Really? My dad sent it to me."

"I sure wish my parents had given me something like that," Jinot says looking intently at the knife as he turns it in his hands.

"You'll find that knife comes in handy," Basil says. "Your dad is right. I can see it's had some use, but I think he used it as his hunting knife. You realize, guys, Cat's dad was a federal warden in this state, working with migratory birds and endangered species a few years ago. He spoke at a warden meeting we had."

Rick and Jinot nod as they look at me with raised eyebrows and acknowledgment.

I look at the knife with renewed interest and wonder what kind of use it's had.

Basil adds with a grin, "Jinot and I will have to behave or you might use it on us."

We drive to the northeast section of the county. The rolling hills and twisting roads are different from the flat sandy areas of the county. It's near dusk as we go around the corner near Wobesan River. We spot a barbed-wire fence up ahead that separates the road from a field. Jinot automatically slows down while my eyes are getting focused. I'm seeing, but not believing. There's an animal hanging from the top wire of the fence. We pull up and get out next to what appears to be a beautiful Labrador retriever. He's big and black and swollen. He's also dead.

"Why would anyone do this to such a beautiful animal?" I ask, shocked and disgusted at the sight.

"Running deer, I'm guessing," Jinot says matter-of-factly. "They're sending a message to the neighbors to keep their dogs under control." Jinot backs away toward the car.

"We just gonna leave him?" I ask.

"Yep; lets the owners know what happened." Jinot looks at me and signals me to get in the car. "Not much we can do, Cat. Damage is done."

I stare at Jinot, disappointed by his lack of emotion. There's a sick feeling in my stomach and a similar feeling in my head… Reconciling what I've seen, its cruelty, is going to take some time to process. Jinot takes the car out of park and moves onto the road.

What is with this guy? Why isn't he outraged? It takes a few minutes to find words. "You ever had a dog, Jinot?"

"Sure. We had dogs on the farm. We had to teach them not to chase animals." Jinot looks at me before he continues. "Dogs love to chase. It's part of their nature. But they can be trained."

Jinot is taking me on winding roads through rolling hills. He's talking about landowners who have called in with complaints of shooting out of season near their homes and fields that normally get hunted. I hear him, but it's barely sinking in. I'm still wondering what kind of person could kill and string up another's pet. *And why doesn't my partner have the same visceral reaction I'm feeling?*

"Cat, tonight will be your first night out working shiners," he starts. "You know it's OK to spot deer at night, right? Some people will have an actual spotlight; others use the headlights of their cars. Deer will come out at dusk to feed in the fields," he continues. "When a light beam shines on them, they freeze in place. It makes them an easy target to watch *or* to shoot. You'll see a lot of families come out with their kids for an evening of entertainment. But it's the people with weapons or shells proving an *intent to hunt* that we are interested in. We'll see the light shine, stop the vehicle, and search it for weapons and ammo. If it's clear of firearms, we let 'em go."

"OK." I'm still thinking about the dog and finding it hard to focus on Jinot's words.

After a moment, he says, "The Chief tells me you aren't qualified yet to carry a pistol."

"True. I'm not sure when I'll go for my qualification, but meantime, I'm pistol-less."

"Well, I don't think it's a problem. You'll be working with a partner at night in case we run into trouble."

"How often does that happen?"

"Running into trouble, or pulling my weapon?"

"Either."

"Hard to say… Sometimes it's a lot. We've had shiners throw their weapons from the window or hide them under their wives' skirts. You've got to be observant and smart. You want to be prepared for anything a person might try."

The sun has left us in the twilight of evening, when most people are settling in at home for a quiet night. My night is just getting started.

Jinot has slowed the car to a crawl and points the spotlight on a field. We see three deer grazing near the tree line. "There they are, momma and her two babies," he says. The doe is not much bigger than her two fawns, now without spots.

We continue down the road a short way, and Jinot backs the cruiser into a woodland drive overgrown with brush and small trees. We exit the car, and Jinot pulls camouflage netting from the backseat. He flings it over the hood of the cruiser, blocking any shine from the windows or chrome that might reflect from passing headlights. "Now we wait," he says.

We stand in front of the car and spray DEET over ourselves as we hold our breath. Until the first frost, mosquitoes will be a constant annoyance. Crickets and bullfrogs are serenading us as Jinot asks about the law enforcement classes I've taken. He went through the same training a few years ago after returning from his Marine Corps tour of duty.

We stop our conversation as a car comes our way. "It's traveling too fast," he says.

Once the car goes by, he continues the conversation and asks about a couple of professors we both might know. We drink our coffee, smell freshly cut hay from the nearby field, and watch for cars. The law enforcement radios chatter away in the background as Dispatch monitors the sheriff's department, the state troopers, and, of course, us. I had never imagined there was this much activity in a rural county evening. Kids are breaking into abandoned houses looking for a place to drink alcohol. A car veers off a road somewhere and hits a tree. It's minor, but the ambulance is on its way. The Chief radios that he and his partner will assist. Jinot reaches in to the radio mike and uses this strange language of ten-codes, as in "Ten-four, I copy that, Chief."

"How am I gonna learn the ten-codes and what they all mean?" I ask with concern.

Jinot smiles and laughs, breaking the tension. "It'll come with some time. You've got a lot to learn, but you're smart."

"If you say so," I reply. "Is there some list I can look at?"

"Yep, there's one on the clipboard inside the car."

"Phew," and I walk over to retrieve it. "Holy smokes, there's a lot of 'em."

"Yeah, but you only use a few most of the time."

As the darkness overpowers us, the night air turns cool and crisp and our noses are filled with the smell of moss and damp leaves. Our attention is still focused on the field.

A car comes into view, and a beam of light scans the field one way and then another. It clicks off, returning the night to darkness. We hear the low hum of an engine at idle, then gravel churning and scraping. We are silent, watching.

The engine rattles alive with the sound of crunching gravel drawing nearer. Another beam of light scans the field closer to us. It stops and focuses. We are close enough to see the doe gazing back, transfixed by the light. We watch the beam and its source, waiting. Voices we hear are indecipherable. The doe moves toward the field's edge, displaying its mocha-brown winter coat, standing broadside—an easy shot. I hold my breath, anticipating the crack of a gun. She raises her tail and turns to jump into the dense brush, safe. The young ones follow. The stream of light clicks off.

The old car rattles to life and moves our way. We hide in the thick underbrush, crouching low and still while the car passes by unaware that we are within feet of touching it. We make our way back to the cruiser as quietly as possible.

"We're going black," Jinot whispers as he throws a kill switch on the dashboard, preventing any electronics from glowing on ignition and giving our position away. We creep onto the road using the moon and fading lights of the old car for direction.

"OK," I reply, adrenaline pumping now. This will be my first stop as a game warden. My new boots and uniform suddenly feel stiff and uncomfortable again. I silently go through my mental checklist and visualize what's about to happen.

"Get your flashlight ready and move up to the passenger side," Jinot advises. "And watch out! I think we've got a live one here. You'll find a gun somewhere, I'm sure of it. If that doe hadn't spooked, she'd be dead right now."

"OK, OK. I got it!" Nervous and excited, I fumble for my flashlight and grip it like I'll never let go.

We're behind the old car in seconds as it slowly idles its way down the road, its occupants unaware we even exist. Our windows are down to catch any noise while Jinot maneuvers us within yards of their bumper. I pick up the radio and call in the illuminated license plate number and wait for owner information from county Dispatch.

"They're stopping… Go, go, go!" Jinot directs as he hits the cruiser's high beams, spotlight, and rotating blues all at the same time. The old car is lit up like it's on a Las Vegas show stage. Four shocked faces automatically turn toward us mouthing, "*What the f—?*"

With flashlight in hand, I'm out the door and running alongside the old car. My boots feel like heavy weights tied to my ankles. I pound the trunk with my fist as I go by, shouting, "Hold it right there!" Suddenly, my body lurches forward as my footing gives way and I belly-flop into the ditch. "Game Warden," I grunt as I land with air gushing out of my lungs. Looking up from my prone position, I see two teenaged eyes peering down at me from the window.

"Whoa, du-u-de…" I hear from above. "She's down, man…" as I quickly right myself, step up from the ditch, and shine my flashlight into bloodshot and highly dilated eyes.

"Gentlemen, please step out of the car and walk directly back to the rear to stand between your car and the cruiser, hands in full view." I open the front passenger door, step away, and watch them exit their clunker and walk to its rear bumper.

The car search reveals no guns or ammunition but smells of heavy smoke with an unusual earthy scent. Jinot is still shaking his head as he calmly walks to the driver's side. The license plate is from a local address matching the driver's license of the docile but nervous young driver.

"We're just cruising the roads, takin' a break from our studies, you know," driver Tom says. He's articulate but a little slow in delivery. "We like checking on the deer."

I notice the other three young men are trying to avert their eyes from me as I check their ID's.

"Smells kind of funny in the car, guys," Jinot says and looks for a reaction. "Fresh air might do you all good. But we aren't interested in looking further for pot." They relax and exchange glances. "Might be wise to roll down the windows on your way home. The county deputies are around," he says, "so, you might want to get off the roads and back to your studies."

They don't wait for any other advice.

Walking back to the cruiser, I begin swiping the dirt and weeds from my uniform.

"Nice first stop, Rookie," Jinot says with a smirk as he swings into the car. He turns off the beams, spotlight, and blues, and steers the car toward a different hiding spot and a different field.

"Why didn't we care about the pot?" I ask.

"More than likely, they had a minimal amount on their persons or we would've found it," Jinot says. "It isn't worth the paperwork."

Jinot pulls into another spot, and we hide in the bushes for another couple of hours before being released to head home around midnight. Jinot tells me he'll be going for a run in the morning and asks if I'd like to join him.

"Sure," I say without thinking twice.

4

FIT FOR DUTY

The calm blue lake and cloudless sky greet me at six a.m., and the cool temperature is delightful. I'm barely awake and dressed when I see Jinot drive in and park next to my car.

"Why waste a beautiful morning with a run and a workout?" I say when he arrives in his sneakers and hands me a cup of coffee.

"I want you to pass the warden test but you gotta run a couple miles and be able to lift heavy weights," he says. "You also gotta swim."

"Swimming isn't an issue. Swimming's my favorite sport. I want you to know, I was a senior lifeguard during my high school summers. Running just isn't fun."

"It's work, Cat, and if you want to work as a warden, you're gonna have to run a mile and a half in sixteen minutes. You won't know when the department will be calling for recruits, so you should be ready. Now guzzle that down and let's hit the road."

Donning our earth-colored shorts and T-shirts, we look like a couple of military personnel rather than civilian runners who sport stylish clothes and sneakers. "We're running around the cove, toward town and back. That's only a five-k, Cat."

"Sounds like four too many to me," I say, only half joking. We head out on the dirt road. "It's also no fair that your legs look better than mine."

"That's from running."

We soon find a similar cadence that feels comfortable. Jinot pops a question: "What made you interested in warden work, Cat?"

"You know my dad was a game warden. He had me band birds with him, took me on bird counts," I say. "I enjoy being in the outdoors more than anything. When Earth Day was created, I realized we had been living the dream my whole life and wanted to continue."

"Did he talk about the law enforcement part?"

"No, not really. But his service revolver and badge were around. He practiced holds on me." I smile as I think about the games we played. "Why did you get in the business, Jinot?"

"I was always outdoors. If I wasn't doing chores on the farm, I was hunting in the back forty acres or fishing in the closest stream. I just couldn't picture myself farming or in a desk job cooped up all day. Like you, I loved the thought of protecting wildlife and the environment. I didn't think we'd be protecting people from themselves as much as we do."

I think about his comment as we run the old trail next to the lake. Chipmunks skitter across our path, incensed that we are intruding in their domain. A doe crosses the trail in front of us and quickly moves into the shadows of the woods. The cool air keeps us relatively comfortable as we catch our stride, and the sun is rising to wake up the world. A float plane starts up in the distance.

"That's Fuller's Air Service. They fly folks into remote areas to fish or stay in lakeside lodges."

"Are they good guys or bad guys?" I ask, huffing a bit with exertion.

"Hard to say. They run a good business, but the people they take to these remote areas probably don't give a darn about catching too many fish or following the law. They're paying for a good time."

"You ever had issues with Fuller's?"

"No. But they're smart not to ask too many questions of their clients. It's simpler that way."

We reach East Cove just as the float plane has taxied close to shore. It's turning to take off, with the lake as its runway. The pilot revs the engine before it engages for takeoff. The plane's floats skim the water at increasing speeds until lift takes the plane off the lake and it rises above the treetops before turning into the early morning sun.

"I wanted to learn to fly," I say to Jinot as we turn to start back.

"Why didn't you?"

"The Air Force wouldn't teach women to fly when I graduated from high school," I say. "I really wanted to fly helicopters. You put me up there and I could do reconnaissance. I would have a bird's-eye view and catch all sorts of bad stuff going on."

"That sounds like a good plan. What got in your way?"

"Veterans coming back from deployment," I say, now more than a little winded. "Hundreds of pilots came back with thousands of hours of flight time. There was no way I could compete for work—even with my pilot's license. So here I am, grounded," I say with a smile.

"Still like helicopters?"

"Yep."

"Good, 'cause we use them quite a bit."

"I'll take that assignment anytime."

"Stand in line, Rookie." Then Jinot sprints ahead, picking up the pace.

Damn.

I need to concentrate on my breathing as we run back. It takes every ounce of energy I have to keep up with Jinot. He's pointing out landmarks on the lake while I'm doing everything I can to breathe. We make it back to the cabins, and I'm sucking wind. Jinot acts like it's nothing.

"I'm heading home to clean up," he says. "The chief wants me to take you to the range. Can I pick you up at three?"

"Sure," I respond. "Will you have a gun and ammo for me to use?"

"Yes, you'll use mine," Jinot says. "And this'll give you a chance to get your heart rate down," he adds with a grin.

Once he leaves, I saunter to the lake and walk into the shallows with my clothes on, just to cool off. It takes some soaking time to get my body temperature down. I thought I was in shape...

But I was wrong...

5

QUALIFYING TO CARRY

"Do you really think I'll need a gun?" I ask. "I'm a little nervous about this."

"You won't be nervous with practice, and I need you to cover my butt if we run into trouble. We need to get you out on the range and shoot. Have you ever even shot a pistol before?"

"Not with real bullets."

"What do you mean, 'not with real bullets'?"

"I shot a starter gun for track once. It was kind of loud and I think I closed my eyes."

"Oh," he says, and his body slumps, like, *You gotta be kidding me.*

"Yeah, I liked the feel of the pop that set everyone into motion; like a toy gun, only louder."

We pull into an old gravel pit with high berms and a few picnic benches in the rear. Down in front, sheets of plywood hold paper targets with human-shaped silhouettes stamped on them. Most have a dozen holes in them, and I think they'd all be dead a dozen times. Jinot parks the car and opens the trunk. He pulls out a small revolver in a holster with a belt wrapped around it. The leather is thick and decorated as if tooled for a gunslinger.

"That's cute."

"I'm glad you think so," Jinot says without further comment.

"Seriously, it looks like it came from the Wild West," I say with a smile.

Ignoring me, he says, "Next is your ammo box."

The green metal box looks like something from WWII, storing hundreds of bullets. Jinot hands it to me, but I'm not quite prepared for its weight and almost drop it. We walk to a picnic table to begin the lesson. Confidently, Jinot pulls the gun from the holster, and in the blink of an eye, he pops open the cylinder to show it is empty of bullets.

"This is a .38 caliber Smith and Wesson, common in law enforcement. It's simple, easy to use…and deadly." Pointing to the barrel, he goes on, "This is the dangerous end. Always have it pointing down and away."

"Got it. Down and away."

"First, I want to work on your grip. Use two hands—none of this Dirty Harry one-handed macho stuff. Two hands will give you stability and readiness for follow-up shots in rapid fire. You'll be timed in the qualification, so you gotta keep control, steady your aim, and squeeze the trigger in rapid succession."

"OK, keep control, steady the aim, and squeeze the trigger," I say as Jinot ushers me to a position facing the targets at the other end of the range.

"Let's just get the feel of the gun in your hands first without loading it. Put both hands around the grip, pointing downrange. Your left index finger should brace the gun as it points toward your target."

Jinot is adjusting my hands and fingers around the grip. The gun is hardened steel, but I'm surprised at its polished smoothness. Jinot's hands are solid and sure, while mine are cool and nervous. I am trying to concentrate on what he's saying, but I can't help notice how warm and nice his hands feel around mine. It's distracting.

"Cat, did you hear what I said?" interrupting the moment. "Stand with your feet hip-width apart and the gun at shoulder height."

"Roger that. Hips and shoulders."

Letting go of my hands, Jinot says, "Do you see the front sight of the barrel aligning with the target?"

"Yep, I do now."

"Good. Now smoothly squeeze the trigger."

I squeeze, but my grip is so tight, the gun trembles.

"Don't choke the gun to death. Hold the grip firmly and squeeze the trigger."

My second attempt is better.

"OK, that's what you want, firm control… Break your cylinder open and let's put some live ammo in it."

Jinot pulls out six cartridges from the ammunition box, hands them to me, and steps away. I fumble with the cold brass as I align them to the cylinder slots and load my first bullets. Turning to the target and aiming as he directed seems to take forever. I'm conscious of him standing behind me, looking over my shoulder, with seconds ticking away.

"Aim and squeeze the trigger smoothly," I hear him say. Trying to comply, I squeeze but the trigger doesn't cooperate. I grip tighter as I try to pull the trigger. "Use pressure on your index finger, Cat, and don't choke the grip."

The gun fires and I jump uncontrollably and yelp, "Holy crap!"

"Well, at least you hit the target," Jinot says safely from behind. "It could've been worse." He patiently offers more advice. "Let's try to cock the hammer back first. This time, keep your eyes open."

I pull the hammer back, aim, and put my finger on the trigger. It releases quicker than expected, startling me with the crack of its blast and the way it jumps in my hand. The target is untouched and I am thankful for a tall backstop behind it. "This might take some time to get good at," I remark.

Jinot demonstrates the prone and kneeling positions. "You'll have to hit the target at least eighty percent of the time to qualify, Cat. You have to fire from standing, kneeling, and prone positions to pass."

I like the prone position. Like lying on the beach reading a magazine, it's natural. The kneeling position, however, is awkward and unstable. Either way, my grip on the gun needs attention.

"We'll work on your hand strength and come back when we can," Jinot offers as we chuck the empty cartridges into a canvas bag and holster the revolver. At the car, Jinot pulls a grip exerciser from under his seat and holds it out to me. "Better start using this today, Rookie." I reach for it and start squeezing it with my right hand over and over again.

As we turn onto the road, I comment, "I suppose this kind of exercise won't burn many calories, though…"

6

DAWN

Clear Lake County Park is a quiet little place nestled along the east shore of a glacial lake. The rocky shoreline adds interest for canoeists and kayakers looking for a serene place to paddle around and enjoy the water. The swim area has a small sandy beach with picnic tables nearby that families can enjoy in peace without motorboats whirring about.

The lake is spring-fed, so bass and pickerel can be found here if you prefer to fish. Rick LePine, the park's ranger and part-time warden, has invited me here to show me around. It's a pleasant place to visit when I'm looking for a change. We drop the canoe in with a little electric motor to check for fishing licenses and ensure folks have their personal flotation devices in their watercraft.

Rick's been the park's ranger for three years, but a county employee for almost fifteen. Most park employees are seasonal and rarely get hired full time. Between May and October, the park is bustling with visitors and employees. After October, when the leaf peepers leave, the park quiets and is placed on the honor system. There aren't enough visitors to pay for an attendant, so visitors are asked to put their money in a box voluntarily. Most comply. But it's now the height of the season and the park is bursting with people.

Rick introduces me to two young girls who work as maintenance employees. Both live locally and are part of a government assistance program aimed at hiring at-risk youth. Celia has fire-red hair and a matching personality. I'm guessing a little hyperactive, she is talkative and lively. Dawn is her co-worker and just the opposite, quiet and keeping to the background. Dawn's long straight hair is midnight black, her eyes are dark chocolate. She's slightly overweight and timid. She looks Native American with her creamy caramel skin tone. The girls might be seventeen years of age.

They are anxious to talk with me about my job. Where did I go to school? What classes did I take? Why don't I carry a gun? They are fun to talk to, but it's Celia who keeps the conversation going. Dawn smiles quietly.

After a half hour, Rick breaks up our conversation. "Time to get back to work, ladies. The latrines aren't gonna clean themselves."

The girls frown but leave willingly. "That's our job!" replies Celia with a wave. "Want to help us, Cat?"

"Not today," I reply with a wave back.

"They're good kids," says Rick. "They *usually* do their jobs with a smile and do them well."

"What's their story?"

"Celia's mom died when she was young," he says. "Her dad has his hands full and she started hanging with the wrong crowd. The school counselor recommended her for this program. Dawn Blackwolf comes from the reservation. She just needs a job and some direction."

"You think she's related to Harry Blackwolf?" I ask.

"Harry would be her grandfather," Rick shares. "As I understand it, Harry's son, Dawn's dad, is lazy and drinks too much. Harry and he don't talk anymore."

"No kidding. That seems a shame for everyone..."

Rick encourages me to return to the park whenever I can. He thinks I could be a positive role model for the girls. But I don't know what I can do to help them. Some days, I'm not sure I'm a model of anything. But a few days later, I'm in the area picking up car kills around lunchtime. I pop into the park with my sack lunch. The girls drop by to eat their lunch with me and chat a bit. Celia talks, we laugh, and Dawn shyly smiles.

"Dawn, I think I know your grandfather," I say cautiously. "Harry?"

"You know Harry?" she asks.

"Not really, but he lives near me."

"I don't get to see him much," she says softly. Her tone is smooth and gentle. "My dad and he had an argument. So they don't talk."

"That's too bad," I say. "Do you ever want to see Harry?"

"I don't have a car, so it's hard," Dawn says. "And if my father found out, he'd be ripping mad."

"Well, if you need a ride to see Harry, I might be able to help sometime," I suggest.

And just days later, Dawn finds a ride from the park after work to visit Harry. The sun is low on the horizon when she knocks on my door, ready for me to take her home.

"How was your visit with Harry, Dawn?" I ask as we travel north.

"Wonderful," is all she says as she stares out the car window.

She doesn't want to share more, so I don't probe. I ask her about her job and if she likes it. Talking with Dawn is like playing the game of twenty questions. I can ask, but she doesn't say more than is needed to answer my question.

About forty minutes later, she directs me onto a road past a sign announcing that we are now on the tribal reservation. I've never been here and immediately notice that the small Cape Cod–style homes all look alike. Neat, gray homes with small wooden steps leading up to the front and side doors are all prefabricated and plopped into the yards.

Driveways were once gravel, but now dirt and grass have overrun the stones. Hulks of cars and rusted parts sit on the driveways or on the grass. Junk of all kinds sits inside the wood line of some homes. A tarp draped over a big engine is half off and blowing in the wind. Each yard seems to have car parts or appliances on display, in various stages of rust and neglect.

Dawn directs me into the driveway of a similar house with its own share of yard debris. Several skinny dogs of unknown parentage are circling the steps to the back door.

"Come in and meet my parents," she says, getting out of the car.

"Sure," I say, not feeling all that sure. I look around and notice there are no neighbors outside. The place looks abandoned.

"Oh, shoo," she says as she picks up a cardboard package from the stoop and kicks the dogs aside. The package is open slightly and I see *Hap...* across the top of a sheet cake and *Daw* in the bottom half.

"Did you just have a birthday, Dawn?" I ask, looking at what's left of the cake after the dogs got to it.

"Yeah, yesterday. I turned eighteen," she says without any excitement or expression.

"Well, Happy Birthday!" I say. "Why didn't you say something?"

"It's no big deal," she says with a shrug of her shoulders. She opens the door and says, "You can have some cake, if you want it."

I look to see if she's kidding but realize she is serious. "Not right now, but thanks," I say as I follow her into her home.

We walk directly into the kitchen from outside. To my right are oak cupboards in a U shape with a white stove and refrigerator breaking up the countertops. That is, if you could see the countertops. On every inch of the white Formica is a stack of dishes, or used bowls, or dirty pans spotted with food. To our left is a round oak pedestal kitchen table with four chairs. It, too, has a myriad of papers, cups, and trash covering its top. I move papers and an open milk carton over so Dawn can set her half-eaten birthday cake down.

Until now, I hadn't realized a television is on in another room. There is no greeting of anyone in the house. The trash is full and stinking of something bad. Dawn moves around the kitchen without acknowledging or apologizing for the mess. She suggests I follow her. "Come this way."

We walk down a short hallway from linoleum kitchen floors onto hardwood with no rugs to protect them. We pass a stairway on our right. I pause in disbelief that an open Pennzoil jug is sitting on the oak treads seeping oil from one stair to another unchecked. I look up the stairway walls to see holes the size of fists every five feet or so marking a trail up to the bedrooms.

"My brother got drunk one night," Dawn says when she notices me looking at the walls.

"I see."

We continue toward the sound of the television in the living room. Across from us sits a woman in a printed housedress. She's interested in her game show and smiles when the audience laughs. A man is sitting quietly to our right in his recliner with an open beer beside him.

"Momma, Daddy, this is Cat," Dawn interrupts. "She gave me a ride home."

Momma gives me a nod before returning her attention to her show. Daddy takes his beer and raises it in my direction, then looks at me with the Blackwolf eyes before saying, "I'm hungry. When's supper gonna be ready?"

"Do you wanna eat with us?" Dawn asks with her dark eyes zeroing in on me.

I feel like running out of the house, never to return. But I look at Dawn. Thinking I don't want to abandon her, even if it is in her own home, I reply, "Why not?"

When Dawn smiles her timid smile, I see relief, maybe gratitude, but a hint of happiness.

We return to the kitchen and its mess. "I can clean up a few dishes while you're cooking," I say.

"OK," she replies as she opens the refrigerator door, and I see venison chops in a bowl. She removes a pan from the stovetop and hands it to me. "I'll need this cleaned first."

"Right," I say, taking it from her and heading for the sink full of dirty dishes. While I fill the sink with soap and water, Dawn chops an onion. I start washing while she puts potatoes on to boil and starts frying up the onion before adding the venison chops. She turns on the oven to keep the venison warm while she makes a thick gravy. In another pan she fries a thick patty of dough. I'm able to clear away a lot of dirty dishware by the time she calls her parents to the table. We have venison in gravy, mashed potatoes, thick slices of fried bread, and water for dinner. Oh yeah, there's dog-chewed birthday cake for dessert.

A younger version of Dawn's dad walks in the back door just as we are seated. He hands Dawn a small brown paper bag as he says, "Sorry I forgot your birthday yesterday."

Dawn opens the package and pulls out a ten-ounce bottle of perfume from the kids' section of a grocery store.

"Thanks, Tad," Dawn says, without any appearance of affection. "This is my friend, Cat."

"Hi, Cat," Tad says, more interested in the food on the table than me. He's a big young man who towers over us at the table. He could be nice-looking, but he needs a haircut and a shower.

"Nice to meet you, Tad," I reply. "It's nice of you to get Dawn a birthday present."

Tad grunts and gets an ottoman from the other room to sit on while we eat. There is no orange of a fruit, or green of a salad, or vegetables at the table. Our food is bland in color and nutrients. I notice the kitchen is without color as well. No curtains, no pretty bowls, just neutral colors of the government-issued house.

There is no conversation among the family members, I realize. No asking what was done during their day, who did what, who did they see, or if there was something to share. There's no laughter or even a smile of acknowledgment between them. I'm not sure how to break the silence. It's awkward, but I can't think of one topic of conversation to bring up, and I'm usually not at a loss for words. The only sounds come from utensils scraping plates or slurps of drinking water from newly clean glasses. With such a focus on the food in front of us, we are done within minutes.

I help Dawn clear the plates from the table, and she reminds us that there's still a little cake that the dogs haven't touched. Mom, dad, and Tad all ask for a piece. While Dawn serves them their cake, I wash the dishes we've just used and politely decline a piece of the cake celebrating her eighteenth birthday.

Once done, the family gets up and moves to the living room without clearing their dessert plates from the table. "It was nice to meet you all," I say. "But I need to get home. Thank you for having me."

Mrs. Blackwolf turns and says, "Goodbye." She even smiles a shy smile.

Dawn gives me a hug before I open the door and let myself out. "Thank you for staying and helping me with dinner," she says.

"I appreciate the offer, Dawn," I reply. "Happy belated birthday."

She smiles her smile. I turn from her and walk to my car, ready to leave this place. Scrawny dogs are still pacing around the house as I turn my headlights on and quietly back out of the yard. The visit has left me sad. I saw no joy or respect for the significance of Dawn's birthday, no pride in their home or a healthy meal for the family. How do kids break out of a cycle they grow up in? I may not see Dawn, now that she and Celia are returning to school next week. This will be their senior year. Will they apply to go to college? Or will the lack of family encouragement settle their direction? Especially, will Dawn stay on the reservation, mired in the life I just witnessed?

"Hi, Mom, how's it going?" I ask in my *almost* weekly call to DC.

"Oh, Cat, it's so good to hear from you!" she says cheerfully. "How's the new job going?" she probes.

"Great. I'm learning a lot," I say stoically. "How's life in DC?"

"Well…you know, I didn't *realize* how many people would be on the roads, no matter what time of day!" she offers. "Your dad goes in to the office at five in the morning and still runs into more traffic than he did in the Northeast."

"Is Dad around?" I ask.

"I'm sorry, Cat. He's been working a case, somewhere on the Chesapeake," she says. "I don't know what's going on, but we wives *know it's big*," she says.

"OK. Well, tell him I'm fine and that I'll try to contact him on my next time off," I say, feeling dejected. There's so much I want to ask him about the job, gun handling, meeting people with different backgrounds. This is all so new to me. But mom wouldn't understand and will just worry. "I love you both," I say just before hanging up.

7

LABOR DAY

It's Labor Day weekend. Wardens from the surrounding territories have joined up to blanket Eagle Lake this Saturday. Concerned about boaters being unsafe, we operate three government boats in the open with each warden in uniform, which screams LAW ENFORCEMENT. Everyone is warned. Operators under the influence are a major concern on this popular lake, so perhaps with our presence, the public will be extra cautious about their behavior. At least, that's the idea.

"Last year," Basil tells us, "we had a boat miss the Narrows and run aground, almost taking the deck off a camp. The driver was thrown backward out of the boat with it still running." He shakes his head and rolls his eyes upwards. "And that happened at noon."

A small island in the middle of the lake is a good spot from which to watch much of the activity. It has a fire pit, a picnic table, and an outhouse. We spend the afternoon choosing which boats to approach, checking for life jackets and open alcohol containers, and making sure fishermen have licenses. Most are happy and having a good time. They don't mind our small interruption. The others are what make our jobs *work*. They aren't pleasant, maybe even snotty, but we grin and go on.

With a break at five that evening, Jinot and Basil fry up bass fillets. Rick LePine opens his ice chest to make up a simple salad. I pull out two store-bought pies.

"You don't even bake?" Punk Lutkins asks. He looks at me with a question mark on his face. The others pause for a noticeable second. Punk is a warden from the county north of us. He's a small man with dirty-blond hair and beady, red-rimmed eyes.

"I see you don't bake, either," I reply as I point to his contribution of paper plates and utensils.

"That's for sure," Basil says.

A quick roundup of trash into a bag and plates into the fire, and we are ready to go back to work. Based on the amount of pie left, everyone is working on a sugar high.

I've been teamed up with Punk today, while Jinot works with Basil. Rick is working alone for a few hours before heading back to the park. The chief wants me to get experience working with other wardens. The life jacket Punk hands me is a men's XL. I have trouble getting it snug, and it's made for a person at least six feet tall. As I sit in the boat, it holds my chin up like a cervical spine immobilizer. Punk is not the kind of guy I share my concerns with. We barely talk. I certainly don't tell him to slow down as we flail across the waves. I bounce continuously and think to myself, *I wish my* boobs *were immobilized.* They are bouncing with each *whap* of a wave. I keep that to myself, as well.

We stop a family to check for life jackets and boat registration. Punk puffs up his chest as he identifies himself. "Game Warden! Checking for life jackets. Hold 'em up for me."

There's no informal conversation, no "please" or "thank you." The family looks at Punk, then at me. "How's everyone today?" I ask. I can't help but try to make the stop at least a little friendly.

"Good. It's a great day to be out," the driver of the boat replies.

"Yes, it is," I say. *Except I'm stuck with this prick.* And smile.

In the setting sun, water-skiers are pulled by powerful boats, young kids in large tubes are dragged screaming through the waves, and kayakers quietly skim the shores with their double paddles. Numerous stops later, we reconvene back on the island. A few citations have been handed out for various offenses, but luckily, no one has been operating under the influence.

The fireworks crew has been setting up on a large flat raft all day. Preparations seem in order, promising the best display ever. As dusk turns to dark, boaters find their spots in the middle of the lake in anticipation of great end-of-summer entertainment.

"Remember two years ago when the fireworks went off ahead of schedule?" Jinot looks toward Basil as he shakes his head remembering. Jinot continues with his story. "The crews had set up all afternoon and were waiting for darkness when one of the crew members lost his balance off the side of the raft. The other guys had been drinking too much and tried to help him up. They weren't thinking too clearly by standing up and pulling him by his arms. His belly was rubbing on the rough boards of the raft. He recoiled and pulled two fellas in right over his head. A boater thought he'd help, bumped the raft so hard it overturned a flare and a bunch of fireworks, setting 'em off in all directions. Everyone ducked, but a bow-rider caught fire and the guy and his wife jumped into the water as their boat turned into a torch. It was pandemonium at its best. But thank heaven no one was hurt." Jinot and Basil chuckle as they recall the scene.

Through my binoculars while listening, I can see kids dressed in pajamas and wrapped in blankets. Teenagers are laughing and loud in their parents' boats. They are carefree and clueless that their voices carry so well across the lake.

"What happened, then?" I ask.

"We rescued the fireworks guys, made 'em sit down and tell us how to light the fireworks that were left. It was a blast." Jinot high-fives Basil as they grin at one another.

"What about the husband and wife?"

"Another boat rescued them, put their boat fire out, and left it on its anchor to smolder overnight."

We stand and watch quietly during the fireworks display. Oohs and ahs fill the air with each colorful rocket. Bursting flares light up the lake above the flotilla. The exhibit lasts about thirty minutes, and the finale is filled with pops and sparkles of all colors. Cheers and applause conclude the event as engines start up and running lights are turned on for the ride home.

We hold our breath, watching the various shapes and sizes of boats leave. Even without streetlights and directional arrows, the boaters find a way to head for their camps without running into each other. Slow and steady, they point their bows to shore.

Dispersed and safe, the lake turns quiet and dark again. Our work is done. Punk reaches in the hold under the seat of one boat and pulls out a six-pack. "One for the road, guys." As he passes a can to each member of our group, no one seems to hesitate. I take the can he offers. "It's one beer, Rookie. Ain't gonna hurt you."

"No problem, Punk. Cheers," I say as I lift up the can to the others. We wind down as we drink our beer. Basil suggests we all get together in two weeks to work deer poachers. Punk suggests we work his area, to the lake's north side where the serious violators live.

Jinot and Basil are the first to pull away from the dock. Punk and I take a look around to make sure our cooking fire is out and all is cleaned up before heading to our boat. I throw my oversized PFD into the bow. Punk sits behind the wheel and starts the engine as I untie the rope from the dock cleats. I have my hands on the bow with my feet on the dock. As I push off the boat's bow and wrap one leg over the gunwale, the motor engages, the boat jerks in reverse, and I'm pulled into the lake.

Plunging deep, I find no bottom to place my feet. My eyes are open, but all I see is darkness. Deep blues and shades of black. I cannot breathe. I turn, looking for something to grab onto. My long hair floats and my uniform swirls around me, fanning in slow motion. My boots become weights. I kick and flounder. But still I can't breathe. My arms flow around me reaching, but not finding…anything. Anything solid. There's a faint swirling sound. It's me and I'm releasing precious air.

The chill of the water seeps through my clothes. My khakis tighten around my legs. The fabric works against me. The weight of the water brings me further down. Down from the air I long to breathe.

Bubbles escape from my mouth and I follow them up. Up to where? I see no stars, no light, just murkiness…vast murkiness. *What have I done? Is this what drowning feels like?* My lungs burn. *Don't breathe…don't you dare breathe.*

I flail. I kick. *Be smart.* I reach up with my arms and pull at the water. My fingers cup above my head. Darkness continues as I look upward. Again, I reach and pull. I feel the smooth bottom of the boat. It's on top of me, but I feel my way to one side and welcome its contour. My lungs are screaming. I push away from the boat and pop to the surface gasping.

The boat hovers above, rolling on the waves. I place my hand on the hull, keeping it from floating over me. I continue to gasp and sputter, pulling in as much air as possible, collecting my thoughts. A hand reaches over the side.

Punk looks down on me as he offers his hand. The boat is to my left, the dock is on my right, about ten feet away. "Well, well, Rookie. You didn't say you wanted to take a swim."

"What the heck?" I say, stunned. "You put the boat in gear before I'm on board?"

"You gotta be quick, Rookie. It's about being prepared," he says with a smirk.

"I'll keep that in mind," I growl before kicking my feet hard, elevating myself just enough to grab his arm and shoulder, pulling him over my head and into the water behind me. I swim away from him to the rear of the boat and pull myself back in. Waterlogged and shaken, I think, *What the heck is Punk thinking?* I reach for my gear bag, making sure the knife is still there while I catch my breath. *Better grab my towel instead of the knife.* I stand above Punk as he treads water, eyeing me with surprise and disdain.

"Now I gotta clean my gun," he sputters as he pulls himself out of the water.

"That's what you get for carrying a weapon," I say, watching him and keeping my distance. "Listen, you little twit, you gonna try anything else, or are we good?"

"How was I to know you can't take a joke?" he says without conceding.

We ride back to the dock sopping wet, trailer the boat, and head home in silence. Thank God it's dark and no one sees how dysfunctional we are. Anger wells up inside me on the drive back. I don't like Punk, and worse yet, now I don't trust him; not a good feeling when I may be partnered with him again in the future. At least he knows I'm not a pushover. He's been around for years and is part of the group. I'm not sure who the others will side with if given a choice…

8

GRANDPA PITTS

Several weeks and many stops later, Jinot and I meet at the boss's house, which I realize now is his primary office. We walk into the kitchen. Basil is sitting at his command post, also known as his kitchen table, with a pad of paper in front of him, pencil in his right hand, phone in his left.

Ranger Rick saunters in to work with us again tonight. His warden uniform looks like he slept in it, wrinkled and shirttail barely tucked. Jinot and Basil tease him lightly.

Then Basil gets serious. "We'll get on to business, shall we?"

I'm in the background, wondering what specific business he's referring to.

"Tonight, we split up into two groups. Cat, you and Jinot will interview Philip Pitts at Riverside Senior Apartments. Rumor has it he is hunting out of season and selling deer meat to big-city restaurants. Could've gone on for years, but neighbors don't like him taking all their game. They've probably just gotten tired of him now."

"He's living in an *old* folks' place?" I asked.

"Senior doesn't mean *old*," Basil clarifies, defensively. "But yeah, he is a senior citizen. Ranger Rick and I will be staged out by Pitts's farm, where his boy lives. We have reason to believe the farm has a butcher shop in the barn. Jinot, you know the interviewing drill. Cat is the observer."

"Yes, sir," Jinot responds, using his military manners.

"So, you're saying Grandpa Pitts is a bad guy?" I ask.

The other wardens smirk and nod their heads.

"We'll find out tonight," Basil says. "Any questions before we head out?" Hearing none, he stands up, indicating our brief meeting is over. Jinot and I head for our cruiser.

Jinot listens and observes people. I could use those skills. I'll need to study, train, and transform into a credible law enforcement officer. I want him to be proud of my progress. I'll be studying him tonight.

It's getting dark as we head for the Riverside Senior Apartments. The night air is a chilly forty-five degrees and dropping.

"So Jinot, what's the secret to interviewing?" I ask.

"Be disarmingly charming," he responds with a slight smile.

I have to look away as I smile back, because *he's* being disarmingly charming, and I'm trying to focus on my job.

I pull down the visor and look in the mirror. I turn my head to show my innocent look. *Not believable.* I try turning the other way and nod like I'm listening and agreeing. *That looks reasonable but needs more work.*

"Seriously, can't we just be direct and call him out? Just say, 'We think you're a bad guy and we want you to admit it'?"

"I don't know that your technique would work so well, Cat," Jinot says. "Someday you should try it. But tonight, you're the observer, so observe and learn."

"I'm just saying we could end this interview quickly and be on our way. What old man is a bad guy? He's probably crippled up with arthritis and barely moves."

Most lights are on at the old folks' apartment house as we drive in. We find P. Pitts on the name plate of Apt. 301 and press the call button. A scratchy voice soon asks, "Who's there?"

"Jinot Rideau, Warden Service, here to see Philip Pitts."

"Yeah, we've been expecting you," says the scratchy voice. "Come on up."

"See, Jinot, they've been expecting us," I say. "What bad guy is gonna invite us up to his apartment? And did you hear that voice? He sounds like he's about to die."

Jinot looks at me, squints his eyes, and points to the elevator.

We make our way up to the apartment only to find the door open and a young family hanging out with a much older couple. Jinot knocks on the door frame and waits for the family to acknowledge him. He introduces himself and me as I'm observing Grandma and Grandpa entertaining the grandson, his wife, and their toddler. *Awww…*

Jinot glides into the room with quiet confidence and the relaxed demeanor of a casual visitor. Jinot says in a friendly but disciplined tone,

"You have a nice place here, Mr. Pitts. Thank you for allowing us to talk with you." He looks around the room, smiles at the family, then focuses on Grandpa.

Jinot, in his charming manner, asks Big P. if he's been fishing with his grandson and the toddler yet. "Well, even at this age, I can tell this little guy will be a good outdoorsman when he gets older," Jinot offers.

I'm thinking, *I didn't know Jinot was up to date on child development.*

The parents are smiling and Grandpa is beaming at the little boy romping between his parents and his great-granddad. Everyone is happy with this gentle conversation.

"It's nice your family is here, but we have some questions for you."

Big P. Pitts sits back in his comfortable grandpa chair and says, "No problem, warden. I have nothing to hide from my family."

I'm thinking to myself, *Of course not; he's Grandpa!* But I'm only sitting on the edge of my chair, observing.

"I don't want to intrude any more than necessary on your family time, Mr. Pitts," Jinot says. "We are investigating some complaints that you have shot deer beyond your limit and that many were shot out of season. Now, Mr. Pitts, I know these allegations may come as a surprise to you, but I do have to investigate—you understand." Jinot continues to watch Big P. with a compassionate and understanding look.

I've got to master that look. It's a good look that could come in handy someday.

Grandma and Big P. are both shaking their heads back and forth. Big P., looking distraught, grimaces before saying, "I don't know who would say such things about me. I'm an ol' family man that can barely get around. You can see that for yourself, can't you, warden?"

I'm thinking, *Yeah, look at those gnarly ol' feet!*

Jinot continues his compassionate look and asks, "I understand, Mr. Pitts. Does your son hunt deer with you?"

Big P. pauses. "It's been a while, I guess. My mind isn't too good either, warden. I don't really remember the last time I was out with Sonny."

Jinot smiles and says, "One last question, Mr. Pitts. Were you hunting deer in the past two weeks?"

"Warden, I've got arthritis, heart problems, and gout. I'm in no shape to be hunting. Plus, you and I both know it's not deer season." Grandpa focuses on Jinot without blinking. He's leaning forward as he speaks—well, as far as his big potbelly will allow.

Unfazed, Jinot continues, "Well, thank you for your time, Mr. Pitts. We don't want to keep you from visiting with your family here." As he gets up to leave, Jinot casually turns and asks, "Would you mind calling Sonny and letting him know we'd like to talk with him as well? It's still early and we could be there in an hour or so."

Big P. asks his grandson to make the call to his dad. We shake hands and thank them all for their time.

"That's the way life should be, Jinot. Grandparents and grandkids getting together for a nice visit. See, innocent gentle folks," I say as we walk out of the building and make our way to the cruiser.

Jinot just smiles at me and makes a call to the boss. "We're done here and making our way to the Pitts farm."

I can hear the boss on the other end: "Sonny got the call and is loading up a carcass from his barn now. Join us as soon as you can."

Jinot smiles at me and turns on the ignition. "Did you hear that?"

"Yes," I say, deflated. "He lied to us in front of his grandson. What kind of grandpa does that?"

Within the hour, we join Basil and Rick at the farm. "Sonny led us right to the burial pit to dump that last carcass. It wasn't tagged, I might add."

The open pit is about five feet wide by twenty feet long and ten feet deep. There are at least thirty deer in this open grave, in various stages of decay. Their hunting has been going on for a while, and it looks like the whole family is in on it.

I look incredulously at my partner. Dear old granddad, with his gnarly feet, is indeed a bad guy. "He was lying the whole time, Jinot. He had me believing every word."

Jinot nods. "We'll spend the night securing the pit until daylight," he says. "Tomorrow we'll see how many animals have been slaughtered by Grandpa, Sonny, and the other family members. You'll find out that bad guys come in all shapes and ages," he adds.

"Hi Mom, how's it going?"

"Cat, it's so good to hear from you!" she says, ever the cheerleader. "We're just doing great. Your dad and the other wardens finally caught those politicians hunting out on the Chesapeake. Their hunting club had a hundred geese in the freezer, and they were continuing to shoot. How are you doing, dear? How's the job going?"

"Good," I say, but I'm really not sure. "Is Dad home?"

"Actually, he's just coming in the door," she says, "Let me put him on."

"Cat, how are you doing?" he asks in the wonderfully warm voice that has always given me great comfort.

"Dad, I'm not sure I know what I'm doing," I pout. "I can't tell a good guy from a bad guy, even when they're lying right to my face."

"It takes time, Cat," he soothes. "You gotta have your antennas up and be suspicious of anyone you come across."

I think about his comment. "There's a warden who doesn't like a woman on his turf."

"So? You'll have to prove yourself, prove that you belong. Right?"

"Yeah."

"Yeah, is right. My daughter better be able to hold her own amongst those guys," he continues. "You working out?"

"Yes, sir."

"You getting ready for the warden exam?"

"Yes, sir."

"Well then, keep studying, be smart, and be a good partner, Cat. Observe and learn from your experiences."

"Yes, sir," I say again, and with that I feel pumped up and ready for another adventure in the warden world. "Thanks, Dad. I love you."

"I love you back."

9

NIGHT HUNTING

In the dusk of nightfall, Jinot backs the car off a gravel road so the trees and brush shield us from passersby. We exit the cruiser into the cool night to wait. Just as most neighbors are sitting down to their evening meal or watching the news, Jinot and I are beginning our watch. Stars seem to brighten as the sky turns from velvety blue to black. There's a fresh chill to the night air as Orion stands bright and bold above us. I love the smell of dew on the fields and the trees around us. The sound of far-off traffic yields a low background noise. Bullfrogs add a resonance of *grippets* close by. Crickets chirp all around us, seeming loud when there's nothing else to listen to.

"It is going to get chilly tonight, Jinot," I say, trying to break the silence. "Can you tell me what we're in for?"

"Good idea," Jinot says in a no-nonsense way. "Basil received a report of shots fired last night, probably by poachers. This road heads east for two miles before it T's at the lane. There's one farmhouse on that corner. There's a stream between us and the house, with an old wood bridge over the stream. Beyond it is a field road that takes the farmer up to his oak ridge. Otherwise, this road is the only way to get to the ridge, where the shots were heard around midnight."

"Got it," I reply as I ready my radio, binoculars, and flashlight. My probationary time has prepared me for some situations, but it's an ongoing process. Each day seems to bring new tests of mental and physical agility. I can dredge up the genus and species names of plants and animals around us, but differentiating the sound of a rifle from a shotgun is still foreign to me. And since they won't let me put bullets in a revolver the chief loaned me, I don't even wear it. I tried to wear the knife on my belt, like I promised, but it's uncomfortable because it digs into my backside.

Lights appear in the east moving slowly in our direction. We watch patiently, trying to identify the vehicle. It's a pickup, but that's about all we can make out at this distance. The truck takes an unexpected right turn into the field toward the oak ridge. It stops at the base of a prominent field oak and parks under the tree's huge spreading branches. The truck doors open and close but the headlights continue to illuminate the tree trunk.

"I can't hear what's going on," I whisper to Jinot.

"Neither can I. Take your radio and binoculars down the road and find a spot to hide. Let me know what you see," Jinot says.

I grab my gear and half run, half crouch down the side of the gravel road, being as quiet as I can. I stop once to listen and look for a hiding spot as I watch the truck. Voices are muffled. The doors open and close again. The truck lurches backward, turns around, and comes back to the road.

Oh crap. It's coming this way, and I can't let them see me. The stream is just ahead, so I scurry forward and jump down the embankment, half sliding until I come to rest on a ledge just above the flowing water. The bridge is next to my head. I hold onto the grassy bank, standing precariously on a small wedge of streambank, and the truck rolls to a stop on the bridge. I shrink into the wet grass to hide in the shadows of the embankment, truck tires just a few feet away.

Holding onto the tall weeds to prevent sliding into the brook, I hear two men get out of the truck and walk along the bridge.

"I don't know where those blasted hounds have gone to. You reckon they would've come back by now?"

"Yeah, and that was a big coon they missed out on," a second voice chuckles. I hear a can being opened and the gurgle of a big swig.

"You want another?" the further voice says as he follows with a belch.

I feel myself slide as the grassy bank lets go and I slip into the stream with a splash and a *kerplop!*

"What was that?" a bearded and ragged old man says, shining his flashlight into the brook. Peering down at the water, the driver has pulled out his shotgun and trained it on the figure below them.

There I am, soggy, disheveled, and standing in the brook with water up to my knees and a gun pointed at me. "Game Warden," I manage to spit out as I point my flashlight back at them.

The man with the shotgun is big and round, wearing a worn and tattered green jacket that barely covers his belly. His dark beard covers most of his face and matches the hair in his ears. His massive arms remind me of burls on a tree limb.

It takes a few seconds to register before he lifts the barrel of his shotgun away from me.

"Well whaddaya know, Bartholomew, we have a different kinda game warden here." Bartholomew drops his can in the grass.

"That's right, gentlemen," I say, keeping an eye on them as I squish up the bank.

Jinot arrives in seconds, jumps from the cruiser, and shouts at the men, "Game Warden!" His headlights and spotlight aimed at the hunters blind them. "Drop your gun."

"Whoa! Warden, no problem," Burly says from the driver's side. He places the shotgun gently on the ground in front of him and both men step back and raise their hands.

Burly's buddy still has a surprised look on his face and pouts, "We're just coon hunters."

Jinot cautiously approaches, watching them for any sign of movement. "Gentlemen, what are you up to?"

"Warden, we're just out doing some coon hunting," Burly says. "We're looking for the dogs, but they've gone off after something."

Jinot reaches for the shotgun, cracks open the barrel and walks back to the cruiser to talk with Dispatch. I ask Burly and his buddy, Bartholomew, for their hunting licenses. Burly reaches down his backside, deep into his pocket, to produce a worn wallet held together with a rubber band. He slides his hunting license out with his thick, crusty fingers.

After looking the licenses over, I tell Jinot they are valid and start to search the truck, dripping creek water as I go. The vehicle has seen better days, rusted fenders and doors barely holding together. Dirty blankets covered with dog hair lie in the truck bed. A six-pack of Bud, half empty, is on the seat next to the box of shells, but no dead animals or other items of interest are found. The boys are just out for a night of fun.

The truck registration comes back to Burly and everything seems to be in order when the hunters begin calling and whistling for the dogs, triggering faint barking off in the distance. Three hounds find their way back to the truck, tails wagging. The dogs make loops around the truck and into the ditch through the water. They pace, slurp water, circle the truck, and repeat their rounds, full of energy. The largest male jumps up, paws planted on my chest. His tongue swipes my lips and nose at the same time.

Ewww.

"That's Carl," Burly says with pride. "He's a good coon dog, that Carl."

"Carl?" I repeat, which encourages the hound to jump and lay another slurp across my face.

"Carl!" the old man shouts. "Get down, you son-of-a-bee-sting!"

"Yuck," I say as I wipe my face with the back of my hand.

"Kennel-up," Burly says to the dogs. Carl and his dog buddies jump into the bed of the truck while Jinot and I talk more with the men.

"Were you out here last night, gentlemen?" Jinot asks as he returns the unloaded shotgun to Burly along with two shells.

"Yeah, we came out. You know, gets us out of the house." Both men nod in agreement. "This big raccoon we seen is smart. We've been after him for a couple nights. Last night, we got close. We saw him take off. I fired several shots but was too late. I didn't get him."

"What time was that?" Jinot asks.

"Probably midnight or a little after," Burly says.

"Well, let's be safe out here, gentlemen," Jinot says.

"Bartholomew, I believe you dropped your beer can," I add. "If you empty it, take the can with you and put the unopened cans in the bed of the truck, I'll be happy."

"That's what we want; a happy warden," Burly says. "Right, Bartholomew?" he continues with a wink.

We say good night to the men, return to our cruiser, and head home.

"Coon hunting isn't illegal at night," Jinot confirms. He looks at me questioningly. "That was an interesting way to get the beer issue taken care of."

"Yeah, I seem to have interesting ways of working with the public," I say, looking for Jinot's reaction. Without size or brawn, I don't intimidate the people I interact with. I don't wear a weapon, which removes a whole different level of power and protection afforded other wardens. My ability to approach the public and confront offenders will depend on my ability to judge the personalities I'm dealing with, use common sense in assessing the situation, and present myself with authority…and maybe compassion.

"Unconventional, but it gets them to comply with the law," Jinot responds, "…and that's the job, Rookie."

"I'll let the sheriff's department know the shots appear to be legal from last night," I say, still dripping on the floor mat. "I'm gonna have to get another uniform. I can't seem to wear the same clothes two nights in a row."

10

THE HOUSE

Two days later, the morning is eerily warm and foggy. I can barely see a hundred yards. Mist droplets are floating in the air. They are gentle and velvety against my face as I head for my car. I'm at the office when a call comes in that a train has hit a deer.

"Come help me find it," Jinot says. "The train conductor called the sheriff's department and said he doesn't think it's dead."

We take the cruiser east of town, following the directions given. "Geez, it's foggy," Jinot says, slowing down. Car headlights can barely be seen coming toward us. Those cars without their lights on can't be seen until they're at our left front bumper. That's OK, I guess, until someone strays into the wrong lane, or you creep up on a car going a lot slower than you are.

After thirty minutes, Jinot turns north, then parks the cruiser just before we cross the railroad tracks. "They think it's to our left, maybe a half mile or so," he says.

Jinot opens the trunk, pulls out his revolver and holster, and places it on his belt without pause. I watch and reach for my light rain jacket. No pistol. The thick fog curls around us as we begin our search. Jinot takes the right side of the tracks, I take the left. Walking over the rocky bed and railroad ties deserves some attention while we also watch the ditch line. The grass and weeds have browned out with the recent drought.

Jinot has taken a couple of side trips into the ditch line to look closer. I'm ahead of him when I hear a shot. I turn and walk back fifty yards until I can see Jinot as he's reholstering his pistol and standing over a dead yearling. He says, "I tried to call you, but the air is so dense..."

"Yeah, all I heard was the shot," I say. "Sorry."

"Well, the fawn's hips and legs were mangled. It's good we found it and put it out of its misery," Jinot replies. "Help me carry it out of here."

"Sure."

Jinot picks up the front legs and I pick up the hind quarters. We carry it up to the tracks and back to the cruiser. "I know where we can get rid of it, not too far from here," he says. We put our rope around the hinges of the trunk and let the ends hang out. Once we lift the deer onto the trunk, we tie the rope's ends around its legs to hold it for the ride.

Twenty minutes later, we slow down at a driveway. "This is it," he says. The fog is still heavy, giving everything in view a silvery wash.

From the road, the house on the hill looks abandoned. I've driven by this place many times without really noticing it. Its gray shingles are stained from weather and age—that is, the ones remaining on the house. Many are missing, and others are barely hanging on. The house is square and bland and in bad need of paint. Concrete steps on the side are broken and lay tilted from years of the uneven ground freezing and thawing. As we drive up to the structure, I notice broken windows on the second floor with pigeons flying in and out. The dirt drive widens on the hill, separating the house from a barn that also lacks paint, or any other care. The once red structure lists to one side and is missing boards that might protect any animal seeking its shelter. This morning's fog and light mist give the place a ghostly appearance. The only signs of life are a few chickens in the yard and the pigeons flying out of the upstairs windows.

"Let me do the talking," Jinot says as a warning.

I seriously wonder who he'll be talking to, but hold back any comment other than, "OK."

"You are about to meet a true skunk skinner," he says as we idle to a stop. "Come help me with the yearling."

We get out of the cruiser and walk to the freshly killed deer lying on our trunk lid. We untie the knots as a side door to the house opens to reveal a frail old couple cautiously peering out from the depths of the house. Both are dressed in drab, worn clothes that hang over their hunched, bony shoulders. Both seem to recognize Jinot at the same time and slowly move out of the doorway and onto the tilted step. Their smiles show a lack of dental care but are genuine as the couple greets us.

"Jinot, what have you brought us?" the old man asks.

Jinot returns the smile. "Hello, Emma, Stanley. We've brought you fresh meat, if you can use it," he says.

I sense Jinot is being carefully polite to the couple. I think to myself, *Of course, they need meat; they look half-starved!* But I remain quiet in the background.

"Sure, sure, we can make use of a yearling," Stanley says. "Can you hang it on the line over here for us?" he asks.

I take the request as a cue to help Jinot lift the deer over to an old clothesline post and hoist it up to hang free.

Jinot takes the opportunity to introduce me, but the introduction is brief. I fall back as the couple graciously engages Jinot in family updates. Their grown children are wonderfully successful in other parts of the country, or so they tell Jinot. Emma offers to make tea, but Jinot politely declines. Emma goes into the house and returns with a jar of canned meat, handing it to Jinot.

Proud, Emma says, "Raccoon."

Stanley follows with, "We thought you might've dropped the 'coon off last week."

I listen to the conversation while watching birds flying in and out of the upstairs. I see in the window of the first floor where two old worn chairs sit near a woodstove. They were once overstuffed, but the frames of the arms are visible through the tattered fabric, along with a little of the original padding. The hand pump of the kitchen sink can be seen through another window, and I now notice the outside privy blending into the trees in the backyard. No running water or flush toilets for this couple, who appear to be in their eighties.

Jinot says, "Thank you for the meat. I can't wait to taste it. But it wasn't me who dropped off the 'coon."

Both Emma and Stanley shrug their shoulders as if it doesn't matter who blessed them with a dead animal on their doorstep. They were beholden to return a gift and not feel like a charity case. Stanley filled Jinot in on the health of the deer herd he sees near this farm and their success at putting meat in their freezer. It was clear they lived off the land and were satisfied with their means. I wondered if I would be as comfortable in these conditions.

We say our goodbyes to Emma and Stanley and back away toward the cruiser. I stay quiet until we drive onto the road. "Oh, my, God!" I blurt. "I can't believe they live like that; I didn't see a car, running water, or indoor toilets."

Jinot keeps driving and remarks, "Those two are nicer and more generous than many wealthy people I know. They are very proud, take responsibility for themselves, and won't ask for help. But when I told you he was a real skunk skinner, I meant it. Be careful if you ever get asked to dinner."

I turn up my nose. "Thanks for the warning."

11

THE BREAK-IN

My phone rings at three a.m. It's Jinot. "Wake up, Cat. We have a bear complaint up on the lake. Get ready and I'll be there in fifteen minutes to pick you up."

"Whaaat?" I say, as my brain pushes through the denseness of sleep.

"Just be ready."

As I pull myself together, I realize the benefit of having yesterday's uniform not yet put away. It makes the choice simple. My gear sits by the door, ready for these special occasions: flashlight, knife, and gun I've been loaned. Oh yeah, badge and bullets, too. But until I'm range qualified, I can't put bullets in the .38, which makes it pretty useless as a weapon. Yep, just like Barney Fife...

I slide into the cruiser with Jinot, who greets me with a brief, "Morning." I'm barely awake, but the coffee he hands me will help—a lot. Jinot has been in this business for a couple of years and always seems "together" no matter what time of day or what the occasion.

"It's still night, for God's sake," I reply. "Thanks for the coffee."

With each sip, I revive as I listen to his briefing on the bear complaint. It appears a bear came to a home and returned after being scared away the first time around midnight. Home owner Meredith Koch called her neighbor, Jack Cousineau, each time to help. He told her to call the sheriff's department after the bear came back. The dispatcher called Jinot.

"We'll be there in about twenty minutes," Jinot tells me as we speed up and turn the rotating blue lights on. The River Road follows the outlet to the lake, twisting with its shoreline, but Jinot is in complete control as we speed through the turns and try to reach the scene before harm is done to humans, property, or the bear.

"Did they teach you speed driving in warden school?" I ask.

With a half-smile, Jinot responds, "No, I learned fast driving with dirt bikes on the farm as a kid."

We reach the lake house in twenty-five minutes, finding lights on everywhere, a sheriff's car nearby, and several people huddled on the porch. Looking past the small crowd, I see a splintered and shattered door barely hanging on its hinges. We walk up to the group on the porch and see a black bear sprawled dead on the deck.

After introductions, we learn that the bear didn't stop at the door the second time around. This time, Jack didn't hesitate to shoot when he saw the bear break through the screen and splinter the door with a of couple swipes from its paw. Meredith is still shaking from the experience. Jack is running on adrenaline.

As we talk with Meredith, she is unsettled at the thought of the bear breaking into her home with her little girl inside. She tells us her story:

She thought she heard a strange sound on the porch as she wrestled herself awake. Heavy on the deck, the sound was *pud-scrape, pud-scrape.* The window was cracked open to let the cool fall air freshen the bedroom. Meredith had never worried about being on the lake without her husband. Her young daughter, Jennifer, slept in the next room, innocently trusting her mother to protect her.

Meredith listened to the noise on the porch, fully awake. Obviously, some animal had found its way onto the deck. She thought back to the precautions she had taken. Had any food been left out? Was the grill cleaned off? Meredith was OK with small critters feeding off the crumbs they might have left behind. She and Jennifer loved watching the squirrels and chipmunks come close to the house. Small creatures were entertaining, using their little paws to nibble away at the treats while balancing on their haunches. But these sounds were slow and dense, not the light quickness of her usual visitors.

The low guttural growl shocked Meredith into reality. She tossed off the covers and moved to the closest window. Seeing nothing, she left the bedroom to get a view from her great room. The sight of the black bear outside her sliding glass doors stunned her where she stood. The bear also stopped at the sight of Meredith, stood to a full six feet, and placed its paws on the glass. The window strained at the weight of the bear leaning into it, its front paws pressing and pushing, scraping and clawing.

"Get! Get out of here!" she screamed. It was a reaction one would use with a begging dog. She knew no other way.

The bear dropped down and moved away from the window toward the back door. Meredith reached for her phone and was glad to have the neighbor's number handy. As the bear knocked a garbage can over, Meredith tapped out the number with trembling fingers.

"Hello," a sleepy voice finally answered.

"Jack! A bear is here. Can you help me?"

"Meredith? You OK? A bear? Where?"

"Jack, he's outside my door. Now he's in the garbage!"

"OK, OK, I'll be right there!"

From outside her door came the unnerving sound of the bear batting the garbage can about. Then the door strained as if the bear would burst into her house at any moment. Meredith hunted for options and decided to push her heavy table against the door, just in case. She was struggling with a heavy cabinet nearby when a shotgun was fired from the property line. The thud of the bear jumping off the porch was a relief. Meredith left the cabinet and looked through the curtains to make sure the bear was gone. She moved the table away from the door and was on the porch when Jack walked to the bottom step.

"That scared him off," Jack said, his shotgun still in his hand. "That's quite a mess he made, Meredith."

"Oh, my God, Jack. Thank you for coming! He scared me half to death. I was afraid he would come right through the door."

"No problem," Jack replied. "I'm glad you called. Let's clean this up so we don't have any more visitors tonight."

By the time the garbage was cleaned up, it was nearly one a.m. "I'll take the can with me and put it in the garage for safekeeping. Garbage shouldn't be kept by your door, Meredith. It attracts bears…"

"Thanks, Jack. It's obvious to me now. I don't know what I would've done if you hadn't been here."

We all agree the bear was probably looking for more food when he returned and couldn't find the garbage can. The house probably smelled of last night's dinner and the doors were only minor deterrents. Jinot takes notes and recommends getting bear-proof containers and storing household waste away from the house.

Meanwhile, I take pictures of the scene while a little girl in pajamas watches intently. I can't help but pet the bear's jet-black fur and study its sharp claws and the width of its great paws. The little girl timidly pets the head of the bear as if it's a sleeping pet. We ask Jack to help with the bear, and we drag it up onto the trunk of the cruiser. No citations are issued. A young male black bear has lost his life for doing what comes naturally to him. But there's not much you can do when he's breaking into a house.

We drive back to town with few words. Jinot drops me off at home. "Get a couple hours of sleep, Cat," he says. "I'll pick you up at eight thirty to drive to the university to dispose of the bear. They have a freezer and biology students who will appreciate studying the carcass."

"So today I'll learn how to freeze a bear," I say. "Who would've guessed that would be a skill to learn."

The call to my parents goes—disappointingly—to voice mail: "Mom, I'm sending you a picture of my most recent work activity. Don't be afraid of the bear. I didn't have to shoot it." *But I did have to gut it...* "Please make sure Dad sees it."

12

MARSH FIRE

Drought conditions have worsened over the last month. Field grasses are yellow-brown, rustling in the wind. Leaves on the maples are looking withered and stressed. Their usual fall colors will be muted, disappointing to all who wait a year to see healthy, vibrant splashes of crimson, yellow, and orange. This year, the colors will be dull.

"The state's taking precautions with a ban on outdoor fires," my forester pal, Ida Dombrosky, tells me. "Fires could start with a spark from a cigarette. I'm putting in so much overtime patrolling camping areas, I'll be able to shop for a month."

"Yeah, but you don't like to shop," I interject. Ida and I enjoy seeing each other when our schedules permit it. But since I work mostly nights and she works days, we don't often get a chance to visit, share experiences, or, for that matter, have fun together.

Ida ignores me. "Signs are posted everywhere banning fires, but I've issued a dozen tickets to campers and homeowners, and I hate issuing tickets," she continues. "If I had wanted to issue tickets, I'd-a been a game warden same as you. I like people…and I like trees. But now I'm losing my patience over dumb decisions made by people who just don't seem to care if they set the whole North Woods on fire."

Ida and I are at Clear Lake's landing, where we share our sack lunches at a pretty spot overlooking the lake. The midday September sun is warm and intense. The water is a pretty blue, reflecting a robin's-egg-colored sky.

"Do people's brains stop working when they're on vacation?" she asks. Her size sixteen body has a size sixteen personality. Quick thinking and sassy, Ida spends a lot of time by herself in the woods building up thoughts and resting her tongue so she can barrage people like a Gatling gun when given a chance to talk.

"Yes—" was all I could wedge in before she starts up again.

"These people think they can come up here and do whatever they want in our backyard. Don't they realize one dumb move puts us all at risk? Why, one small spark can blow into a flame that takes off in the wind."

"Speaking of wind—"

"I got it, girl, this wind isn't gonna help matters. Why, we probably have that Santa Ana wind problem right here."

"I don't know about Santa Ana—"

"Santa Ana, Schmanta Anta. Whatever! These winds are a problem!" Ida's working herself into a frenzy.

From the radio in the truck, Dispatch makes an emergency announcement. "All forest firefighters and emergency personnel are to report to headquarters. A fire has been reported in Sand River Marsh. Repeat: Fire reported in Sand River Marsh. All forest firefighters…"

I join in multiple responses to Dispatch. "Three twenty-two to Dispatch. Roger emergency."

"Roger, Three twenty-two," is the reply.

"See, I don't even get to eat my lunch," Ida says as she bundles up her sandwich.

We jump into our vehicles and head south to headquarters. We are on the opposite side of the lake from the fire, so it will take us a half hour to get to headquarters, check in, and get our assignments. I take a mental inventory of items I'll need for an afternoon of firefighting. I think I'm set, except for water-can backpacks that will be issued on site, or until I'm told where to report for the fire. Dispatch acknowledges that the command post has been established a short distance from the fire and heavy equipment is on its way. I have never been on a forest fire, but "heavy equipment" doesn't sound like a backyard barbeque. Ida is following a short distance behind me in her truck.

Headquarters is bustling with equipment being loaded and personnel being assigned. Several forest service folks, dressed in green, are attaching a big bucket to the belly of the Huey. Basil is easy to spot in his snug gray uniform, his dark hair combed back into ducktails. Several other wardens are listening to him as he points to the map on the wall. Assignments include traffic control on roads surrounding the fire.

"Cat, grab two backpacks of water and put them in my cruiser. You'll ride with me to the fire's starting point and get pictures of the scene."

"Got it, Chief," I respond as I grab my gear along with the backpacks and put them all in his cruiser. I check the camera and ensure we have extra batteries. Within minutes, we're heading west to where the fire started.

Sand River landscape is 2,500 acres of peat moss and a few lonely tamarack or black spruce trees breaking up the landscape. Red maple and balsam fir outline the marsh with only a few inches of topography differentiating the wetland from where those trees can survive.

"Normal years, this low area would have standing water," Basil says as we look out over the marsh. "I've canoed down the river running through it in a *normal* year."

Minutes later, "Look at this, they've got dozers driving right through the marsh!" Basil says. We watch one bulldozer churning up the marsh grass to expose as much dirt as possible. "This fire line they're dozing will place a natural break between burning grasses and the edge of the tree line. The idea is to prevent the fire from moving beyond the marsh and control the burn in short grasses rather than letting it reach treetops where the wind can blow it out of control."

A tanker truck is pulling up behind us as we watch the fire line being built. The driver leans out and hollers to us, "I can use a man up on the nozzle, Basil."

"Cat can help ya," is the response. "It's her first fire, Dan, so let her know what you need."

Basil turns to me. "See that water gun on top of the tank? You'll water down the fire line from the truck as Dan drives behind the dozer. Take your water pack and radio. Once the other volunteers show up, I'll come back for you."

I jump out of the cruiser and ask Dan, "Where do you want me?"

"Climb up top and get on that nozzle gun. We need to douse any flames and wet down any flammable debris in the fire lane in case the fire edges up here."

After climbing on top of the tanker, I tie my water can to the truck, and taking hold of the gun, holler to Dan, "All set!"

Dan shouts a warning: "Hang on tight and brace your feet! It's gonna be a roly-poly ride!"

The truck edges into the fire break and I spray water in the lane, wetting down anything that might burn. The truck lurches and sways even though we're moving at a snail's pace. Dirt and churned grass blow onto the truck and into my face. It is hot with the sun beating on me as we creep along this newly made path. I am now inhaling the smell of smoke along with rising dust. Plumes of dark-gray smoke rise above the tree line. Darker gray billows indicate another pine has caught fire. I keep one eye on the smoke, the other on the constant stream of water I spray along this perimeter. After several hours, I'm parched. I place my hand in the stream of water and rub my wet hand on my face. It's somewhat refreshing but dries quickly. Stale water from the tanker truck quenches my thirst even though it tastes metallic.

"How ya doin' up there, Cat?" Dan calls up from the cab.

"Good!" I manage to say with sediment coating my tongue.

"We gotta make this next bend before we stop. Can you do that?"

I look at the distance and have no idea how long the water will last. "We'll try."

As we round the bend, the river flows close to the tree line. We stop and I climb down, anxious to stretch my legs, massage my backside, and see what happens next. Dan pulls a hose from a roll attached to the tank. The hose is long enough to reach the river. A metal strainer covers the end of the hose and will act as a filter for debris, bacteria, *or whatever else* might be sucked in from the stream. Dan plops the filtered end into a deep pool of the river and starts pumping water back into the truck, replenishing our supply. I'm thinking, *I don't even want to know what I drank or splashed across my face right now.*

The pump chugs in the background while Dan fills me in on our location and next target. "We're here," Dan says as he points to his map. "We're about halfway through this fire line ending at this old lane. By the time we get there, it'll be close to sunset and we'll meet up with the other crews. Wind typically dies down close to sunset, but the weather report says the wind will creep up after dark. We don't want to get caught out here after dark..."

Who am I to disagree? Dan is confident and reassuring.

Also, I don't have a choice.

I wash my hands and face and take a drink from Dan's water jug before climbing back on the truck and into position holding the water gun.

"I'm ready when you are," I holler to Dan and brace myself for another rough ride.

We reach the old lane just as the sun is setting. The other crews have arrived, and we all head for the command unit, which is set up on Turkey

Ridge, a safe distance from the marsh and with a view over the valley. This time, I get to ride in the cab.

Sandwiches, water, and coffee have been delivered for the crews. We swap a few stories as we gulp down our food and drinks. The commander joins us with his update on the situation and our next assignments.

"At this point, the fire remains contained in the marsh," Commander Klau announces. "You all did a great job surrounding the marsh with fire breaks. It's calm now. Unfortunately, Mother Nature is going to challenge us…"

Reinforcements have joined the fight, including local fire departments with their equipment. Crews are being assigned to areas surrounding the fire with the mission to protect homes and outbuildings overnight. Winds are going to be blowing at ten to fifteen miles per hour with gusts to twenty-five. Half the crew from the afternoon is sent home to get rest for the next ten hours but are reminded they are still on call if needed.

I am not so lucky. My name shows up with the Porter Fire Department, consisting of one pumper truck and four older men with ruddy complexions and quick smiles. We are assigned to guard the Nelson house down this road on Turkey Ridge.

"You're with us, sis," says a man I would later learn is Harvey. "The Nelsons have been called and know we're coming," he says to his crew, which now includes me. "Grab another sandwich for later. It's gonna be a long night."

Once in the Nelson yard, we introduce ourselves to Claire and Hank Nelson, fifty-somethings with a nice home overlooking Sand River Marsh. From this ridge, we can smell the smoke even though we can't see it. A westerly breeze is light. With it blowing in its current direction, the house should be safe. If the winds shift, however, we'll be called into action quickly. We get to know one another while we wait and watch. Harvey and his crew are a jovial bunch, joking and teasing in a friendly way. It is easy to see that they know and like each other.

"We depend on one another," says Harvey. "We trust that each of us knows our assignment and will cover a fellow crew member if need be."

Darkness deepens and envelops us quickly. The air cools to the point where I need a firefighter jacket on. Its florescent colors make me visible from 500 yards while we stand shoulder to shoulder watching in the direction of the marsh. Sharp gusts of wind exhale at midnight. Wisps of clouds blow across the light of the moon as we brace for the smoldering coals to breathe back to life.

By one a.m., a reddish glow blossoms in the valley. Our eyes are fixed on it as we stand by and watch it grow. Command confirms the danger over our radios.

"Winds have reignited our marsh fire, people. Emergency crews, evacuate all residents between Sand River and Marsh Roads. Repeat: Evacuate all residents between Sand River and Marsh Roads."

"We're *currently* out of harm's way," says Harvey. "We don't have to evacuate, but winds are known to change course and vigilance is essential."

About two in the morning, winds blow sparks into the tops of a patch of pine trees directly across from us on the opposite ridge. Within minutes, the fire grows and rushes red and rough through the treetops carried by wind as if this firestorm will never stop.

Burning branches sizzle and crack, and burning treetops fall as we watch the yellow flames merge with oranges and reds, their colors rolling fluidly through the trees against the backdrop of a dark night sky. The beauty of the fire belies the devastation. Contradictions of smells, with the nutty scent of pine and wood smoke, are masked by the sootiness of death. We are momentarily safe on our ridge but are watching a natural disaster that can't be stopped. We're in awe of Mother Nature and feel helpless for now.

The fire burns large and long while it has a pine forest to fuel its progress. But as it flows into the marsh again, it drops, hiding from the winds, and slows. By daylight, the fire hasn't hit the southbound cross-over road. We are tired but determined to stop the fire's progress.

"Fire breaks will start from the crossover road around the low-level marsh area," says the commander in our early morning brief-ing. I see Ida standing with another group looking equally dirty and tired. "Containing the fire in low areas so it can't reach the treetops is key, people," Commander Klau is reminding this group. "Focus on cut-ting through with fire breaks around the higher terrain. Then we'll begin building back-fires to burn any combustible material. We expect winds to pick up again tonight... Don't let it cross our lines!"

Our fresh replacements are listening to the orders and eager to get started on the lines. Those of us who had manned the night vigilance are running on caffeine and sugary donuts. Basil finds me with the Porter crew and rescues me from another shift on the fire.

"You've done enough here, Cat," Basil says as I return the jacket and a smile to the crew. "Did she learn anything about fires, boys?" he asks.

"She did well, Basil," Harvey replies. "She can work on our fire crew anytime."

Basil nods and walks away with a slight wave, while I follow, hoping to get a shower and a few hours of sleep before returning.

"You smell like a well-used woodstove, Cat," Basil says as we get into his cruiser. He, on the other hand, is clean, with not a hair out of place, and appears rested. I lower myself into the warm seat, smile, and close my eyes for the ride home.

"I can even smell myself," I reply, but I'm too tired to care. "I might have to air out my clothes on the porch for a week." I'm not sure if I say or just think it. *Most of all, I'm looking forward to a hot shower and my nice comfortable bed.*

Basil wakes me up and drops me off at my cabin. I try to wave, but my arm is too tired. I slowly climb my porch steps and reach for my door, then decide to unbutton and drop my uniform right there on the porch before proceeding to the shower in my underwear. Tons of soap, shampoo, and hot water feel heavenly before flopping into bed.

I don't even hear the train come back from the mills.

In the next few days, fire breaks are completed and the winds stay down. Forest fire crews from away have arrived, relieving the emergency crews from fire duty until the rains come and tame the last flame. Ida tells me fire can smolder in the peat underground until winter snows smother the last spark. She also tells me that teenagers had started a campfire, but never checked that the coals were out before leaving it. Thank heaven, an inch of rain is forecast for later in the week.

13

BLACK BEAR

Bessie's knocking on my door and it's not even six thirty. "Cat! Cat! Wake up, dear! It's Bessie."

"Bessie? Hold on, I'm coming," I say, trying to clear the cobwebs from my mind. I climb from my nice warm bed and plod to the front door. "What's going on?"

"Sorry to wake you, Cat, but I need your help this morning," she says, in somewhat of a dither. "That pesky bear's been back, and he got into our trash barrels last night. It's a mess!" Bessie extends a cup of coffee to me. "I thought you might need this."

"Thanks," I say reaching for the cup. "I didn't hear anything…"

"Well, *you* can sleep through a freight train roaring about. That bear kept me awake since three this morning! It either got its fill or got tired about five o'clock, thank goodness. Anyway, we gotta clean up the place or we'll have all sorts of critters in that trash before he comes back tonight."

"OK. I'll get dressed and be right there." I don't bother to tell Bessie that I didn't get home from work till midnight last night.

"Good. I'll have another coffee for you when you show."

It's the end of September, and a slight chill is in the air. As I walk toward the shed, I notice that the trees are starting to turn colors. There's Bessie, pointing to the shed door, torn off two of the hinges and barely hanging on the third. Two big steel barrels used as trash cans are dented and turned over. Trash is strewn all over the shed floor and outside in a radius of at least fifty feet.

"I don't see one ounce of food scraps left behind," I say, as I assess the damage.

"Me either. It looks like he even licked the wrappers clean," she adds. "He was hungry!"

"Once we clean up here, I'll call the biologist and see if we can set a trap for our unwelcome visitor," I offer.

"He's only unwelcome when he does stuff like this."

"I don't like the fact that he's bold and hungry enough to do this," I say, "but we're also close to town. At best, he's a nuisance to us, but he could get dangerous to others."

Later, Bessie and I watch the local wildlife biologist, Gus, set a big live trap made from two barrels welded together, with steel doors on each end. Gus baits the trap with enough pastries, bacon fat, and honey to feed a bear for a night. "He found a good spot last night, ladies. I'm sure he'll be back for more," he says as he works on the trap.

Gus is a nice man in his early thirties, totally committed to studying wildlife. Totally. No small talk. No wife or family in the area. "*Ursus americanus*," he says, "eastern black bear. Which is a different subspecies from the Olympic black bear, the California black bear, or the New Mexico black bear. No matter, we'll get him. They're omnivores and opportunists, meaning they'll eat anything."

Gus sets the trap and provides a word of caution: "Let's just hope he's a small one."

"Why is that, Gus?"

"If he's too big, he won't fit in the trap, then he'll get mad when he can't get the bait. You don't want a big mad bear around."

Bessie and I look at each other nervously.

That night, Bessie and I keep each other company on her porch with a bottle of wine and a flashlight. By midnight, the wine is gone and there's no action, so we decide to say good night and good trapping—of a *small* bear.

Bessie is at my door the next morning banging away again. "Cat, we got him!" she hollers. "Ya gotta come see him!"

"I'm comin'!"

"How can you sleep through that bawling?"

"I thought it was a dream, Bessie, for God's sake! And I hope you have coffee," I say, as I make my way to the door. The smell of java helps my eyes to open. "What time is it, anyway?" I accept the cup without hesitation.

"Five. Let's call Gus. He'll want to be here. And, quite frankly, I don't know what to do with a bear in a barrel!" she laughs.

The bear is moving around in the trap and bawling like a baby. Coarse black hair sticks out as he brushes up against the air holes of the drum.

"Oh, my God, Bessie, we got a bear!"

Gus drives in the yard within the hour. "I was waiting for your call," he says. "I knew we were gonna catch him." From the passenger side of his truck comes a gangly young lad, dressed like Gus but thirty pounds lighter and at least ten years younger. "This here is Tyler, my intern. He's gonna help me get some measurements on this-here bruin."

"Nice to meet you, Tyler," Bessie and I say. Tyler shyly waves hello back at us.

The bear is agitated, crying like a baby, and then snarling like the caged animal it is.

"I'm gonna tranquilize the bear first," Gus announces as he pulls a huge syringe from his truck box and fills it with some liquid from a bottle. "This-here sleep serum will calm him down," he adds while jabbing the needle into the bear's backside through one of the holes in the barrel. "Nap time."

It's about twenty minutes before the bear appears sedated. Bessie provides coffee for each of us.

"Tyler, reach in there and put this rope around whichever end you can," Gus directs. "We'll pull him out from here."

"Yes, sir," Tyler says before he dutifully crawls in with the sleeping bear, attaches the rope, and backs out. He emerges covered in honey, bacon grease, and bear pee. "Phew! He stinks!"

Bessie and I exchange a glance. Tyler doesn't realize that he's picked up the same odor he's complaining about. "It's good you can fit into the barrel, Tyler," I say as he spreads a canvas tarp in front of the trap.

"That was part of Tyler's job description," Gus says. "Must be skinny enough to fit in a barrel. Say, can I get you ladies to help pull on this-here rope with us?" All four of us get a good grip on the rope, and Gus shouts, "Pull!" In a couple of yanks, the steel drum gives birth to the sleeping male bear. "He's a young one, thank heaven. We can easily move him." With that, the bear is pulled further onto the canvas, and Gus adds, "I'm guessing he's last year's cub and Momma has kicked him out of the house."

Tyler grabs a tripod and a backpack of equipment from the truck. Gus instructs him on how to set up the tripod so a scale can be attached just above the bear. Grommets in the canvas conveniently hook onto the scale as the bear is winched off the ground. "A hundred and eighty-two pounds," Gus says. "Let's count the teeth next, Tyler."

We watch Tyler stick his fingers in the bear's mouth without hesitation. I'm watching the bear's big black paws, including its two-inch claws. I feel the bear's fur, thick and coarse like a horse's mane, as I pet the sleeping beast. It's jet-black, but the fur reflects light as though shiny blue threads are interwoven. Gus straddles the bear, taking a vial of blood from its front shoulder. Next, he places a tracking collar around the bear's neck, giving it a number, and the measurements are attached, too. Gus's movements are efficient, so there's time to get the bear back into the barrel before it wakes.

"OK, Tyler," Gus says. "All the measurements are done. Let's put Sleeping Beauty back in the trap."

Tyler threads the barrel in the opposite direction where the back of the trap is now open. We all grab a part of the rope and pull the bear back into the barrel. Tyler brings more food and places it in the trap before the doors close. A winch on Gus's truck pulls the bear-filled trap onto the truck bed. They secure it with chains so it doesn't bounce or roll around on the way to its destination.

"Where you going with him, Gus?" Bessie asks.

"Top of the lake where there's plenty of food and space for him," Gus responds. "Thank you for helping us, ladies," Gus says as he and Tyler wave goodbye.

I look at Bessie. "It's not even eight a.m. yet, and we've done trapped ourselves a bear, loaded him up, and gotten rid of him." I put my arm around her shoulders.

"I'm ready for breakfast, Cat. How about some more coffee?"

"I'm always ready for more coffee, Bessie, but this morning I feel like I've really earned it. Just let me wipe off the bacon grease first."

14

BEAR SEASON

Days later, I've turned down a little-used road on paper company land, alders scratching the dirt off my car. There's a break in the bush where I stop. My goal is to find bear bait sites. Bear hunters use bait to lure black bears to a spot that has a blind or a tree stand nearby. This affords the hunter a good view and the ability to shoot their target cleanly, whether with bow and arrow or gun. Baiting can also be a nasty business when a rival guide or anti-hunting fanatic dumps gasoline into another's bucket of bait. Some baits are simply a family's garbage thrown into the woods. Bags broken and strewn about with the rest of the garbage ruins my day. I do my best to find an envelope or address that names the owner, but I often come up empty-handed, which frustrates me even more.

I follow a foot trail past the alders and into the shade of the young forest. The moist ground is pocked with fresh boot prints, assuring me that I'm headed in the right direction. The thin canopy of beech is still dark green. Massive oaks reign first in gathering the day's light, standing tall and gnarly along the trail. Their roots have grown in a similar fashion to fan out in the soil below. Anchoring the trees into adulthood, the winds over time have blown them this way and that, pruning the roots as they stretched across any rocks, only to grow twice as thick, ensuring that the mighty trees will withstand the next storm. Beech nuts and the oaks' acorns are prime food for deer, squirrels, and bears.

I watch the canopy as well as the trail, looking for signs of man and bear. There's a snag of a pine off to my right with its bark rubbed off. A smaller game trail is nearby. An old thick log is torn apart about a hundred feet away—all bear sign. Looming above me is an ancient oak with a thick limb angling out over the trail. Small pieces of wood have been nailed to the tree as steps to climb the oak. Man sign.

Surprisingly, I see no bait. But the trail continues, so I follow it. Soon I hear a muffled grunt and snarl. Something is being battered about. It takes me a second to realize I hear plastic banging. The slight wind is blowing at me, which means my smell is pushed away from the sound. It gives me confidence that I can get closer. I step beyond a knoll blanketed with ferns to watch a young black bear sticking its head into a five-gallon pail. Watching her slurp the insides and turn the pail with her large paws makes me smile.

The bear's black claws catch on the handle, moving the bucket about. The pail suddenly flies free of her head and ears. Intent on slurping more, the bear playfully jumps at the pail and sticks her head inside it once more. She has no clue I'm watching…yet. I look overhead and see another tree with a manmade tree stand nailed to it. If the owner has put his name on it, which is required by law, I won't know it today.

I am focused on the bear. She seems to be frolicking about with the pail as a toy, the bucket teasing her with tasty treats. The bear's big paws swipe it right, then left. She bites the pail and with little effort punctures the edges with her huge canines. Concerned that the bear is still hungry and frustrated without more food, it's time for me to back away slowly and head for the car. I've found the baiting site and will come back another time.

The rest of my day finds other bait sites, but they remain untouched by slurping bears. I see hunting platforms ready for hunters, but most have been tagged with names of local bear guides. The season opens in a few days, and the guides are hungry to open their businesses to out-of-staters. This is their time to earn the majority of their annual income, so it's a big deal to them. Most guides play by the rules because it's their livelihood. Others don't care about rules, the environment, or the wildlife, including some of their clients.

Jinot picks me up later that evening. "What did you find today, Rookie?" he asks casually.

"Lots of bait sites in that Burnt Mountain area," I report. "I watched a yearling wrestle with one of the bait pails. It was fun to watch."

"Yeah, I'm sure it was. Easy food will make the young bear a ready target. The hunting guide will visit these bait sites at least once a day to refill the pails with food, giving their clients an unfair advantage over an inexperienced bear."

"Let's just hope the hunter is a poor shot and the bear survives the season."

"You know we have an overpopulation of bears, right?"

"Who says?" I retort.

"You've had a nuisance bear around. Multiply that by a hundred and numerous beehives being ripped apart, and you've got too many bears coming into people territory."

"Why isn't it *people coming into bear territory*?"

Jinot glances sideways at me before he looks away and grins smugly.

"I do have a story you might like from two years ago, Cat."

"I need a good story."

"One of the local guides had a new young client and his dad. These clients were from the city, and this was the kid's first bear hunt. So the guide takes the kid to a tree stand that can hold both of them. The guide was able to talk to him, guide him through the hunt, and make sure the kid didn't hurt himself. The guide spends several hours with him, but no bear shows up that morning. They return that evening, same spot, but the kid says he's fine and would rather have the stand to himself. The guide agrees but watches him from a tree not far away. About an hour later, here comes a young bear, maybe two hundred pounds. The kid drops his candy bar to the ground in his excitement to get his gun ready. The bear eats the candy bar, looks up at him, sniffs the air and in three seconds shimmies up the tree coming face to toe with the kid, smelling his shoes and pants."

"Oh, my God!" I say.

"Oh, my God, is right. The kid screams! The bear drops to the ground as easily as it had climbed up. The kid drops his gun from the stand. He screams again, and the bear takes off into the woods to live another day."

"What did the guide do?"

"It happened so fast, he barely had time to holler. He had to help the kid down from the tree stand, the kid was shaking so bad. Poor kid was embarrassed; he had peed himself and never went back out."

"Holy crap, I probably would've done the same thing."

"Anyway, we don't have an alternative method to cull the bear population, according to the wildlife biologists," Jinot says. "And with the bears' sense of smell, the biologists say there isn't really any better way of getting a bear in range during hunting season. Distasteful maybe, unsporting. But that's what the biologists say...and I don't like dealing with bears in camps at night."

"Yeah, that's what Gus told me, as well," I reply with a sigh. "I certainly don't want any more nuisance bears coming around breaking into homes. I just like knowing smart bears have a chance—you know, survival of the fittest."

15

FIRST DUCK HUNT

Gus invites me to join him on opening day for my first duck hunt. He has agreed to take me along and show me how it's done, but only if I leave my badge at home.

He picks me up in what feels like the middle of the night to drive to his favorite slough. As I close my eyes in the passenger seat, he's explaining how he has scoped out this particular area because the marsh is pretty dry. The slough is good habitat for puddle ducks and geese, and they've concentrated in river backwaters and ponds that still have enough water.

"Are you awake?" he says, pushing at my shoulder.

"Hmm?" I manage to say as I ease my heavy eyelids open.

"We're here," Gus says with gusto gained from a gallon of caffeine. "Get your gear ready and put it in the boat."

"It's so friggin' early. It's not even light out yet."

"That's how duck hunting works, Cat. Hunters get their butts up in the morning and are out in their hunting spots before the birds start flying."

"I think my butt prefers a warm bed right now," I say, reluctant to leave the warm truck.

"You begged me to show you how to hunt ducks. Now, I'm pushing the boat in. You ridin' or swimmin'?"

"Yeah, yeah, I know. Like that water will feel good in October..." I say with a shiver.

"You sit in front while I take us to our hunting spot," Gus says as we shove the boat into the snuff-colored water. "It's not far from here. Shine the light ahead of us so I can see where we're going."

The electric motor isn't fast, but it's quiet and won't disturb any nearby waterfowl.

"We're heading for that hummock of tall grass straight ahead of us," Gus whispers. "Let's put out a few decoys first. They have to be in a natural-looking pattern to birds flying above." After we unfurl the lines attached to the plastic birds, we toss and plop them into the water. Gus turns the boat around and motors toward the mound of dirt flagged by an old tree snag. "We'll pull the boat around back, and if you'll tie the bow up to that ol' snag, we'll be in our spot."

Once in position, Gus stabilizes the boat and continues in a low voice, "Let's drape the netting over our gear so it will camouflage us from any waterfowl flying over."

I look at what we're wearing. Not only are we both wearing camouflage jackets, pants, and hats in various tones of green and brown, the boat almost matches us. "Aren't we camouflaged enough?" I ask.

"Nope," is the cryptic reply.

I watch Gus ready his gear. He pulls two shotgun shells from his jacket and loads them into his .12-gauge, keeping the breech open. I've brought my recently purchased, very much used .16-gauge that I bought from Gus. It's still cozy in its soft gun case. "You won't mind if I don't shoot anything, will you?" I ask.

Gus looks at me briefly but shrugs. "As long as you don't disturb my shooting," he replies as he scans the horizon.

I relax and take in the scenery. "Look at the halo of yellows tinting the dark-blue night sky," I say, watching the beautiful morning unfold.

"It's called dawn," Gus says in a whispery tone as he readies his shotgun. "It's the legal time to start hunting."

"Well, it's lovely and so quiet in the early morning," I remark, quietly. "Oh, and here come two ducks flying right for us."

The shotgun blast next to me shatters the moment.

"Ahhhh!" I jolt, teeter the boat, lose my balance, and fall sidelong into the cold, murky water. Frantically popping up, I sputter, "Theeww," spitting out the debris-filled water. I take a breath and add, "I wasn't expecting you to shoot."

Gus, still holding the shotgun and now, the side of the boat, looks down at me. His face looks stunned, then worried, and then, chuckling, he puts his shotgun down and steadies the boat. As I pull myself up onto the gunwale, Gus grabs my belt and hauls the rest of my sorry self into the boat. As I get myself upright, he hands me a towel and a thought:

"Maybe duck hunting isn't your thing..."

I sit sopping wet and sullen in the boat while Gus watches for more birds to fly. Gus had missed with his shot but doesn't seem upset. The slough actually comes alive as the sun rises and casts a pink glow on the clouds. Ducks are flying in the distance, and Gus points out the flight differences between blue-winged teal, with a fast wingbeat, versus the slower wingbeat of the larger mallards. He calls to them using his small wooden duck call. A pair of birds fly close, interested in his sound and the decoys we had set in front of us. The patches of light blue on the birds' wings are flapping at us like flags.

"Why didn't you shoot?" I ask.

"Sometimes, I just like watching 'em."

The sun is climbing in the sky and it's getting warm.

"You had enough duck hunting, Cat?"

"It's up to you."

"Birds don't fly much after the sun's high," he says. "But it sure is nice to be out on the water at sunrise."

"I can't argue with that, Gus."

At that, we pack up the netting, pull up the decoys, and head for the boat landing.

I'm not disappointed to get out of my wet clothes but decide I kind of like witnessing the slough come to life in the morning. "Thanks for bringing me, Gus."

"No problem, Cat."

"Hi, Mom, Dad," I say to voicemail. "I went duck hunting for the first time today. It was amazing to be out there at sunrise. Now I know why you like it, Dad. Hope to talk with you soon. Love you."

16

BE SAFE

It's early evening and warm for the second week of October. The dry weather has dulled the normal golden oaks and coral-colored sugar maples. Staghorn sumac displays its dull red leaves topped with velvety twigs and rust-colored cones.

The dirt road I'm traveling is very rural and only connects to the camps and cottages surrounding several small lakes. Many are shut down and locked up for the cold months. The road doesn't lead to a town, shops, or other attractions. Land beyond the camps is being harvested for timber, which rattles the camp owners, who love solitude and a canopy of trees to rest their eyes on.

But animals that graze love the openness of the cuts and the new sprouts growing in after a harvest. Timber cuts bring succulent, tender shoots to ground level and a respite from insects that haunt the woods. Camp owners *do* like seeing the wildlife. I'm patrolling the area to see if night hunting might become an issue here.

I can see the outline of a truck down the road from me. Traveling slow and coming my way, it appears there is a camper on the truck and something else I can't quite identify. I slow to watch for a beam of light or any kind of action that might be illegal. The truck is traveling very slowly. No dust kicks up. I now recognize that a canoe is on top of the camper. My eyes are trying to focus on an object on top of the canoe. I am idling toward them and see two little outlines in the fading light.

I take my portable red flashing light, plug it into the lighter, and after rolling down the window, I place the magnetic bottom of the light on the roof of my Corolla. This light probably dates back to the fifties.

Once I meet up with the truck, I block its progress. The truck stops and an older man with a white beard opens his door and steps down from the driver's seat.

"Game Warden, sir," I say, exiting my car and walking toward him.

"Evening, Warden," the man replies.

I'm guessing he's in his late sixties. Dressed in a worn flannel shirt, open to a dingy gray T-shirt, and faded jeans, he seems comfortable with me. "Sir, I'm watching these two little kids straddling the canoe on top of your truck. Please help them down before they fall off."

Watching these two youngsters perched precariously on top of the canoe with nothing to hold onto is a first in my experience. At thirteen feet above ground, one minor bump of the truck would send the unprepared kids over the edge to the road below.

"You heard the warden, kids," the old man says with disappointment. "Fun time's over. We won't get to see any deer tonight."

"Aww," two young girls say in unison.

They appear to be seven and nine, or thereabouts. The girls climb down from the canoe and camper top to the hood of the truck. Grandpa reaches for each little body and lifts them easily to the ground. My visceral reaction is hard to contain. I'm ready to lash out at this incompetent, unthinking older man who is so reckless. I take a deep breath before I blast him with my thoughts.

"Sorry to spoil your ride, ladies. But riding on top of the canoe is not safe." I'm talking to the girls, but aiming my remarks at Grandpa, who ought to know better than to put his precious cargo in harm's way. "Big log trucks come hurtling down these roads, and they have the right of way. When Grandpa tries to move off to one side where the road is soft, the truck may tip. I hate to think what might happen." Looking at Grandpa with disgust, I continue, "What's your name, sir?"

"Otis," he says while scratching at his weeks' worth of gray beard. "Otis Carlyle. You know, Warden, Grandpa's just showing the girls what fun we can have at the cottage. Ain't that right, girls?"

"Yeah," they say in unison. They are eyeing me as if I am the Grinch Who Stole Christmas.

"Ma's back home cooking supper. We're just entertaining ourselves meantime."

"I understand, Mr. Carlyle, but let's make sure these cute young ladies get home to Grandma safely." The girls are sidled up to Grandpa, their protector. "Did you get to see any deer along the way?"

"Naw, just getting started," Grandpa remarks.

"Well, if you promise to keep the girls in the cab, take the next dirt road to your right and you'll find the remnants of an old farm. I think that's the best spot to watch for deer in the next hour. Deer usually feed in those fields."

"Thanks, Warden. That seems like a good plan, doesn't it, girls?"

"Yeah!" With a squeal of little-girl excitement, they are ready to go.

"Be safe," I say as I shake hands with Otis and head back for my car.

After forty minutes of thinking about Otis and the possibility of two little bodies lying along a dirt road, I am home. I need to eat something and take a shower before meeting Jinot for night duty. A hot shower helps me clear my head.

The golden glow of lights in the cabin adds warmth to the darkness. The refrigerator is pretty bare other than condiments and a half gallon of milk. I opt for a glass of milk and a peanut butter sandwich. I make coffee to fill my thermos and pack an apple for later. Jinot drives in just as my gear is packed.

Jinot calls in to Dispatch that we're 10-8, in service. "Destination is County Trunk V, Northwest."

"I thought we were working close to town tonight," I say, confused.

"We are," he says, looking at me with a smile. "Chief thinks we have the offender listening on a police scanner. They find out where we're working and move to a location in another part of the county."

"Well, that's pretty smart."

"Yep, but I called Dispatch on the phone and told them what we were doing tonight."

"Very good, Jinot. Let's see if we can outsmart the bad guys."

Our location is just outside of town, where potato fields are all around us. We're parked in a windbreak of pines. Windbreaks are planted by farmers to slow the drying winds of summer and the drifting snow in winter. It provides a good cover for us in the dark. We put a camouflage net over the hood and windshield to prevent reflections.

A new housing development is not too far down the road. We can see the lights of the homes from where we are, and it appears there might be a party gearing up at one of them. Cars are traveling past us, unsuspecting, and turning into the development. Hints of music and laughter can be heard sporadically.

Jinot catches me up on his court appearance yesterday. "Remember ol' Grandpa Pitts?"

"Of course; he's the old guy with gnarly feet. I'm still mad he snookered me."

"That's the guy. The judge took his hunting license away for life with a fine of fifteen hundred dollars."

"That's good, isn't it?" I ask.

"Yep," Jinot says dismissively. "But do you really think it'll stop him from hunting?"

I think for a moment. "Probably not."

"Let's face it. He doesn't need a license to hunt on his own property, and it's too easy to walk out back to some salt lick or bait and pop off a deer whenever he feels like it."

"We're just a small deterrent, aren't we?" I say, a little deflated.

"You could think that way, but I choose to think that if we *weren't* here and catching *some* folks, publishing their names in the paper, and putting some in jail, poaching would be rampant."

"I like the way you think, Jinot. That's one reason, I want to be a warden. Law enforcement provides some protection of our natural resources."

It's nearing eleven p.m. when a car turns in our direction from the development. "Party must be winding down," I say. The car is slowing down as it nears our location. We step behind the nearest tree and watch the car travel in front of us and stop. The driver is a young man, midthirties. He looks to his passenger, who opens the door, leans out, and pukes.

Eww. I could take a few steps and reach the car, but there's no need. His passenger, a young woman, withdraws into the car and closes the door. The car continues down the road.

"It must've been some party," I say.

More cars exit the development over the next half hour. Then it is quiet. The lights turn off at the houses and the development appears to go to sleep. And we're still on watch.

The coffee is gone and the apple I packed is eaten. A few cars have passed us coming from town, apparently heading for home. Nothing for us to worry about.

"How long we working till tonight?"

"I'm thinking our problems will start at bar time, Cat."

"Really?"

"Yep. I'm thinking that at bar time, guys will be looking for something to do, not ready to go home, and have enough alcohol in 'em to dull their good judgment."

"Great."

About 1:30 in the morning, a truck slowly rolls our way. Our eyes are focused intently on the cab of the truck. There! A beam of light turns on and scans the field across the road from us. The truck is close enough, and we can see four deer in their beam of light, standing still in the field.

Ka-boom! The shotgun blast cuts through the air and thankfully, the deer flee unharmed.

"Let's go!" Jinot says as we throw off the netting and jump in the cruiser.

I call Dispatch. "Shotgun fired on Field Road half a mile north of River Road. We are in pursuit of a Ford pickup. Stand by."

Jinot screeches to a stop with high beams shining and a spotlight focused on two fellas yelling at each other and moving something below their feet. I jump out and have my flashlight in my left hand, lighting the inside of the truck cab. "Warden! Put your hands on the dash!" They are slow to comply. "Now!"

"Yeah," I hear a slurred, slow voice. Both sets of hands are visible. A shotgun is nowhere to be seen.

"Where's the shotgun?"

The driver slowly answers without looking at me, "I don't know what yer talkin' 'bout."

Jinot has called in the license plate and is now at the passenger side.

"You see the shotgun, Jinot?"

His flashlight beam is scanning the floorboards and the lap of the passenger. "Not yet."

"One last time: where's the shotgun?" I say to the driver.

"Don't know what yer talkin' 'bout. I don't know 'bout no gun."

"Keep your hands where I can see 'em and get out of the cab, real slow." I open the door.

A portly man in his forties turns his legs out and slides his butt off the driver's seat with a heavy plop of boots on the ground. "Move to the front of the truck and place your hands on the cruiser," I tell him. His red plaid shirttails hang over his worn and dirty jeans. His massive hands are dry and calloused. No wedding ring, but that's not unusual. His unkempt beard is thick and black.

Jinot is moving the passenger to the front of the truck with similar instructions. He shakes his head. "No shotgun yet."

"Black Beard, what's your name?"

"Earl. Earl Mansfield," he says in a slow slur.

"Where do you live, Earl?"

"Down near Pine Ridge, Sandy River Road," he replies, several beats slower than I'd like.

"You got identification?"

"Back pocket."

"Real slow-like, reach back and pull your ID out for me with your left hand. And I better not see that right hand move an inch." Black Beard pulls a wallet out of his jeans pocket. "Put it on the hood, move away, and return your left hand to the hood."

Black Beard is having trouble with his balance while he tries to follow my directions. I move to his left side and pick up the wallet, shining the light on his face. He is slow to respond and turns away.

"Now that we've been properly introduced, Earl, you gonna tell us where the shotgun is?"

Earl leans over the hood and rests his forehead on his forearms, head bowed, silent.

"Jinot, if you can watch Earl the pearl, here, I'll comb the ditch."

"Call for a transport first," Jinot says. "We need a blood alcohol on this pair. Shotgun or not, we'll get 'em for OUI. I found half-full beer cans in the truck."

With a call to Dispatch and a transport coming, I follow the ditch line from the truck back a few hundred feet. "Found it!" Pictures are taken, and the shotgun is unloaded and marked as evidence. Earl is charged with OUI. Earl and his buddy, Calvin, are charged with night hunting and will spend the night in the drunk tank.

Jinot drops me off at home about three in the morning. I stoke the woodstove to take the chill out of the air and grab a beer. I've got too much adrenaline flowing to fall asleep. Watching the flames catch and crackle gives me something to focus on while I think back on the day's events.

The two little girls are hopefully snug in their beds, dreaming wonderful dreams, at Grandma's house, innocent and dependent on Grandpa and Grandma to keep them safe.

And as for Earl and his buddy? Their targets are safe and they can just enjoy the drunk tank tonight.

I take another sip and think, *Cheers!*

"Hi, Mom and Dad," I say to voicemail. "Sorry I've missed you again. I just gotta say, I can't believe how many dumb people I meet who need direction and common sense!"

17

BURNING SKIES

As I patrol the county, I see parched leaves of trees lining the roads. It still hasn't rained much, and the normally lush green should be turning to vibrant fall colors. Now they are dull and limp. Streams are trickling over stone beds where rushing water is more the norm. Farm fields are turning dusty brown, and cornstalks rustle lifelessly in the wind. Summer rains were few and far between, and September's never-ending winds contributed to the dry conditions. I pass the familiar Smokey Bear sign pointing to the warning: "Extreme Fire Danger." Outdoor fires have been restricted for weeks, and watchtowers are on full lookout for wisps of smoke signaling a source of fire that could take off quickly in these conditions.

It's midday when a call comes through: Smoke has been spotted near Sandy Creek. I radio my position and announce that I'll respond to the call. Jinot calls to have me meet him at headquarters.

I try to sound official: "Ten-four, Three-oh-seven. ETA of fifteen minutes."

Jinot is ready with his gear as I pull into a bustling headquarters just as the Huey lifts off. I pull my gear from my car and throw it in the backseat of the cruiser. He quickly turns the car south as he shares the latest information on the fire.

"A farm tractor caught fire, sparking the initial blaze," he says matter-of-factly. "Wind carried the fire into the fields, and the farmer barely escaped harm. Fire departments and the forestry crews have all been called to respond."

We see smoke miles before we arrive at the command post. Gusting winds are carrying the fire beyond the fields and into the adjacent properties. Neighbors close by have been notified to stand watch, but farms at risk need to be evacuated now.

Jinot and I are assigned to block traffic from entering the area. He drops me off at the junction of two county roads, then rushes farther south to the next intersection. I stand alone at the intersection watching smoke rise and furl not too far away. A farm to the west of me is being evacuated. The family station wagon drives by me with precious belongings thrown into their vehicle and panic written on their faces. A fellow in a truck follows them with oak bureaus, a table, and chairs bouncing in its bed. The furniture looks to be dated, perhaps handed down from generations before.

I can smell the heaviness of smoke as I watch it billowing upward. The wind is now steady, carrying flames and smoke with it. A patch of tall pines between me and the farmhouse is in the fire's path. I radio the fire commander with my report. He orders Jinot and me to fall back from our positions. Jinot is at my post to pick me up in seconds, but I tell him I'm not sure if everyone has left the farm.

"Two vehicles came from the farm, but I didn't talk with them. I don't know if everyone has gotten out."

Jinot doesn't hesitate. "Get in. We've got to find out!"

I barely hop into the cruiser before it's moving again. Up ahead, I see the fire rolling through the tops of the pines to our left. It's sending sparks and fireballs across the road and into the field on our right. Our road disappears behind a curtain of thick black smoke. Anything beyond is screened from our view. I brace myself as we drive under the arch of fire and dense smoke roiling above us. We are going through what looks like the gates of hell. The fire sucks in the surrounding air, swirling around us. *Whoomph!* Flames of orange and red produce a heat that licks and swallows what moisture remains in the trees. It roars around us with cracks and sizzles of burning twigs. The heat penetrates the cruiser. I instinctively hold my breath and shrink from the door as Jinot drives through this inferno. The darkness of smoke and flame consumes us before we break through to see a smoke-filled road, hazy fields, and an imperiled farmyard beyond us.

Escaping from the raging tree fire, we focus on a grass fire sweeping toward the farm with its jagged line of yellow flames lapping up what vegetation lies in its way. Next to the old white farmhouse, a dilapidated garage and chicken coop lie in the path of this relentless enemy. Now in the dooryard, Jinot and I exit the cruiser. I rush to a water spigot outside the house and turn it on. Jinot uses the garden hose to squirt water on the house, wherever it will reach. I hear chickens clucking in the coop and presume they'll be better off fleeing from the fire on their own. I open the gate and shoo them from their cage. Feathers and dust fly out with them. Rabbit cages hidden in the back of the coop are filled with frightened bunnies. They are so cute…and helpless. I reach for the scared creatures, releasing each of them to fend for themselves. These docile animals will be better off free than left to burn in their cages. They might actually survive.

The fire is moving around the yard with the driveway acting as a barrier to the approaching flames. Sparks flying in the wind, however, are jumping from bush to bush scattered through the adjacent fields. A swirl of wind gathers little fireballs and sends them flying onto the roof of the house. Jinot can barely get the water from the hose to reach the ignited roof. He yells that he hears a dog yelping in the house. I run to the back door and free the dog, and two frightened cats run out as well. *Who would leave their pets to die in a burning house?*

I spot a small pail and dunk it in the kiddie pool. I throw the first pail of water onto the house when the fire reaches the empty chicken coop. I keep refilling the pail and tossing water as I watch the garage begin to burn. Burning debris and ash continue blowing onto the roof of the house just as a local fire truck turns into the yard. In seconds, a fire hose is unwound and aligned to send streams of water to douse the roof fire before it burns through. Jinot turns the garden hose onto the grass, knocking out small blazes and setting up a wet perimeter in the yard. A tractor is driven into the yard from a nearby farm. It drags a disc behind it to turn the burning grasses underground and leave dirt and sand exposed around the house, creating a protective border.

The larger fire is beyond the farmyard now, moving on to other victims. This house has been saved, though barely. A few animals return, terrified, to the yard. The crew puts out the last of the garage and chicken coop flames, preventing a re-spark later on. They won't be housing cars or animals anytime soon, but they won't be kindling anymore, either. The firemen have this fire under control and let us know our job is done here. We get in the car and call Command for our next assignment. Leaving, we realize the unburned yard is a small island in an extensive blackened landscape.

Acres of fields and forests burn into the dark night. Standing next to a fire crew stationed on Hawk's Ridge, Jinot and I watch the wind roll the crimson flames through the treetops on the adjacent hillside. As the fire jumps from aspen saplings to the tinder of a pine plantation, the fire boils through the tops creating its own windstorm and movement. Charred leaves and twigs blow through the air acting as fire starters igniting whatever's in their way. I am witnessing the uncontrolled devastation of a wildfire, feeling momentarily helpless. Fiery reds, yellows, and oranges fluidly roll and lick the midnight sky. It is mysterious and breathtaking from this distance. The reality of its power is unchecked hungry destruction.

"Why aren't we doing anything?" I ask.

"Nothing we can do," says one of the fire crewmen. "It's uncontrollable right now. We can only monitor its direction and get everyone out of the way."

Jinot tells me, "Fire needs oxygen and fuel to feed it. After months of drying wind and the summer's drought, the dried vegetation is prime fuel for this beast. A tiny spark can ignite it, and the slightest breeze will carry the flame to its next source of fuel. Containing the fire usually means snuffing it out with water, sand, or some manmade fire retardant. The only other option is for the fire to run out of fuel…and that's not happening anytime soon."

We stand in awe of this firestorm. Jinot points to a doe and two young fawns running away from the flames in their woodland home, into the open field. "They'll run until they can escape the fire's path. If they're lucky, they'll cross a stream where the fire can't cross."

Small flames continue burning the charred bones of the forest after the main firestorm rolls through. Hazy smoke wisps apart allowing moonlight to shine through. Ashen tree trunks are still burning with glowing coals at their bases.

"In the morning, we'll see where we can mop up any hazards," says the crew chief. "But I think we'll find that this area has been burned clean and there's little more damage that *can* be done here. We'll move on to where we can make a difference."

"If you've got this covered, guys," Jinot says, "Cat and I will take off for our next assignment."

"It's almost one in the morning, Jinot, and I stink," I say, sliding into the cruiser.

"Yes, it is and yes, you do," Jinot says as he rolls down the window.

"Three-oh-seven to Command," Jinot radios.

"Go ahead, Three-oh-seven."

"Three-oh-seven looking for next assignment, with fire down at Hawk's Ridge."

"Three-oh-seven, you're relieved for tonight. Please check in at oh-seven-hundred for next assignment."

"Thank you and good night."

I struggle to keep my eyes open on the forty-five-minute drive to headquarters. A hand shakes me awake. I slowly pull myself from the cruiser, remove my bag, and throw it in my car.

"I'll pick you up at seven," Jinot says as I turn and shuffle away.

I start up my car and, after smelling myself, roll down the windows for the short ride home.

Thank heaven I live in the woods and no one's awake. I get to my door, strip my clothes off, and once again leave them outside to air. I grab a beer from the fridge on my way to the shower. A quick soaping and rinse feels heavenly. I think I could fall asleep standing right here. But I find the energy to dry off and comb out my hair before flopping into bed feeling sheer relief.

The winds die down the following day, allowing the fire crews to build firebreaks and contain many fires. But it isn't until weeks later, when clouds open up with much-needed rain, that the fires are finally defeated.

To experience the challenges of firefighting with Mother Nature working against us gives me a sense of citizens working together to thwart disaster. Hundreds of civil servants and volunteers collectively worked together this week. We are bone-tired when crews of firefighters from distant towns come to relieve us. In the end, thousands of acres burn, but only two homes are lost.

Only two.

18

WOOD THEFT

It's been almost two weeks since the fire. Ida and I are enjoying our breakfast at The Landing. Locals fill up the booths and tables, talking among themselves, swapping stories and the latest news. Our waitress, Julie, is cute, friendly, and good at lugging coffee pots and balancing plates of hot eggs and hash while carrying on multiple conversations. The mouth-watering smell of bacon drifts from the kitchen. We're the outsiders, having come from away and transferred here for a time until our jobs take us somewhere else. We're made to feel welcome but will never truly belong without a local history.

From outside, a big bear of a man fills the doorway, barges in, and makes the aisle his own as he finds a seat at the counter. His red wool shirt is worn at the elbows and smudged with dirt. His jeans are saggy in the butt yet too small to fit over his protruding belly. The café seems to quiet while conversations turn to low whispers. The intruder finds a stool, his bulk covering the vinyl seat. Julie rushes to put coffee in front of him without a word.

In time, Julie brings our check.

"Who's that?" I ask.

She huddles in low. "Donny Thomas. He owns a logging company."

Ida perks up and says, "I've never met him, but his crews work on some jobs I have." She adds, "I was told to watch them closely."

She motions that we should leave. We pay our bill and head outside, where Ida continues, "Rumor has it he steals wood. Loggers are set up on jobs but move over to more valuable timber and have trucks come in the middle of the night to haul it away before the owners ever know it's gone."

"Sounds like we need to set up a sting, Ida girl," I say.

"Come with me this morning, and I'll introduce you to one crew I'm working with."

"Let's go."

We travel north for thirty-five minutes before running out of blacktop, then turn east on a gravel road past camp lanes. The road narrows, and overhanging trees block the little bit of sunlight that's shining.

"I've developed a management plan for the state land they're harvesting now," Ida explains. "The cutting is done with a permit that specifies what types of timber can be harvested. I lay out the area to be cut with boundary tape. I also mark trees to leave uncut as seed trees. Then the site can regenerate into a healthy future forest."

We make one last turn, and I spot a truck being loaded in front of us.

"That's Lonnie Case on the loader," Ida says.

We get out and watch this thirty-something-year-old twitch levers and swing his grapple over to the pulp pile, pick up four trees, minus stumps and limbs, and swing it back onto the truck like they were Tinkertoys. It looks like fun work until I see his calloused and grimy hands. They are covered with hydraulic fluid and grease, matching the stains on his worn jeans and jacket. Lonnie looks like he hasn't seen soap in a month.

Ida motions him to stop. "Morning, Lonnie. You got trip tickets for me?"

"Yep, in the truck," Lonnie says without elaboration. There's no smile or familiar greeting.

We hear a chain saw up on the hillside. "Who's cutting for you?" Ida asks.

"Lucien Daigle is up there now. The other guy didn't show today. Lucien's better than nothing, but not much."

"This-here's Cat. She's the new warden. We'll walk up and see how Lucien's doing while you finish up your load."

"Good enough."

Walking through stumps and tree limbs is tough. "When a tree is cut high off the ground, it scrapes your shins, and hurts like hell," Ida informs me. It doesn't take long for me to confirm her wisdom. "The first log from each tree is also the most valuable, so you want the logger to cut as close to the ground as possible. Foresters don't like to see high stumps..."

We crisscross the harvested site to ensure all the marketable pieces are picked up and winched to the road. The smell of fresh sap and evergreen fills the air with the scent of Christmas. As we near the whir of the saw, we watch a lanky man de-limb the tree he's working on. He's not very stable on his feet, tripping and stumbling as he moves about with a running chain saw. Chain saws are meant to cut wood, but when they hit a human part, it's like running into the jaws of a grizzly bear. Nasty.

Ida whistles and motions for him to stop, and we walk closer. "Lucien, how's it going?"

"Fine," says the young man without conviction. His handsome face is covered with sweat and sawdust. Lucien pulls his hard hat off, tosses it to the ground, and walks to a water jug. Blond hair falls in wet curls around his ears. From beneath the dirt, his blue eyes are the color of the sky on a cloudless day. He flops back onto a felled tree to rest.

"Lucien, you OK?"

"Well, it doesn't help to have a hangover and no breakfast..." Lucien guzzles from the water jug, not caring if it drips down his shirt. There's a noticeable pause. "You ever cut wood?"

"Nope," Ida answers.

"Well, it's a helluva way to make a livin'." Another gulp and deep breath. "But since I can't find other work, I'm out here busting my ass." Lucien takes another big swig of water.

"Hangovers aren't good anytime, let alone when you partner with a chain saw," Ida says. "I got a lunch in the truck. You want it?"

"Sure. Never turn down a free lunch," he says with a smirk.

"We'll leave it on your truck's tailgate before we take off. Hey, and don't forget to pick up some wood in that direction about a hundred yards." Ida points back across the cut. "Might as well get paid for it."

"OK."

We leave Lucien a lunch and pick up the trip tickets from Lonnie. The trip tickets describe the volume of wood delivered to the mill. Most loggers get paid based on the volume of wood delivered, so if you cut it and leave it in the woods, no one gets paid—not the logger, the trucker, or the landowner.

The phone rings as I'm cooking my supper of green beans. It's Ida. "Lucien had an accident after we left him today," she starts. "He tripped and fell into his saw, Cat. It cut him clear across his face."

I wince, thinking about it. "Oh, my God, Ida. That's awful."

"Lonnie got him to the hospital," Ida says. "He's got stitches from his left eyebrow down his nose and across his lips. Thank God, it missed his eyes."

"It makes me hurt just to think of it." I can't imagine an angry chain cutting into you…especially the face.

"He was an accident waiting to happen when we saw him, Cat. We should've told him to leave."

"It wasn't our call, Ida. Dumb kid made a couple of bad decisions and it cost him."

"Yep, a helluva way to earn a livin'," Ida repeats before hanging up.

I don't sleep well that night. Lucien is on my mind, picturing his handsome face before and after the chain saw raked him. Sometime between three and four a.m., I hear tractor-trailers running on the highway. You can tell they have a heavy load by the way they gear down to make the hill. The direction they're heading doesn't have much in the way of commerce except sawmills, and I'm thinking, *These are log trucks hauling in the middle of the night under the cloak of darkness.*

I call Ida. "You awake?"

"Yep, thinking about Lucien."

"Yeah, me too. But I'm hearing trucks hauling heavy loads."

"Yeah, now that you mention it, I heard 'em, as well."

"I'm pretty sure they're hauling logs to the mill up north, Ida. We can't catch up to 'em now, but we ought to be waiting for 'em tomorrow. Does that sound right to you?"

"I wish we knew where the logs were coming from, though. It's one thing to catch the truckers at their destination, but another to find out who the wood belongs to."

"OK, so think about it. If they're loaded and coming through at three a.m., we ought to be in place to catch 'em empty and follow them to the logging job. That means we need to be in place by midnight, Ida. You up for that?"

"Yep, I suppose another night without beauty sleep won't kill me."

As daylight spills over the treetops, I put the kayak in the lake. Listening to the lake come alive in the early morning is comforting. My strokes are in rhythm with the bird songs above me. The first rays of morning sunlight create a sparkle on the canvas of water. It calms me after the last twelve hours of disturbance. I'll need to report to the chief. He might actually like the idea of a timber theft sting operation. And he does. At midnight, Ida and I are parked at a crossroad with a clear view of four routes the trucks could take. Ida fills me in on Lucien. They didn't keep him in the hospital without health insurance, so they stitched him up with sixty stitches, put him on pain meds, and shipped him out.

"Treat 'em and street 'em, I guess," she says.

"No kidding. I've been thinking about him all day."

It's cloudless, so the stars are shining bright. Being a weeknight, the roads are empty at this hour. "Night work has its benefits. With less noise from people, it's an opportunity to focus on nature," I say to Ida as I pour a cup of coffee from my thermos and offer it to her. We pick out constellations and watch for shooting stars. Orion is standing guard over us as we wait.

Around one in the morning, two trucks make the corner and head north on the east side of the lake. We toss our coffees and follow in behind the eighteen-wheelers at a safe distance. I call Dispatch to tell them what we're up to.

We're a little surprised when the trucks take a turn to the east on a familiar road after thirty-five minutes. We hang back a bit more and turn off our headlights. The fog lights point down and won't be as obvious to the trucks. We travel around a corner just as a big buck is crossing the road. Ida skids to a stop, dredging up dust and gravel. The buck looks at us, annoyed, and saunters confidently into the woods.

We proceed down the road, now in search of the trucks. The settling dust clues us as to their whereabouts. It's the same road we met Lonnie on and where Lucien got hurt.

"Ida, turn off your engine and let's listen to what's going on."

We exit the truck and lean into the silence of the night. "The trucks have stopped," I say.

"Yeah, but what are they doing here? When we were on site, Lonnie barely had enough logs for half a load. Remember?"

"I do. Maybe the trucks are lost," I say, but within seconds, we hear a loader being fired up. "Well, they're loading something. Let's wait a few minutes before moving in to see what's happening."

After listening to the loader for about seven minutes, we climb into the truck and make our way onto the spur to witness two eighteen-wheelers, one being loaded by none other than Lonnie Case. We turn our headlights on and see Lonnie looking back at us, wide-eyed and still. As he recognizes us, we can almost hear him curse.

We get out of the truck and Ida gives him the sign to shut down. He cuts the motor but doesn't move. "What're ya doing out here, Lonnie? Can't sleep?" Ida says, as she walks toward the loader and a stack of valuable sugar maple logs. "Boy, nice logs you're loading. Too bad they're not yours, you sack of crap."

"Ida, we just cut these today and were planning on paying for 'em tomorrow."

"That's BS, Lonnie, and it's gonna cost you big-time."

I watch the two drivers while Ida chews on Lonnie. "Let's see some identification, fellas," I say. Both men are cooperative and just doing a job they were assigned to. Now they'll return empty to their boss rather than to the mill. I'm sure the boss won't be happy.

Ida tells Lonnie that he and his crew are suspended from cutting on state property until further notice. "You go tell Mr. Thomas he'll be hearing from the State about fines after the investigation's done."

"You better tell him yourself, Ida. I don't want to be anywhere near him when he gets mad."

"We catch anyone on this site, we'll charge 'em with trespassing. You got that, Lonnie?"

"Yep."

"Unload those trucks, *now*," Ida commands in a voice I've not heard her use before. She's downright mad—and clearly in charge.

I've taken the truckers' information, and Ida releases them along with Lonnie, telling them all to leave. We spray the butts of the logs bright orange and measure the length and height of the pile that will determine their volume and relative value. Ida and I mark the road with plastic tape that warns, "No Trespassing!"

I call Dispatch to have any cruiser in the area keep watch on this road. Tomorrow, the investigation will begin, looking at the site and all tree stumps found to determine the value of the illegally cut timber and who will be charged for the wood theft.

19

POLKA IN RUBBER BOOTS

The county is known for its German, Polish, and French-Canadian influences. Descendants of these strong ethnic groups are known to work hard throughout the week and play just as hard on the weekends. Local establishments cater to their clientele by providing entertainment on Saturday nights, playing lively tunes where patrons can socialize, dance, and go crazy after a long workweek.

For the few months I've worked with Jinot, I've noticed he doesn't seem to have other interests beyond those ending in *–ing*, like fishing, hunting, and boating. I'm learning a lot from him, which is good, because I have a lot to learn. We've been working sixty-hour weeks, which is OK when you don't have a social life. But at ten o'clock on this night, it starts to rain and Jinot smiles. "Cat, we've just been given the rest of the night off. No one hunts in the rain."

I return the smile as we decide to head for Pulasky's Bar and Grill. Jinot throws me a shirt to put on over my badge, while he removes his uniform shirt and replaces it with a flannel one from the backseat. We hear a country-and-western band rocking the place as we pull into the parking lot. It is midway into the band's second set, so the locals have had plenty of time to lubricate themselves.

We weave our way through the parked cars to the door. Unprepared with other footwear, I stride along in my unbecoming rubber boots from working in wet grass. It's dark and no one will see them anyway, I figure.

We walk in the door and see that the dance floor is wall-to-wall people. Jinot signals the bartender and orders two big Pabst Blue Ribbons. He seems to know the bartender and another guy in the corner. With a nod his way, we move to the corner to unwind and watch the party. Jinot introduces me. "Doug, meet Cat." We clink the butts of our beer glasses and turn to the action on the dance floor.

People are rocking and swaying, enjoying the tunes. It's fun to watch dancers of different ages and styles trying to match the beat. Several women dancing together are comfortably flamboyant, with I-don't-care attitudes. One of them is Ida. I quietly wave to her from my side of the bar, a little embarrassed that my friend is swinging all over the floor. But, then again, *I'm* the one in uniform pants and rubber boots hiding in the dark corner of the room.

The second beers taste as good as the first. A break between sets allows for another round and laughter. Ida makes her way over to say hi and stand next to Jinot. Pop Pulasky is taste-testing his own supplies and enjoying his customers. He is a pro behind the bar and makes sure no one waits long to be served.

A few women spot Jinot and like what they see. "Look at those hungry stares," Ida says. "Ooh, baby, they are jealous of us."

But Jinot is oblivious to the attention as he carries on his conversation with Doug. Ida and I, on the other hand, are free to scan the floor at leisure and watch the ladies watch the men. Their eyes move to us and they stop smiling.

The band is heading back to their instruments to play their third set. They know how to get the crowd to move and shake like Mexican jumping beans. As the band strikes up a familiar tune, some girls shriek and dart for the dance floor. Others twitter in the background, swaying to the song, yearning to be asked to dance. I see them looking wistfully at Jinot and Doug. But they have to build up their courage and walk past Ida and me to ask the men to dance. More beer flows and dances get danced. As their last tune of the night, the band launches into the "Beer Barrel Polka." The crowd goes wild, emptying the bar stools, partners holding hands and dancing to their old favorite, left-right-left-skip, right-left-right-skip. This is one tune where no one misses a beat, probably because they've danced the polka since childhood.

"Come on, Cat. Ya gotta dance." Ida pulls me onto the dance floor with her. No one gets away with not dancing a tune symbolic of the Old Country.

Despite my dirty rubber work boots, I move around the floor in step with her. For her size, she moves gracefully. Bouncing and jostling with other dancers is like riding bumper cars at the carnival, and we're all having a wonderful time. The music concludes with everyone cranked up and not wanting the night to end. Jinot is still sitting in the corner but is now more attentive to the ruckus on the dance floor, his face half smiling, half unbelieving.

Ida gives me a warm hug of appreciation. "Thanks, Cat," she says, sauntering away as the floor empties. "That was fun!"

I move back to Jinot's corner with a warm feeling, maybe from the beer, maybe from the warm bodies laughing and gyrating away. "That made my night!"

Jinot replies, "Yeah, you guys make a great couple. Welcome to Pulasky's."

He ushers me quietly through the lively crowd, which is still reveling in their fun and saying their parting goodbyes. "It's going to be an early morning tomorrow," he reminds me.

The cool air hits us in the face as we walk out the door. Jinot drives me home, filling me in on some new field intelligence. "Doug tells me he's hearing early-morning shots in the river's backwater, thinks they're getting a lot of ducks coming south. Be ready at four thirty when I pick you up."

"In the morning?" I blurt. "That's in four and a half hours!"

Because there's no reaction, I continue, "And I need my beauty sleep!"

"You had some time off tonight," Jinot replies, unfazed as he pulls into my driveway. "See you in the morning."

As Jinot drives off, I drag myself into my little cabin still wearing my dirty rubber boots.

At least they'll *be ready for the morning.*

20

DOGS AND DEER

Several days later, a call comes in about six in the evening. I am about to head out on car kill duty when the sheriff's dispatcher calls. "We have an angry taxpayer watching farm dogs chasing deer."

"What's the address and status?" I ask.

"Route 128, east of town about seven miles. Mailbox number is one-five-three. Two dogs, shepherds, chasing a yearling out behind her place."

"Ten-four, Dispatch. I'm heading her way now. See if she can keep an eye on them until I get there."

"Ten-four, Three twenty-two."

It is still light out at this time of October. The leaves are tinged in fall colors and the fields are dull green with crops. With working folks home and the roads clear, I make my way to the scene in no time. I'm thinking about dogs on the loose and chasing deer for the fun of it. I realize now that for most big dogs it's natural to chase and grab, bringing animals down and killing them. That's why we have laws against letting dogs run free and chase wild game.

As I near mailbox 153, I slow down and scan both sides of the road. Driving slowly in the breakdown lane, I pass the mailbox, continuing to look for the dogs. It's been at least twenty minutes, so I may be too late. There, to my right, in the ditch, is movement. I stop and quietly get out to see what's there.

Lying in the ditch is the young deer. Two shepherds eagerly gnaw on its hind flank. Their ears perk up, but they are not interested in me. The yearling is still alive. It lifts its head and looks at me, pleading. The sight leaves me sick.

I get back to the car and radio Dispatch. "Three twenty-two asking for assistance on Route 128. I need a deputy with a loaded weapon." It'll take some time to get a deputy there, and I am thinking of what I can do in the meantime. A warden can shoot dogs in the act of chasing or mauling deer, but I don't have a gun. I check my backseat for supplies and then check my trunk. I come up with a can of orange spray paint and a stake.

Walking toward the carnage, the dogs are so busy gnawing, they don't move. I spray a line of orange paint across the head and back of each dog. Now they're marked for later identification. I raise the stake threateningly and scare them away from the fawn. They back off, but still have a challenging look, as if they might take me on. I raise the stake above my head and bellow at them, "*Get out of here!*" They cower and reluctantly leave, hesitating again before taking off. The poor fawn, bleeding and exhausted, is trying to move away but has no use of its back legs. I am helpless to do anything for this poor animal, my stomach wrenching at the situation.

The deputy arrives shortly and puts the poor creature out of its misery. Then he helps me load it on my car to dispose of later. I'm able to visit the complainant with the victim in plain sight.

As I pull in the driveway, a woman I'm judging to be in her sixties greets me on her outdoor step. "I was afraid they'd catch the poor thing," she says as she points to the fawn on my trunk. "I'm sad to think nice well-fed dogs will do this for fun."

"Yes, ma'am," I reply, holding in my anger and frustration as best as I can. After all, I'm not angry with *her*. "I'm Warden Higloss, ma'am," I say as I extend my hand to the woman. "Thank you for making the call to us."

"Nice to meet you, Warden. I'm Lilian White. Friends call me Lily."

I hesitate, thinking I may have heard wrong. "That's a nice name."

"Thank you, but it really isn't. My parents thought it was cute, but only when you're a baby..."

I drop the subject and move on. "Ms. White, can you tell me who the owners of the dogs are and where I might find them? I was able to chase the dogs off, but they got the taste of blood and will probably do it again, when given the chance."

"Sure, it's Blake and Emma Schneider down at the next farm on your left. You'll find them to be nice people, but they have their hands full with the farm animals and a young family."

"I appreciate the information," I say as I head for my little Toyota that now doubles as an animal hearse. The next stop will not be as friendly, I'm sure.

"Three twenty-two to Dispatch."

"Go ahead, Three twenty-two."

"I'm stopping at mailbox one-six-one on Route 128, regarding dogs running deer."

"Ten-four."

I pull in the drive of the farmyard and see activity in the milking parlor. I park my car as close as I can, climb out and take my heavy metal flashlight with me. I raise my voice to be heard over cows mooing, hooves stomping, and a man's voice talking to them. "Hello? Mr. Schneider? Game Warden here."

"In the barn, Warden. Busy. But come on in."

"Thank you." I walk in the barn and see two lines of Holsteins being milked. The smell, a mixture of fresh hay and manure, permeates the air. "Mr. Schneider?"

"That'd be me," he says, harnessing a can with suction tubes to the udder of a cow.

"I need to talk with you about something."

"OK. Hopefully we can talk while we work. These cows can't milk themselves."

"No problem," I say as I watch a barn filled with black-and-white dairy cows lined up in stalls, munching on fresh hay while being milked, content as can be. As one cow finishes, the canister is removed and the suction tubes placed on the udder of another cow next to it.

"What can I help you with?" says the busy farmer.

"Do you own two shepherd dogs, Mr. Schneider?"

"Depends on what they've done."

"We caught them in the act of taking down a deer, sir."

"Well, that's not good. Did you shoot 'em?"

"No, sir."

"If you caught 'em, why didn't you shoot 'em?"

"I don't carry a firearm, Mr. Schneider."

"A warden without a gun?" he pauses briefly to look at me.

We hear a growl, barking, and disturbance from outside. I turn to head outside, with farmer Schneider close behind me. A shot is fired. We hurry and hear a second shot.

We stop outside the barn door to see the fawn dangling halfway off my trunk with two German shepherds lying dead beside the vehicle. At the back door of the house is a young woman holding a .22 rifle in her hands. "They were pulling that poor thing right off the car," she says.

"Well, you got 'em, Emma," Blake Schneider says. "Now we don't have to worry about 'em bothering anybody anymore." Blake looks at the dogs and points to the orange paint on their fur and then toward the matching paint on my hands. "Looks like we caught the right villains, Warden."

I look at the couple, in disbelief that they could shoot their own pets. What do you say to a woman who can do that? *Wow, nice shot?* or *How could you do that?* or *That took courage...* I choose to say, "I admire your ability to do that, ma'am."

"Thank you, Warden. Sorry they got your deer."

"Warden, I think our problem is fixed," Blake says.

"Yes, Mr. Schneider. I see no reason to issue a citation on top of your loss. I'll even take the dogs with me, if you want. I see no need to bother you anymore."

We place the dogs on top of the fawn and tie them down. My little Toyota is now a car of carnage. Driving out of the farmyard, I shake my head, frustrated and sad.

What the frig?! Dogs chasing deer is, unfortunately, natural behavior. The dogs' owners are hardworking folks who slipped up by not containing their pets. The fawn loses its life and so do the dogs. *Damn it! Were there other victims of the dogs that we don't know about? Would the Schneiders miss their dogs now, or were these pets just expendable?*

I bury these creatures thinking about how they lost their lives due to the unfortunate circumstance of being at the same place at the same time and following an order of nature. It didn't end well for any of them.

Including me.

"Hi, Mom," I start. "How's it going?"

"How nice of you to call," she says automatically.

"It's good to hear your voice. Is Dad around?" I say too quickly. I hear the phone being handed around.

"Cat!" he says eagerly. "How's it going? Your mom says you're doing well."

"Dad! It's so good to hear your voice."

"My contacts back there tell me you're doing good work."

"Well, that's good. Dad, did you ever think there were so many dumb people who needed saving from themselves?"

"Cat...where did you ever get the impression people would be responsible for themselves? Isn't that why there's a need for law enforcement?" The phone dies before I can answer.

21

RUNNING IN THE DARK

The night air is cool and damp as the late-summer warmth fades and the October chill takes over. The moon is almost full now, and the sky is clear. Fall is my favorite season, when evenings are crisp and clear. I'm snug in my jacket, lying on a sleeping bag spread over the hood of our cruiser. The windshield props me up just enough to gaze at the stars while we watch the fields on the other side of the road. Jinot is beside me pouring a cup of hot coffee from his thermos. The aroma is enticing, and I am fully aware of the handsome gentleman sitting next to me. He is more relaxed around me these days. He seems to enjoy the times when we're together.

"Want some?" he asks.

"No, not yet," I say. "But thanks. I think I'll hold off for a while. This may be a long night." I can't help but feel close and safe with this guy—OK, even attracted—but I am ever so aware that this is a professional relationship and I don't want to blow it.

"Maybe," Jinot says. "The caller said the shots were between ten and midnight. It's not real clear how close we are to the spot where they hunt. We might be on the wrong side of the ridge, but we'll see."

"Well, it's a great night to be out; so clear, the moon and stars are bright against the dark sky," I say, wondering what he thinks of me… I don't dare ask, though, because I'm not sure I want to know the real answer. This way, I can be in my own little dream world and remain close.

"Yep, perfect night hunting conditions."

"Ah, look, Jinot, Cassiopeia has come out to brag about her beauty," I say looking at the constellation.

"Oh, yeah, I see her."

"You kind of wonder how the Greeks came up with their myths. Kings and queens willing to sacrifice their beautiful daughter until a handsome prince comes along and saves her..."

"The storytellers were probably shepherds," Jinot says matter-of-factly, "tending their flocks late at night and trying to keep the wolves away. What else would they be doing but making up stories while the action's slow?"

"Oh, kind of like us tonight," I say.

"Yep... Kind of like us."

We have watched the darkness take over the sky with a bright moon highlighting anything in its way. "What was that song?" I ask. "Leaves are falling all around...the autumn moon lights my way..." But the lyrics without the tune and context don't seem to fit the moment. The smell of the air is fresh and cool. I love the feel of brisk air against my cheeks while my toes and fingers are still nicely comfortable.

"Well, I gotta get up and move a bit," I say, stretching my muscles.

"Me, too," Jinot says as he swings his legs off the hood and stands between the car and the trees that conceal our position while we wait for any sign of poachers.

As usual, the cruiser is backed into some brush. Jinot and I pace in front of the car, swapping stories about the week and testing each other's knowledge of wildlife biology and laws. A car comes down the road but at a speed too fast for shining deer. We step closer to the cruiser and watch it go by. The riders are unsuspecting.

Minutes later, we see a light scan the back side of the ridge. *Shiners...* Jinot heads to the driver's side while I grab the sleeping bag and throw it in the backseat. Jinot flips the blackout switch that shuts off all lights on the cruiser, including the dashboard. We will not use headlights but will navigate by the light of the moon.

"It's amazing how your eyes adapt to so little light," I say as I see the roadway in front of us. We approach an intersection devoid of artificial light and take a left to get over the ridge. All is well until the ridge blocks the moonlight. I can see a yard light at a distant farm and moonlight beyond. But we are entering a darkness that makes me nervous.

Jinot is calm but cautious. "I'm using the edge of the road to navigate, Cat. Open your window so we can hear better."

I focus straight ahead but find myself clutching the edge of my seat. "Stop, Jinot!" I tense up at a shadow ahead.

Jinot is quick to respond. We hear a shuffle of bodies bumping each other and a muffled moo. Jinot throws his headlights on a group of Holsteins standing in the middle of the road. Within fifty feet of us are twenty pairs of eyes staring at us staring back at them. Each cow weighs over a thousand pounds and is worth over a thousand dollars. You don't want to drive into them.

"That was close," he says taking a breath. "They probably came from the farm up there." Jinot points down the road to a lit farmyard and calls Dispatch to reach the farm owner. In thirty minutes, we are rounding up cows and herding them toward the barn.

"Thanks, Warden," the farmer says as we shake hands. "It helps to shut the gate after milking." His young son quietly looks at his shoes in the background. "We appreciate your help, don't we, son?"

"Yes, sir."

Jinot and I get back in the cruiser and breathe sighs of relief. "OK, Cat, now that we've entertained ourselves, let's get back to work."

"Sounds like a plan."

Jinot drives away from the farm. The road is empty at eleven p.m. Our windows are down as we listen for shots. We're driving to fields known to have deer feed in them on this side of the ridge. Jinot has the cruiser traveling at a cautious speed while our lights are blacked out. A rifle shot rings out. We stop. There's movement on our left, and a deer runs within feet of our front bumper. It's a mature doe. Jinot throws the headlights on. We see blood stains on her hind quarter as she passes in front of us, barely missing the now stopped car.

"She's been shot," Jinot says. "I'm going after the shooter. Park the cruiser and call it in. This guy is on foot." Before I can respond, Jinot has his flashlight in hand and is out the door.

I go to the driver's side and pull the cruiser over to the side of the road and mark the spot where the doe has crossed. Dispatch is called to bring out backup, and I can't help but tell 'em I'm in pursuit as well. I'm armed with a flashlight, a radio, and my Ka-Bar. I still have no gun.

Following Jinot is not easy. Woodland shadows dapple the ground, but I can hear footsteps and follow the sound. Moonlight hits the ground in places, and I'm able to move quicker toward the sounds of my partner busting through branches.

Then there's quiet. I don't move but listen intently. Nothing. I turn my flashlight off. Who knows how far I am into the woods. I don't know if Jinot is close, or how far away he could be now. I'm frozen in place and wait for a sign to move. My heart is pounding in anticipation. There's a hunter somewhere. Jinot is in pursuit. And they both have guns. Patience… Let the others make a move. I wait and listen and hear nothing but silence. The tree canopy keeps me in the dark.

"He's running, Cat!" I hear Jinot shout. "Follow me!" I hear the footsteps again and pursue them. A field lies ahead of me, and I make out two dark figures running across it in the moon-shine. A man, with Jinot in close pursuit.

I stop and pull up the radio I'm carrying. "Dispatch, we've got an armed suspect in sight. We're in pursuit. Requesting backup, *now*." I update our location, then I try to catch up to my partner and his target.

Jinot reaches the guy, jumps on him, and drags him to the ground. I see Jinot draw his pistol. He has the poacher sitting in the field with his hands behind his head before I'm near them. Jinot's chest is heaving as he tries to catch his breath. His arm is extended with his pistol pointed. His arm moves up and down with the rhythm of his breathing. I take his pistol from him while he catches his breath and handcuffs the guy.

"Wow, that was some running, Jinot," I say.

Jinot picks up a rifle lying nearby and replies, now able to talk, "It's warm, recently fired."

We get a little information from the shooter as we walk him out. Wes Parnot is hunting on his own land out of season. "You know, Warden, gotta feed the family," he says. We turn ol' Wes over to the sheriff's deputy, who has arrived just in time to transport the hunter to jail. Jinot and I take the weapon and cartridges to the squad car and mark them as evidence. It's after midnight. No matter how much moonlight there is, we won't find the blood trail of the doe tonight.

The next morning, we find the trail that takes us to her carcass. The bullet wound slowed her down enough to make her vulnerable to coyotes in the night. Jinot is just as disappointed as I am to find her this way. We settle for a picture of her body to add to the evidence and slowly walk away.

Later, we find out our shooter is pretty well known locally. He holds venison barbecues for his friends and family every October, inviting close to a hundred people. The judge *might* take that into consideration if it goes to court.

22

HARRY

"Bessie, what do you know about Harry?" I ask while she pours our coffee. I sit at her kitchen table, which is next to the window, where we have a view of the lake.

"Harry Blackwolf is mysterious, Cat. He pretty much sticks to himself. You notice his eyes? Dark. Dark like caves. Deep. So deep you can get lost in them."

"What's his story?" I ask, taking the cup from her.

"He lived on the reservation at the top of the lake most of his life. He was a tribal elder, I hear. One day he's knocking on my door. It was a cold and blustery November day. He stands there straight up looking' at me with those eyes. He's dressed in woolen layers, but it was odd because he had no coat on. His leathery hands were bare and he stood before me without a twitch or a shiver. Like he was invincible against the elements."

"What did he want?"

"He asked for a cabin to rent," Bessie said, thinking back.

"Is that strange?" I ask as I sip the flavorful dark brew.

"It is when he has government-paid housing up north. I told him what the rent was and he said OK. He's been here for two years now, comes and goes without fuss. In fact, most days you don't even know he's around."

"Does he have any friends?"

"Not that I know of."

"Any family come visit him?"

"Not that I've seen."

"What does he do every day?"

"He seems to fish, hunt, and trap. You'll notice the fire pit behind his cabin with a big pot dangling over it."

"Yeah, I've noticed it. What's that about?"

"He's boiling traps now; leg traps, actually."

"What do you mean?" I ask.

"Smart trappers boil their snap traps in spruce or cedar to get the smell off 'em. They must have some dye to disguise the metal and I think they use a little wax to make 'em spring better."

"Hmm, makes sense. I just never thought of it. Trapping's not my favorite sport; can you tell?"

"Not mine either, Cat, but you know fur trapping is as old as Native American history. It was a big part of early life and the settlement of North America."

"Yep. I'm just glad I don't have to trap for my clothes and dinner."

"I second that thought. But Harry is quiet, doesn't cause any problems, and so I can tolerate his strange ways and boiling brew over there."

That evening, I see Harry near his fire pit. His movements are fluid and silent. He reaches for a stick of perfect width and length to stir his pot. Like an ancient shaman stirring his herbs into potions, he stands back and watches his concoction simmer before him. The blaze throws an eerie light on his angular face and prominent nose. His black hair drapes around his dark eyes and high cheekbones. These features are highlighted by the flames of the fire. The shadows add contrast that is enhanced by the darkness of the coming night.

I listen as I move closer. A low hum seems to come from Harry. Like an incantation, he continues to hum slow, melodious, ritualistic tones. I'm not sure if I will approach, after all. I'm curious, but hesitant. *Am I intruding? What will his reaction be?*

But I'm pulled closer, attracted to the unknown like a moth to light. I silently move among the shadows, not wanting to commit myself. The scent of the boiling cedar reaches me where I stand. It's both familiar and intoxicating. I'm lost in the smells and the sounds of the unusual song.

Harry stops stirring. "Come out of the shadows," he says in a low tone.

Did I hear that right? I tense, tucking into the darkness.

"You. Do not hide amongst the shadows." It's a low voice of authority. "Stand where I can see you."

I slink out from behind a tree. The glow of the fire throws amber light across me as I move cautiously through the distance between the fire and the trees. He watches me approach, his body unmoving.

"Sorry to disturb you," I say hesitantly. "I was just curious to find out what you're doing," I say, trying to excuse the awkwardness of the moment.

"Stop."

I stop in my tracks. "Harry? I'm Cat, your neighbor."

"I know who you are. This is my space. Do not intrude," he says stoically.

Taken aback, I look at Harry as he looks at me. "Yes, this is your space, sir. I didn't mean to disturb you."

Harry continues to stare. "Good night, then," he says.

I turn and retreat to my cabin, enter, and close and lock the door behind me. The situation now catches up to me and a nervous shiver shudders through my core. A flash of his eyes flares up to haunt me. I look around my little place, then move to each window ensuring they are locked and the curtains are pulled tightly together. I'm not quite sure why I'm reacting so fearfully to the situation, but Harry Blackwolf has deeply unnerved me. It's different from anything I've encountered. Sleep doesn't come easy.

I wake cold and uncertain, needing to shake away my thoughts of Harry. It's cool outside, but I dress warmly and take the kayak out onto the lake. The water is quiet and calm. The warmth of the water against the cool air creates a wispy fog that rises from the lake. I focus on my paddle, thrusting it into the water and pulling hard to build speed. The workout is just what I need to dissipate some tension from the night before. As I return to the dock, I see a figure before me.

Harry stands on the shore, tall and still. He watches me with those dark eyes, his arms crossed in front of his chest. He's waiting for me to float into the cove. I'm not sure how to approach him. The kayak floats toward him, but I'm not ready to put it ashore.

"Good morning, Harry."

"Last night was bad," he says. "Meant no harm."

I'm not sure how to respond, but I realize this is his way of apologizing. Harry, not waiting for my response, turns his back and glides away in the direction of his cabin.

"Harry!" I call out to him. He either doesn't hear or is just ignoring me. I put the kayak on shore and run after him. "Can you teach me about trapping?"

He turns. "Why?"

"I gotta learn something about trapping if I'm gonna work as a warden," I respond.

He looks as me silently. "Come at four," he says, then turns and walks back to his cabin.

I watch him walk away from me, but don't hear him break a twig or rustle a leaf. It's eerie how he can move through the woods without making a sound. No matter what, I'll be there for my four o'clock lesson.

"You must watch to learn," Harry says, shortly after four. He's taken a small leg trap in his hands. A short length of chain is attached to what looks like a handle with slides around the semicircular jaws of the trap. The metal is all blackened by the boiling process the traps went through these last couple of days. Other traps are still hanging to dry.

Harry demonstrates how to open the leg trap by applying pressure on the handle. He fits a thin strip of metal, called a dog, over one of the jaws to hold it in an open position. He carefully holds the trap from underneath the splayed jaws and lowers the trap to the ground so it doesn't spring shut.

"That looks easy enough," I say, watching Harry withdraw his hands easily.

He takes a stick to apply pressure to the trip pan, quickly releasing the jaws and snapping the stick cleanly in two quicker than I can blink. "Holy crap," I say, while instinctively withdrawing my fingers from harm and flinching at the same time.

"Watch again," he says as he demonstrates the smooth and knowing art of setting a leg trap. "This size is for mink. Muskrat, too." Again he trips the snap trap and the stick is another three inches shorter. "Now, you try."

"I wanna go home with all my fingers, Harry." I wince as I take the trap in my hands.

"You will," he says. "Get caught? It'll only break 'em," he says.

I am nervous and slow, thinking through how to keep from getting caught in the snapping jaws of the trap. I hold the spring down on the ground and feel how smoothly the metal parts work against each other with a little bit of wax coating each piece. The jaws of the trap splay open, and I take the dog over the jaw and hook it in a notch of the pan mechanism, holding the trap open. I carefully pull my hands up and away in an exaggerated movement, being twice as careful as I probably need to be.

"Good," Harry says. "Let's set a real one, close by." He hands me a pair of gloves, grabs a wicker basket that's meant to be carried on his back, and motions for me to follow. We don't walk too far up the shoreline before he spots an animal footprint in the mud and points it out to me.

Harry digs a hole just big enough to lay our trap in. He anchors the trap and covers it with the dirt we've just removed. Like other artists, he's careful to mimic the natural setting with leaves, twigs, and moss, disguising the trap from unsuspecting animals, including humans. He has bait and places it in a hole the size a mouse might make just at the head of this artwork. Just when I think it's perfect, he places small branches on either side of the trap. "This is a runway to the trap from the lake. It deters land animals and focuses on mink coming from the rocks here on the shoreline."

"Smart," I say.

"We watch every day," Harry says.

Harry comes knocking on my door the next morning. "We have a mink," he says before walking away.

"Give me a minute," I say pulling my jeans and sweatshirt over my pajamas. I slide my boots on and finish zipping my jacket as I clamber behind my silent tutor. The air is cool, so I'm pleased to find gloves in my pockets. Fog hangs in the air over the lake and hovers among the trees on the shore. The dampness gives me a chill.

I see movement on the shoreline before Harry stops. The small shape is long, charcoal-brown, and hugs the rock. As I get closer, I see a black-and-brown tail flicking back and forth. Harry motions me forward to see the small triangular face and two scared black eyes looking up to us. Its front paw is caught expertly by the steel jaws of our trap. Harry looks at me. "Good catch."

But he can see I'm feeling the pain of this poor animal. His eyes catch mine unblinking.

"Don't watch," he mutters. I turn away and hear a *whack!* As I hear him pull the chain of the trap, I turn. He's releasing the leg of the lifeless mink, and it drops from the trap. "Do you want to see how to take care of the animal?"

I look at him unable to respond. Then I nod yes.

Harry and I walk silently back to his cabin. He skins the animal expertly, and the pelt is clear of the carcass in minutes. He wraps the carcass in paper and throws it in his freezer. Next, he pins the fur to a wood contraption that reminds me of an ironing board frame, stretching the pelt before it's allowed to dry.

"Harry, thank you for the lesson," I say. "You're very good at this."

"You gonna trap?" he asks.

"No, I don't think so," I say before getting up to go home. "But I've learned a lot."

23

SHOT!

Vernell Ledoux walks into the warmth of Ms. Janelle's kitchen. He's here from the state office to work with me during deer season. Although it wasn't mentioned, he'll be assessing me, and I know it. Vern is a lot of fun to be with—in a friendly-teddy-bear kind of way, easy to talk to and lighthearted. He also likes food, so I know I won't go hungry when we work together. He is an environmental law instructor. Last year, I was one of his students.

"Vern, welcome to paradise," Basil says while shaking hands.

"Thanks for the invitation, Basil," Vern says cordially. "It's nice to be relieved from headquarters so I can do legitimate work."

"That's why you're here," Basil says, smiling. "We do nothing but legitimate work in this county. We're gonna have you team up with Cat. Keep her straight and see if you can work in some target practice. I want her to qualify at the shooting range so we can put some bullets in her gun someday."

"You're talking like I'm not even here," I interject. "And I'll bet I can qualify within a couple weeks, once I get some practice and a few tips."

"I'll take that bet," Basil says.

"What, you have no confidence in me?"

"Like I said, I'm willing to take a bet."

"I don't know about that, Basil," Vern says. "She seems pretty confident."

Basil is smiling. He changes subjects, chatting up Vern, asking about news from headquarters and around the state.

The coffee tastes wonderful this early in the morning, but it makes me have to pee, and there's nothing worse than looking for a place to pee when there are no leaves on the trees and you're wearing fluorescent orange. I gauge my intake with caution.

Basil asks us to take the southern section of the county where the public lands are. "You'll have a lot of traffic there this morning, I'm guessing. The hunters will be around, but the deer have scattered after three days of hunting season. Hunters will probably get antsy and shoot at anything that moves."

"You're probably right, Basil," Vern says seriously. "Won't hurt for us to make ourselves known and maybe the *tourists* will take some extra precautions."

We put our cups in the sink on the way out. I grab my gear, including my blaze orange coat, hat, and gloves, and place them in Vern's cruiser. Although the sun is shining brightly, it's cold. Vern knows the county pretty well, but I'm pleased to be able to direct him to the public land through some back roads I know. We pull into the parking lot where signs advertise public land that is open for hunting. The parking lot has a dozen cars in it, and a slim, geeky-looking guy is just walking into the brush with his shotgun.

"Sir? Game Wardens," I say as I hop out of the cruiser. The man turns and steps closer to us. "We'd like to check your license before you head into the bush."

"Sure," he says, clearly nervous as he walks toward us while reaching for his wallet. He's bow legged, has a wisp of a beard, and smiles shyly. He needs dental work.

Vern walks around the cruiser. "Sir, is your shotgun unloaded?"

"No, sir," Wispy responds nervously.

"Break open your action to be safe, son," Vern says emphatically.

"Oh yeah, sure." He replaces his wallet in his pocket and fumbles with his action. The barrel swings toward us and Vern grabs it to point the barrel down and away.

"How long you had this fine weapon?" Vern asks.

"Oh, I just got it for the season. Trying to put food on the table, ya know. Bought it from a friend of a friend."

"Anybody give you instructions on how to use it?" Vern asks.

"No, but I did look at pictures on how to load it," the man offers as he succeeds in breaking open the breech and exposing two unspent shotgun shells

Vern focuses on the shotgun. "Let's pull those out while we talk," he suggests. The man offers Vern the two shells, but Vern gently declines and suggests he puts them in his own pocket while they continue the conversation. "And while your hand is near your pocket, why don't you pull out your license, give it to Cat, here, and we'll get properly introduced."

"Oh. Oh, sure, I'm Tom Ditts," the man says handing his license to me. I see his hand is now shaking.

The license confirms his real name is Thomas Ditts, and he lives nearby. I check it against his back-tag numbers. "Thanks, Mr. Ditts. Your license seems to be in order."

"Good, Mr. Ditts," Vern continues. "Have you ever heard of Hunter Safety Courses?"

"No. Heck, never thought about hunting till last week."

Vern says, "Hunter Safety Courses are highly recommended and help new hunters get familiar with their firearms and safety precautions. We hope you'll consider it before you get hurt or you hurt someone else. Where did you buy your license, Mr. Ditts?"

"I got my license at the bait and tackle shop," Ditts said. "They offer a class somewhere tonight?"

"Not that I'm aware of, sir," I offer. "I only know of the six-week course they offer throughout the year in preparation for hunting season."

"Well, that's not gonna help me this week, Warden. Maybe they ought to offer crash courses for folks like me."

"Yep, Mr. Ditts. I'll make that suggestion," Vern says. "And keep you in mind. Until we can make that happen, just be careful and make sure you know what you're aiming at. I'd also keep those shells in your pocket till you find your sittin' perch. That way, if you stumble, you won't shoot yourself in the foot."

"I'll do that, Warden."

"Cat, let's leave Mr. Ditts alone and get out of his way," Vern says as we back away.

"Good luck, sir," I say keeping a close eye on him while I get into the cruiser.

Vern and I back out of the parking area while continuing to watch Mr. Ditts make his way into the bushes and out of sight. "Well, let's hope the good Lord looks after him this week," Vern says.

"And everyone around him," I say.

We make our way to the Mill Stream public lands in the very southwest corner of the county. Public lands have a history of community ownership providing hunting and outdoor access. Land management is generally for forestry, wildlife, or recreational purposes. During hunting seasons, these areas see a lot of visitors.

Mill Stream is no exception. Vern drives the cruiser down its road. From our vantage point, we count eight people decked out in flaming orange: hunters within view of the road. Turning west, we cross Mill Stream and spot three more hunters. All are perched in their spots waiting for some poor deer to make the last mistake of its life.

We stop and pull out our field glasses to watch each person individually, making mental notes of descriptors and anything remarkable about each one. The notes aren't lengthy. A short stocky guy with glasses is eating a candy bar. He, thankfully, put his wrapper in his pocket. An old guy is leaning against a tree with his eyes closed and mouth open. A twitch of his head lets me know he is still alive. A third gent is in a tree stand about fifteen feet in the air. He has a rope tied around him holding him close to the tree. *Wow,* I think, *someone who actually prepared for the possibility of falling out of his tree stand. Impressive.*

We compare notes and put our field glasses away. The usual squelch on the radio clears the air for a call to Warden 301, Vern's call number. "Warden Three-oh-one here," he says. "Go ahead."

"Three-oh-one, we have a hunting accident victim being transported to University Hospital by a family member. You are to meet them in the ER. Roger?"

"Roger that, Dispatch. ETA is thirty minutes."

"Roger, Three-oh-one. Out."

Vern puts the cruiser in gear and rushes north toward the hospital.

"How often do you have people get shot, Vern?" I ask.

"We get two to five per hunting season. Thank heaven they are seldom fatal. At least half of them are shot by a person in their own hunting party. Some are inexperienced, some are disoriented, and others hunt too close to their buddies. Occasionally, alcohol is involved."

We arrive at the hospital's emergency room entrance. As we go in, we spot a hunting party still wearing fluorescent orange. It's a stark contrast to the white, sterile environment of the hospital. Vern strides over to introduce himself.

"Warden Vernell Ledoux here about the hunting accident. You all a part of the hunting party?" he asks.

"Yes, sir," says a tall, thin, dark-haired boy who moves forward and is anxious to talk. "It's my Pa. He's been shot."

I estimate the young man to be seventeen or eighteen years old. He can't stand in one spot and is wringing his hands, clearly nervous.

"OK, son. What's your Pa's name?" Vern takes out a small spiral notepad from his shirt pocket and begins taking notes.

"Michael Terriault," he says moving from one foot to another.

"And what's your name, son?"

"Andy…André, actually…Terriault," he says.

"Where do you and your dad live, Andy?"

"We live near Porter, on County K, Terriault Farms."

I'm also taking notes and keeping my mouth shut.

"Good, Andy. Thank you. Can you tell us what happened?"

"Sure. Pa, me, and my cousin Joe are walking through our woods trying to kick up some deer. Uncle George and Uncle Richard are set up on the field posts waiting to shoot 'em. I was a little behind Pa, working my way through some brush when the shot came. I hear my Pa groan as he's hit. I run over to him lying on the ground. He says to me, 'Why did you shoot me, son?' I told him I didn't shoot him. But he fainted. I hollered to everyone to come help us. We brought him here as fast as we could."

"Good, Andy. Where did he get hit, and how's he doing?"

"He's shot in the right shoulder. The docs are looking him over now."

"Andy, can you introduce us to your hunting party?"

"Sure. This here's my Uncle Richard," Andy says touching the shoulder of a big middle-aged man at his side. "He's one of my dad's brothers."

"Hi, Richard. What can you tell us about the accident?"

"Andy told you like it happened. I was sitting on a post in the field waiting for deer to come through. I was tired of standing so I sat down and was reaching in my sack for something to eat when the shot rang out. Shocked the crap out of me."

"Thank you, Richard. We're gonna need to see everyone's hunting licenses for identification. Anything else we need to know?"

"Sorry, Warden. That's all I got."

"This here's my Uncle George," Andy says pointing to a slight, shaggy guy to our left. "He's my dad's older brother."

George is sitting in the lounge chair and doesn't bother to get up.

"Hi, George," Vern says, extending his hand to shake George's hand. George reluctantly lifts his hand to take Vern's. George has long, stringy, mouse-brown hair and an unkempt beard that's taken years to grow. Unlike the others, George doesn't make eye contact and is gazing in another direction.

"George, what can you tell me about your brother's shooting?"

"Can't say much. I was on my post when I heard the shot," George says as he continues to keep his eyes elsewhere.

I can see George shifting in his seat. He's got a nervous personality and wants this conversation to go somewhere else. He has a slight hiccup.

"George, where do you live?"

"Porter. Next farm down from Mike's. You know, Warden, I recommend you get out of here and go catch whoever shot him."

"We'll do just that shortly," Vern says patiently. "Cat's gonna take licenses and contact information from all of you first. While she's doing that, anyone bring their weapons here to the hospital?"

Three different voices say, "No."

Andy offers, "Joe took them to his farm. Joe's there and can show you."

"Thank you, Andy. If you think of anything else, please get in touch with me. Here's my card with phone numbers on it."

"Yes, sir. Thanks," Andy says.

Vern and I leave the hospital. It's cold and gray outside. It feels like it's gonna snow; the air is damp and raw.

"I didn't like George's behavior," I say to Vern.

"Did you smell alcohol on his breath?" Vern asks.

"No, but that makes sense of why he turned away from me."

"My guess is he didn't want to give away the fact he's been drinking. Let's go have a look in the truck."

I follow Vern to a vehicle that looks like George: disheveled. Sure enough, there are plenty of silver beer cans strewn around the floors. But who knows how long they've been there.

"Looks like his truck doesn't get a regular cleaning, Vern."

"No, I'd say it's probably never been cleaned, but it'd be nice to think the beer cans were just picked up on the side of the road, wouldn't it?"

"Yeah, but I don't think George is much of an environmentalist."

"Let's head for the farm, Cat."

"Good idea. Maybe we can get Joe to take us out to the scene."

Gray clouds roll in from the west, threatening snow. It gets darker as we head to the Terriault farm. Dispatch calls the farm and Joe agrees to meet us.

Joe is waiting when we roll into the farmyard. He seems pleased to talk with someone after being left behind. Joe is probably sixteen or seventeen years of age, thin and about six feet tall. He's polite and shy, keeping his hands in his pockets.

"How you doing, Joe?" Vern asks after the introductions are made.

"I'm OK, sir, but darned if I know what happened."

"Well, maybe we can figure this out together," Vern says, putting a comforting hand on the boy's shoulder. "Can you take us out there and walk us through what you remember?"

"Yes, sir."

Joe directs us to a dirt road about a mile from his farm. "Down this dirt road, you'll see a fence line on your left with a gate. Pull into the gate and park." Vern parks by the gate, and Joe jumps out of the cruiser to climb the gate. "This is where dad was posted."

"Richard is your dad?" I ask.

"Yes, ma'am."

Vern and I climb the fence with a backpack of gear we might need during our investigation.

Joe points to his right. "Uncle George was posted down at the other end of this fence line. This field is about forty acres. And in the woods ahead of us is where Uncle Mike, Andy, and me were walking this way."

Walking the field isn't easy with the uneven ground and frost heaves. The two men have longer legs than I do and stride easily across the field. I follow with twice as many steps, ankles twisting and turning. We reach the woods edge and stop.

"Who was walking where, Joe?" Vern asks.

"Uncle Mike was on our right, then Andy, then me," Joe responds.

"Show us where your Uncle Mike took the bullet."

In minutes, Joe has us standing around a blood stain. We tape off the immediate area with yellow "No Trespass" tape, the only marking tape we have.

"Everything was fine as we walked through the woods from over there," Joe says as he walks away from us, pointing. Joe seems to be concentrating on his thoughts. "We were walking along cautiously, watching for deer, listening. Uncle Mike heard something I didn't hear. He trotted forward a little, hollered something—didn't wait for Andy and me to catch up. That's when the shot rang out. Uncle Mike groaned and I heard him fall. I couldn't see him, but Andy yelled for me. Uncle Mike was bleeding pretty good, and we just wanted to get him some help, so Andy and me lifted him up and carried him out while we hollered for my dad and Uncle George to come help us."

"Did you see anyone around here earlier this morning, Joe?" Vern asked.

"Nah... Nobody."

"Did you hear any other shots this morning?"

"Nope, because I would have known the deer were spooked and they'd be moving."

"Good. You've been hunting for a while, haven't you, Joe?"

"Yep, since I was eight, I've been comin' along. At twelve, I could shoot well enough to have my own gun," Joe says proudly.

"I can tell you seem to know what you're doing."

"Yes, sir, I've shot a couple small bucks, which helps fill the freezers."

"Has anyone in the family got their deer yet this year?" Vern asks.

"Yes, sir. Both Uncle Mike and Andy have their tags filled. That's why they're walking with me. Uncle George and my dad have to fill theirs yet. I can hunt before or after school."

"I see," Vern responds, looking over the area. "How tall is your Uncle Mike?"

"About two inches taller than me, near six feet two, I'd guess."

"And the bullet hit him in his right shoulder, which would put that height about five and a half feet from the ground. How tall are you, Cat?"

"Five five. Why?"

"Good. Come over here, right behind the blood stain. Look out toward the field. Can you see where Uncle George was posted?"

"Yes."

"Let me look over your head in that direction for a moment," Vern says, putting the binoculars to his face and spotting the post. Then he dials the focus so he can clearly see what he is looking for.

"Well, Joe, we won't take up any more of your time. Cat will get you back to the house. She and I will continue our work here for a little while, if that's OK."

"Sure. Looks like I'll be doing the chores myself today, so I gotta get started anyway."

I walk Joe back to the cruiser. *He seems like a good kid, likeable.* "We appreciate you coming out here with us, Joe," I say. "You must be worried about your uncle."

"Yes, ma'am."

"Andy told us at the hospital that you have everyone's weapons from the hunt. Can you show them to me?"

"Sure, if Andy told you about 'em."

We arrive at the farmhouse, and Joe invites me into the enclosed porch. The porch is long, the width of the farmhouse. Windows line up like soldiers, allowing natural light to shine through. To our left are gun racks hanging on the wall. Each rack is filled with different models of rifles and shotguns. Below the racks are boots of every size and degree of muddiness. Coat racks on the other side of the door are filled with camouflage jackets with thick insulation.

"Looks like you have a militia living here, Joe."

Smiling shyly, he says, "I never thought of it that way. Our family likes to hunt, I guess."

"Well, there's no law against that. Whose guns are these?" I say pointing to the wall.

"This .12-gauge shotgun is my dad's," says Joe, pointing to the top rack and then to each rack below it. "This old .12-gauge is mine and this one is Andy's. The .30-06 Winchester is Uncle George's, and at the very bottom is Uncle Mike's .308 Winchester."

I take a hanky from my pocket and touch each barrel. "This is quite an arsenal, Joe. Would you mind if I take a picture of them? I like the looks of the rack and how well they're displayed."

"Sure. Dad made it so we'd have a safe place to store 'em."

I stand away from the rack to get the full view and snap the picture with Joe proudly displaying the family firearms. "You OK here, Joe? I gotta catch up with Vern and help him figure this out."

"Nah, I'm OK. I gotta get to the chores anyway. The family will call when they know something."

"OK. Thanks for helping us, Joe. We're pulling for your uncle to come through this all right."

I exit the porch and go to find Vern, which doesn't take long. He's blowing warm air on his hands and rubbing them as I trudge toward him. "Have you figured anything out yet?" I ask.

"Come see, Rookie, and tell me what you think." Vern takes me back to the blood stain where Mike Terriault dropped after being shot. He hands me the field glasses. "Look at the two posts where Uncles George and Richard were standing or sitting. Line it up and dial in the focus to look closer. Do you see anything?"

"Ah… Looks like a clipped branch straight toward the right post."

"Correct. Now take that alignment straight behind you." I turn around to find a large oak tree. "What do you see?"

I peer closely at the oak's bark. Just about eye level, the bark's been shattered and a hole has been bored into the trunk of the tree. I walk toward the tree, step in front of the hole, turn 180 degrees, and put the field glasses up to my eyes. The alignment to the right post is a straight line to the broken branch. Vern and I place markers near the blood stain and in the hole of the tree trunk to take pictures. Vern has a hand drill and a sharp knife to dig the slug from the tree.

"Do you know the caliber of the slug?" I ask.

"Not for sure. We'll have to send it to the experts, but it's definitely from a rifle."

"Now's my time to contribute," I say. "Joe showed me the hunting party's weapons back at the house. There were three shotguns and two rifles.

"Who owns the rifles? Do we know?"

"Joe told me one is Mike Terriault, the victim. The other belongs to Uncle George. And guess what?" I say proudly, "I got pictures!"

"Nice work, Rookie. Based on what we know so far, let's get Uncle George and bring him in."

"You did well today, Cat," Vern says driving back to the hospital. "What's your take?"

"I love the detective work, Vern," I respond. "But I can't get over how stupid people can be, drinking around firearms. And around those young boys. Not good role models."

"I'm not happy with the number of folks who drink and hunt, but I believe most of the hunters are law-abiding citizens," Vern says. "We hear about these because there's a problem. Don't let this taint your assessment of all hunters."

"I hear you, Vern," I say as we pass by many fields. "Then again, let's pray for God to keep people like Mr. Ditts safe as well."

Uncle George is found to have a blood alcohol level still above the legal limit four hours after the incident. George is charged with reckless use of a firearm and operating under the influence. His hunting license is immediately revoked and we're not sure what the District Attorney will seek for other charges and punishment. Mike Terriault comes through surgery just fine, but he'll need help with the farm chores for a while and will certainly need another hunting partner next fall.

24

INCOGNITO

Deer season is in full swing. It's midweek and my turn to patrol the southwest end of the county. I am alone and undercover driving my beat-up old Toyota. My bold fluorescent orange outerwear is toasty warm on this chilly day. My binoculars are handy. I can spot hunters by their orange uniforms across the fields and try to determine who is law-abiding versus lawless. The morning has been pretty quiet, which is good. Unfortunately, six cups of coffee are beginning to bloat my bladder. Without leaves on the bushes, finding a private spot to pee is equivalent to finding one in a desert. Florescent orange doesn't make for good camouflage, either.

I turn south onto Wolf Run Road and look left toward Fog Hill, trying to find a good pee spot. A dark pickup is parked near the crest of the hill. As I drive by, I slow and see two men standing near the truck, waiting. Both are dressed in hunter orange and holding rifles. If their guns are loaded, it's considered hunting from a road and therefore illegal. I keep driving but watch the hill as much as I can without going into the ditch.

A turnout provides needed privacy and a chance to watch the hill from the edge of the woods. I park and quietly get out. As I move to hide in the brush behind the car and drop my drawers, a beautiful buck spooks into the field and runs parallel to the hunters. Within seconds, I hear the crack of a rifle, once, twice, three times. I rise from a crouch and see both hunters have rifles raised. The buck is down and not moving. *Oh crap.* I take a moment for myself, pull my orange back on, and pack myself back into the car, driving toward the hill and the hunters.

As I pull in and park behind the dark pickup, the two hunters smile broadly and catch their breath. They have dragged the big animal up to the road and are admiring their trophy. I turn the county radio down and step out of the car with my orange blazing and credentials nestled in my pocket, looking more like a hunter than a warden. They greet me, anxious to share their good fortune. "Lookie what we got," says a tall lanky guy. His dark, greasy hair escapes from his cap and he needs a shave.

"Congratulations," I say as I approach them both. The buck is a handsome eight-pointer. "Wow. He's a beauty."

"Yeah, he sure is!" says the shorter of the two. "He's the biggest one we've ever gotten here."

"Really?" I say watching them. They are flying high on excitement and talking up a storm. I let 'em.

"Yeah, we've been hunting here for years," says Stretch as he finishes dressing the buck.

"No kidding... Where were you when you got him?"

"We hunt right here every year; hunt right off this road," says Shorty. "Don't even have to get off the blacktop. Nice and easy." He can't contain himself. "We've been violatin' like this for years and never been caught."

"No wardens come around," says Stretch enthusiastically, "so we just wait for the other hunters to move the deer around."

"Wow..." I say with a nod and a smile. "Well, this is pretty cool."

"Yeah," says Stretch. "We travel a couple hours 'cause it's so easy to hunt here. No wardens, no hassles."

"We get our deer every year, too," Shorty adds with a chuckle.

The boys are high-fiving, hugging, and admiring their new trophy. While I watch, I spot spent casings on the road and the drag line of their effort to bring the buck to the truck—all evidence. Both rifles are leaning up against the bumper of the truck, safeties off, and I resist the urge to point out my safety concerns.

"Yeah, this is a perfect place to violate," Stretch comments with a smile that suddenly turns to concern. He looks hard at me and goes quiet. Shorty's still admiring the buck and taking pictures. But Stretch puts a hand on Shorty's shoulder and he also stops smiling. Now both boys are looking at me with puzzled looks. "Yeah, this is a perfect place to hunt." He pauses. "Unless you're a warden." Shorty and Stretch glare at me quiet-like.

I assess the situation. They seem like otherwise OK guys, have a nice truck that's registered and been washed in the last month, and I don't have many options at this point. I can't let 'em go. They'll be bragging for the rest of their lives. And I won't deny I'm a warden. They are hunting from a blacktop road. And they've made a big deal of violating here for years without seeing wardens.

"You're right, gentlemen," I say as I pull my badge and credentials from my pocket. "I am a game warden, so this is your unlucky year. Let's see your hunting licenses."

Both men drop their jaws and let their faces go slack for several seconds before they regain their composure.

"Holy crap," Stretch blurts out. "She's a warden!" He slaps his leg, shoves Shorty; half grins, half grimaces.

"Nobody's ever gonna believe this," Shorty says with a shake of his head. "We finally get caught, and it's by a woman game warden!"

I take their hunting information back to my car and radio in the stop. Shorty's real name is George Trembless, who lives in a small town to the east. Stretch is really Carl Stock from the same small town, both in their early forties. As I hand their licenses back to them, they are talking about the story they'll tell their friends at work.

"I gotta take the evidence, gentlemen," I say picking up the casings and placing them in a bag. "Now let's take a look at your weapons."

They look at each other as if they just want to fold up and go home. They reach for their rifles and let me take down the make and model of each one, muttering something about not believing this is happening.

"I should confiscate these," I say and notice an odd silence.

Carl's grip on his rifle tightens and his knuckles go white. His body tenses and I realize this pushes him too far.

I give him a weak smile and suggest, "Well, on second thought, you still have a couple days before the season ends and one more tag to fill. Why don't you keep the weapons and try to fill your other tag—legally, of course."

Carl's body relaxes and George nods his agreement.

I look at the big buck lying at my feet and guess he weighs close to 180 pounds. I try to pull him toward my car but barely move him two yards. There's no way I'll be able to lift him onto the trunk of my car.

The boys are watching me struggle when Carl says, "What the heck." He reaches down and picks up two legs of the deer to help me move him to my car.

"Thank you, Carl," I reply, then finish tying the animal securely to my trunk.

With a handshake and a wave, Carl says, "Wait till the boys hear about this. They ain't gonna believe it."

I drive away with their beautiful trophy hanging over the trunk of my old car. Two citations have been written and it isn't even noon. Wait till I tell the chief. He *ain't gonna believe it*, either.

Traveling farther south, I tuck into a couple of dead-end roads, looking for hunters. Blaze orange can be spotted off in the woods line in a few spots, but it looks like the deer aren't moving, so the hunters are patiently waiting.

Nearing a public hunting area, I spot three hunters standing in a field. They are coated in blaze orange and hovering around something on the ground. I park and walk toward them. "Hey, how's it going?" I ask, still incognito. As I near them, I see a nice buck lying on the ground at their feet. The older gentleman has his tag in his hand.

Each of the men wears a week of beard growth. But one gentleman's is certainly more salt-than-pepper-colored. He's also shorter and thicker around the middle. The other two resemble him with dark features and dark eyes. Their eyebrows are noticeably bushy under their orange hats.

"Nice buck," I say. The rack has only four points and the body is on the small side, but you always compliment the hunter on his prowess and trophy, no matter how small.

"Yeah, thanks!" says the younger hunter, still gawking at their kill, almost in disbelief. The three are standing over the animal, minds trapped in the moment.

"What's going on?" I ask.

"It's our first deer," the older man says sheepishly. "We're not sure what to do."

Looking at the three of them, helpless and confused, I say, "Let's put the tag on the deer first," as if I'm an expert. "Who's got a knife?" They look at each other questioningly. "No one brought a knife?" I ask. But they shake their heads. "I'll be back." I walk to the car and get my gear bag. *Who would've guessed I'd be so prepared today?*

I walk back to the group, reach into my pocket, and bring out my credentials. "By the way, gentlemen, I need to identify myself as a game warden. Let's check licenses and make sure we're legal."

"I'm the shooter, Warden," says Salty Beard. "Leo Abrahms." He finally steps forward and hands me his license. "This is my brother, Joseph, and my son, Gabriel."

Leo is from Chicago and has his out-of-state license. "Good to meet you all," I say as I reach into my bag, "Now, here's a knife." I pull out my Ka-Bar and hold it out for them to take, like the Wizard of Oz offering the Tin Man his heart. They look at the knife with wide eyes and step back. "Who wants to do the honor of preparing your animal?" I look at each of the men, expecting them to take the knife and tag the buck. Nope.

"OK, have any of you even seen what happens now?" Three negative responses and helpless looks. "If you give me permission, I can show you how it's done."

"That would be great, Warden," Leo says. The other two nod in agreement.

I was afraid they would agree to this. Little do they know, I've never prepared an animal without a more knowledgeable person by my side. Here I am, nervous, with an audience who's looking to me as an experienced outdoorsman. Go figure.

The Ka-Bar is big and heavy in my hand. It quickly slices through the leg between tendon and bone. I can hear the men grimace and gasp, but they say nothing. I ask Leo for his tag, slipping it conveniently into the hole I've created in the leg and snap it closed. Done and tagged.

"Now comes the gutting of the buck," I say, looking at the men. They look at me, frozen. As I slice into the animal, steam escapes when the warmth of the organs hits the chill of the morning. The knife cleanly cuts through the hide of the animal from rear end to rib cage. The serrated edge makes cutting through the lower ribs easy. I reach up to the windpipe and gently guide the sharp tip along my left hand so the windpipe is cut and not my fingers. I pull the entire gut bag out of the carcass and lay it on the ground at the feet of the hunters. The knife has made the job look easy, and all three men look at me like I'm a hunter goddess as I wipe my hands off ten minutes later.

"He's ready to go, gentlemen. If you can drag him up to your car, we can load him up and you can get him registered."

"Where can we register him around here?" the son asks.

I look at the three of them and smile. "Why don't you follow me to the registration office?"

"That would be great, Warden," Leo says.

The son and his uncle pull the buck up to their car. They spot the big buck on the back of my car. "Oh, my word, is that yours?" Gabriel asks.

"It is now," I reply. "Two boys were hunting off a blacktop road and got caught. They will miss not taking this magnificent animal home with them."

The Chicago trio doesn't have a rope or a tarp in their rented sedan and have no choice but to place the warm carcass in their trunk with the legs sticking out, more than likely forfeiting any deposit they made on their rental. They do find a bit of wire to secure the trunk lid down onto the legs. They follow me to a gas station and market with posters and signs boasting sales of worms and lures along with beer. The clerk tells the visitors of a local butcher who will package the meat and send it to them for a reasonable price.

I shake their hands. "Are you done hunting or heading back out, gentlemen?"

"To be honest, Warden, I think this is it," Leo says. "I don't think we were meant to be hunters."

"Well, it was nice to meet you," I say, somewhat relieved. "Be safe getting back to Chicago."

25

BEYOND THE THICKET

It's just before sunrise on a November day in the north, twenty-eight degrees and gray with sunlight ineffectively trying to peek through the clouds. Winds have blown most leaves from the trees, leaving only a collage of twigs. The smells in the cool fresh air tantalize my senses as I make my way into the bush armed with my .16-gauge shotgun, a few shells, and my license to hunt deer.

My insulated boots keep my toes warm, but these boots are not built for silence as I crunch through the freshly frosted grasses and lightly frozen puddles. My blaze orange, gaudy as it is, will highlight my presence to others in the area. I'm making my way to the edge of nearby woods near a known deer trail. It's on an esker, and there's a large oak stump that will act as my perch. From there, I can monitor a wide area of these public lands. Throughout the day, I will watch hunters and their activities without revealing that I'm also armed with a badge.

It's also my first deer hunt as a hunter, and I'm alone. I've been out a few times with others, but only carried my own weapon once. Gun season is now just a few days from ending. The chief has confidence in me to be on my own. Or maybe he just doesn't have the manpower to team us up when we have a big territory to cover. Nevertheless, I'll have backup if I need it.

My shotgun is still fairly new, at least to me. The shells are actually slugs, made for killing large animals. Gus and I took it to the range to sight it in and ensure that it fit me properly before I handed him a hundred-dollar bill. I don't plan on using it much.

I find my perch and place my rucksack beside it. Just as I had planned, the wide view in front of me allows me to watch a vast area, and already, I spot a patch of florescent orange to my left in a deer stand. It's hard to say how far away the hunter is, but I'm guessing at least 500 yards. At this point, it's only him and me.

The clouds part, leaving the morning sun to warm me as I sit idly and listen to the chickadees behind me tweeting *chickadee-dee-dee.* Squirrels are rattling around in the oak leaves looking for acorns to cache. I can hear a grouse nearby, drumming his presence on some log I cannot see. Along with the sun's rays, these sounds give me comfort.

I focus on a wetland not too far away. The vegetation is scrubby, with vines growing over the young pines and alders, weighing them down. Even lacking leaves, the gnarled and intertwined twigs and branches are so dense, I'm unable to see through to the other side. Like a curtain of growth, it shields whatever lies beyond.

My thoughts float away to what might hide in that brush. I picture mink, pheasants, or fox. I smile, thinking that more than likely it will be snakes, a skunk, or mice; less pleasant thoughts. My mind snaps back to the moment as I witness movement on my right. I focus on the dense thicket.

Eyes catch movement faster than they can distinguish color changes. Scanning the brush, I look for *that which does not belong*, like a child's game learned long ago. Incongruity among the tree forms, the flick of an ear, curve of a rump, flash of a tail.

In a few seconds, a handsome buck trots into the open, his antlers floating above his head like a crown. I count six points and appreciate the size and beauty of this animal. He stands majestically in the wheat-colored grass. I slowly bring the stock of my shotgun to my shoulder and cheek and release the safety.

This is the first deer I've ever had an opportunity to shoot. He stands there, broadside to me, regal, providing a perfect target. Many hunters dream of this day. My eyes focus along the sights of the gun, aligning on the area of the heart of this proud animal. He is still and paused, but I see movement in my line of fire. My focus changes to see beyond the buck.

There, farther from my target, is the thicket with a slight opening that signals dull orange. My attention widens to see an outline of two arms at chest level with a shotgun aimed at the buck from the other side, and in the line of fire is...me. It takes a moment to register that my first deer shot could be aimed at another person, and that *that* person has the same opportunity and the same dilemma.

My heart skips a beat. My stomach tightens. My head screams *Danger!* as my body tenses.

I raise the barrel of the gun, with the buck still in place. Beyond him, the arms in orange raise the barrel of their firearm, as well. I slowly stand, now with slight tremors. I raise my hand to the other hunter in a gesture of thanks. An orange forearm rises similarly. The buck takes its cue and leaps off to safety.

I sit briefly, taking a deep breath before deciding to pack up my gear. I try to settle my nerves but can't shake the thought of this close encounter with catastrophe. If I consider myself observant, cautious, and safe, and still find myself this close to peril, I am surprised we don't have more accidents during hunting seasons, especially with those who are less observant, and trigger-happy or under the influence. It would've been easy to miss that small visual change that marked the other hunter. My job is to prevent accidents and advocate for safety. I certainly don't need to be a part of the problem. I love being out here, but my shotgun doesn't need to be loaded.

I just won't tell the chief, nor will I tell Big Mike…

26

POST-SEASON FEED

There's a sense of relief at the end of deer season. We wardens have worked long hours for months and are ready for the pace to slow while the snow is flying and ice is forming on the lakes.

The chief arranges a game feed to celebrate the end of the hunting season and to thank everyone for their contributions. Our close-knit group of wardens will be hosting our local district attorney, county judge, town selectmen, and a few of the sheriff's deputies who work extra hard to help us during the season. We've gathered a number of confiscated animals that have been dispositioned through the courts and remained frozen until now.

The 4-H camp, built in the 1950s, is used for these special occasions. We just need to clean it up, as it's been closed since summer. With a good cobwebbing, a wipe-down of the grill and tables, and a last sweep, it's in pretty good shape to host this illustrious group. Large enough to feed a week's worth of campers and a kitchen big enough to cook all the food, we could host a lot more than will be joining us tonight.

The main course will include bear meat, venison, and geese prepared in several different ways. The chief shows me how he cooks up bear meat with plenty of onions, peppers, and garlic sizzling in pools of butter. It smells delicious. We've all brought sides to share, from green salads to simmering Crockpots of beans.

Ida is my guest. She listens to Basil give his cooking advice while Jinot assists by chopping and building a bowlful of peppers and onions for the chief to use. Punk is off in the corner watching the rest of us with a beer in his hand. Even from across the room, he gives me the creeps with his constant staring and ever-present sneer.

We greet our guests as they arrive, and the mood is light and fun. I like the district attorney. He's got a great sense of humor and tells stories of defendants saying dumb things that seal their fate. The judge is more conservative but smiles at the stories. Ida and I laugh out loud.

It's not long before we move through the buffet and take our seats to enjoy this wonderful meal. The bear meat is a bit gristly, but the flavor is surprisingly good. The chief takes an opportunity to thank individuals and gives a couple of statistics on the season. He pokes fun at a few people, bringing more laughter, and concludes that if I can now focus on my shooting, they might even let me put bullets in my gun next year. *Ha-ha, real funny.* I laugh with the rest of them.

Except Punk. I can hear Punk, at the next table to my left, with his nasally laugh and jeer. "Won't happen," he says to a person next to him that I have yet to meet.

When Basil's finished, many people clear their dishes and say good night. Ida and I help wipe down the tables, then grab a beer. Our hosting and chores are done, so we can relax.

Punk ushers a short round man over to me and introduces Selectman Thompson. "This man made your position possible, Rookie," Punk says. "The selectman spoke on your behalf and voted to fund the trainee position."

"Nice to meet you, Mr. Thompson," I say, watching this sixty-something-year-old eye me up and down. I shake his hand and introduce Ida.

The man is pale and sweating. He looks like a heart attack on two feet. Wispy strands of hair have been combed over to cover a large bald spot. It's not attractive. Punk slaps the selectman on the back, saying, "Excuse me; I've got to catch the DA before he leaves." He scurries off leaving Ida and me with Mr. Thompson.

"I've heard a lot about you, Catherine," Mr. Thompson says in a nasally voice. "I was hoping to meet you." He reaches for my arm and lightly holds it around the bicep, then gives it a squeeze. "I'll bet you're building up these muscles every day." His fingers are massaging my right bicep, which is uncomfortably close to my right breast.

I laugh nervously. *Is this happening? Is this porky old man hitting on me? What did Punk say to him? If he loosens his grip and touches my boob, I'm gonna deck him.* "I'm working on it, sir," I say with clenched teeth. I slowly move my arm away and, thank heaven, he lets go.

Ida looks at him, then looks at me. Moving between us, she says, "Nice to meet you, but we gotta go." And she pushes me away from him and toward the door. I look for Jinot and Basil to wave goodbye. Just before I'm shoved through the door, I catch Jinot's eye with hand signals that I'm leaving.

"That creepy ol' man was hitting on you, Cat!" Ida says from the passenger side of the car.

"I need a shower," I say, as I start the engine and put the car in drive. "Have you ever met him?"

"No, never seen him before," Ida replies. "Never have and don't want to ever again."

"You think Punk set me up?"

I feel Ida turn to look at me. "Wouldn't surprise me, now that you mention it."

After dropping Ida off at her apartment, I head for the comfort of my little cabin. The front porch light welcomes me home and illuminates the keyhole for me to unlock its heavy door. Once inside, I turn to relock the door and set the bolt as well. The warm glow of the side lamp is somewhat comforting, but a fire in the woodstove and a beer are more of what I need to calm my nerves as I make my way to a hot shower.

I can't get my thoughts straight about Punk's intentions. The way he conveniently introduced the selectman, like I owed him my job, then slithered away. I throw another stick of wood on the fire thinking, *Take that, you snake!*

The shower is as hot as it gets. My skin turns pink, but the warmth is welcome. The smell of the shower gel is soothing as I breathe in mint. I lose track of time, washing myself several times and turning as if to wash all my nasty thoughts down the drain. I towel off, wrap the towel around me, and make my way to the bedroom.

From my bedroom doorway, I can see out my back window a brief flash of car lights. *What the frig?* I can see better with the lights off. I stand to the side and peek around the curtain panel. Nothing. *Did I really see lights or did I imagine it?*

I fumble with my chest of drawers to find and put on underwear, jeans, and a sweatshirt. I move out to the living area, find my rucksack, and reach inside to find the comfort of my Ka-Bar. Its sheath protects my fingers as I grab the knife and hold it close to my body. I move quietly back to my bedroom window as I hear car tires rumble gravel, stop, and then spin away. I reach my window just in time to see taillights take off into the night.

Shit. What was that all about?

I call Bessie. "Bessie?" I ask as she picks up. "Did I wake you?"

"Just dozing in my chair, Cat," she says softly.

"Sorry to bother you, but did you just see a strange car parked outside in our drive?"

"No, why? What's up?"

"I could swear someone was watching my place," I reply. "I don't know if they were looking in my windows or what."

"Were they there long? Did you see what kind of car it was?"

"I didn't see much in the dark," I admit.

"Well, I wouldn't worry about it, dear. They probably took a wrong turn," she reasons.

"Maybe," I say. "Sorry to wake you, Bessie."

"No problem, dear," she says in her calm tone. "Sweet dreams."

I put the phone down, close all my curtains, check the locks one more time, and put the Ka-Bar under my pillow. I finally doze off about one.

The next morning, I call Jinot.

"You left in a hurry last night," he says.

"Yeah, I had a brush with Selectman Thompson," I say. "What do you know about him?"

"Not much; just that he's a big supporter of our warden program," Jinot replies, a little distracted. "Why?"

"I don't know," I say uncomfortably. "He got a little too close."

"You sure?" Jinot says. "It doesn't sound like him. His wife is the school librarian."

"Well, I just hope I don't have to be near him again."

"Doubt it. Look, Cat, sorry, but I gotta go," he says.

"No problem," I say, unable to tell him about the car or the details of my close encounter with the selectman.

Ida and I decide to drive out of town for the day to catch a show and spend the night in the city. By the time we get back on Sunday, it's late afternoon and I have some chores to do. "I'll catch you sometime this week in the office," I say, waving to her before I drive away.

Laundry has to wait till after supper. I make a sweep of my clothes, gathering them up in a basket, then grabbing the detergent and a roll of coins for the laundromat. Sunday nights are a perfect time for me to do laundry. Most folks are home with their families, leaving the machines empty for me. With a little music or a good book, I have the place to myself.

The laundromat building is old and shabby. It has big storefront windows that look out onto the street. Stand next to one and you can feel the cold air seep through the single pane of glass. I wonder if this building used to house a general store. It looks like old pictures of a store that once would have held canned goods, or hardware, or bolts of fabric. Now it holds massive dryers along the wall and washing machines in the center of the floor, whirring around, swishing clothes and sending warm air into the middle of the space.

I pick up a tabloid to distract me. I'm lost in the photos as the machines churn my clothes. I look up to stretch my neck and see headlights turn on, then off. I walk cautiously to the window. A big sedan is sitting across the street. No other cars are around it. I don't recognize the car, but its headlights blink on and off again.

It's signaling me.

Who would do that? And what do they want with me?

I pull on my coat, wondering if I'm doing the right thing. I'm in a building with no one around. It's dark and the streets are empty. I open the door and walk cautiously to the waiting car.

Before the window is rolled halfway down, a familiar voice calls out, "Catherine, how nice to see you."

"What are you doing here, Selectman Thompson?" I ask, confused.

"Oh, I just saw you in the laundromat, by yourself, and thought you might like some company," the selectman says, sitting behind the wheel of his fat-cat car. He's puffy and sweating. His comb-over has blown into his face, looking pathetic.

"Are you following me?" I ask, feeling the adrenaline start to pump. "Because you better *not* be following me." I try to pick my words carefully before I let loose and punch the guy in the face.

"Catherine, I just thought we could get to know each other better," he says without a hint of decency. "We didn't have much of a chance to talk the other night."

"Selectman, I have no desire to get to know you better," I respond, feeling the heat rise to my head. "Does your wife know you're here?"

"Now, Catherine. There's no harm in us talking, is there?" he asks with a syrupy-sweet tone that disgusts me. "You do know that I help to fund your position, right?"

"If you don't stop following me, I will make sure the chief and everyone in this county knows you're stalking me," I say emphatically. "Stay away from my home and me!"

He shakes his head as he at least thinks about what I'm saying. "Catherine, you may be sorry," he says with a threatening look and rolls up his window.

I watch the selectman drive off, leaving me alone in the street. I shiver from the experience rather than the chill of the night and walk back into the warmth of the laundromat. I stand alone with my thoughts, looking out the window.

27

THE INVITATION

"My parents want to meet you," Jinot calls to say. I'm tingling as I hear, "Mom will make her world-famous venison pot roast."

My partner and I have been strictly professional, but I like him. I like him a lot. He's smart and sexy and kind. We've become comfortable with one another. He seems to enjoy our time with easy conversation and light teasing back and forth. He shares his smile and twinkling blue eyes when we meet. I think we have a connection that seems like good chemistry. I'm attracted to him. I'm just not sure how he feels.

"Wow, that sounds nice," I say, but my heart is fluttering and I'm nervous. "What time?"

"Plan to be here about four in the afternoon," Jinot replies. "We can talk a bit before we eat at five."

"I look forward to it, Jinot." My brain is muddled with thoughts about what he might have in mind. "What do I need to know about your parents before I arrive? What have you told them about me?"

"I've told you about them; they're just hardworking farmers," he says. "Simple people. They know I like working with you and are anxious to meet this crazy person I've been talking about." Jinot is smiling through the phone. "I gotta go. See you tomorrow?"

"OK. I'll see you then," I say as the line goes dead.

My thoughts are swirling: *I'm meeting the parents! What should I wear? What should I bring?* Standing there alone, my mind races: *How can I make a good impression? Will they like me? How come Jinot has never asked me out, but now I'm meeting his parents…?*

I pick up the phone. “Ida! I need your help. I’m meeting Jinot’s parents tomorrow.”

“Are you kidding me?” she responds. “What’re ya gonna wear? When’re ya goin’? What’re ya takin’?” She pauses for a second. “Oh… my…God!”

“Can you come over?”

“I’m on my way. Oh, my God!”

I retreat to the shower for the time it’ll take Ida to get here. The water’s hot and relaxing as my excitement moves from ecstatic to schoolgirl joy. By the time she arrives, I’m pulling my only two skirts out from the back of my closet. I have to dust them off and they’ll need pressing.

“Geez, Cat, I haven’t ever seen you in a skirt.”

She’s right. I lay the green print miniskirt on the bed and pull a black V-neck sweater off the shelf. “What do you think?” I ask Ida as she looks the outfit over.

“Better try it on,” she suggests.

“Good idea,” I say as I slip off my robe revealing my Sears bra and panties. They’re a little gray from mixing with my jeans. She looks at me and shakes her head.

“What?”

“You might have to visit that Vickie lingerie store, if this romance gets serious,” she says.

“One step at a time,” I reply. “God, after all these months, I barely get a day to prepare to meet the parents?” I slip on the skirt and pull the sweater over my head. Ida and I look at my reflection in the mirror.

The skirt and sweater are loose on me. “I guess I’ve lost a little weight.”

“But it looks good, Cat,” Ida says. “Better loose than tight, and I never seem to have that problem. You’re meeting the parents, so you want to look nice—like the girl next door. Right?”

“I guess that’s the idea,” I say, turning sideways in the mirror and around so I can look at my backside. “What should I do with my hair?”

“You gotta put some curl into it, girl,” Ida says. “You never have curl in your hair. Put a barrette off to the side so your bangs slope mysteriously over your right eye.” Ida stands to the side of me and brushes my bangs over to one side, demonstrating a new look.

“I can’t see,” I complain. “And I don’t have curlers.”

“My college roommate tied rags in her damp hair overnight.”

“I don’t have rags, either. Any other suggestions?”

Ida pauses. “Socks. Long socks, or dish towels would work.”

"Good, I can do that." I slip off the skirt and sweater and hang them on the door. "Want to go help me pick out a bottle of wine and some flowers?"

"Sure, but the only store open nearby is the grocery store."

"Good, because I need pantyhose, too."

We decide to buy a second bottle of wine for us, as well, then return to my place to cook dinner and plot my strategy. *How will we date and work together? What will the first kiss taste like? Heck, we haven't even kissed and I'm meeting the parents!* We giggle.

In the morning, my hair is oddly deformed, but I'm able to brush out the most seriously deficient curls. Later, I put the barrette in place, but this time I can see. The skirt and sweater suggest I have some curves. Pantyhose gives my legs a suntanned look, according to the package, and now I add a little mascara and tinted lip gloss to finish the look. There's no choice in shoes. I only have good shoes, sneakers, or work boots.

With a bottle of wine and a store-bought flower basket, I drive to Rideau's Farm practicing how I will introduce myself and anticipating their questions of me. My stomach is in knots, and I've bitten off a couple of fingernails. The farm comes into view. It is well-maintained, with the barn freshly painted red, the house solid and welcoming. All farm implements are nicely put away and not used as lawn ornaments. I like that.

I park behind Jinot's car and walk up to the porch entry to knock. A gentle woman with a gray bob answers the door. "Oh, you must be Cat!" she says in a lyrically pleasant voice with a warm smile. She's wearing a periwinkle-blue dress that peeks around her printed apron. Her face is sun-kissed with wrinkles that form when her eyes smile.

The kitchen is warm and smells of spices and wood. The planked wood floors remind me of the 1950s, but they're polished to a sheen.

Jinot comes to the kitchen, welcoming me with a warm kiss to the cheek. His lips are soft. *I never thought his lips would be soft.* I return the kiss to his cheek and hope that he feels the same way. He takes the flowers and wine from me.

"Nice touch," he says with a smile. Then follows with, "Cat, meet my mom, Nadine."

"Nadine, nice to finally meet you," I say. "Thank you for having me."

"Oh, I've been looking forward to meeting you," she says, again with a lyrical tone. "I want to get to know you."

"That makes two of us," comes a voice from the other room. "I'm joining that party," says a man coming through the hallway to meet me. He stops in the doorway, just a few feet from Jinot. The same clear blue eyes are looking at me. Although older and grayer, Jinot's dad cannot be mistaken. "I'm Michel, Jinot's dad."

"Nice to meet you, sir," I say, seeing more resemblances between these men in their smiles.

"Well, let's go into the parlor and get comfortable," says Michel. "I need to take a load off my feet." With that, he turns and walks away to another room and we follow.

Like the kitchen, the parlor floor has wide-planked wood floors polished and buffed to a shine. Two chairs and the sofa all have slipcovers protecting them. The side tables are simple and solid oak. A television is at the far end of the room, center stage on a small bureau.

Above the TV is a mounted buck head with antlers that reach to the ceiling with a wide span between ten points. A handsome male pheasant is mounted and sitting on the floor next to the TV stand. Other walls are adorned with cross-stitched and framed flowers. Everything is clean and well cared for. The room is simple and comfortable.

"You have a beautiful home," I say. "Did you shoot the buck, Mr. Rideau?"

"No. Call me Michel, please. Jinot shot that buck as a young man, here on the farm. I think it weighed more than Jinot did at the time."

I smile seeing father and son look at each other with love and the same twinkling eyes.

"I shot it early one evening when I was fourteen," says Jinot. "I couldn't drag it home, so I walked back here and got the tractor. Dad couldn't believe how big he was, when I finally got him back to the house."

"I had been feeding him for years," Mr. Rideau says. "No wonder he was so big!"

"He filled our freezer," Nadine chimes in. "Jinot was always putting something in our freezer," she says with a laugh. "Including squirrels and rabbits." Everyone chuckles at the memory.

"Let me go check on our dinner," Nadine says and leaves the room.

A car rolls into the dooryard and stops. Jinot stands and walks to the kitchen. I hear Nadine's, "Hello, Lizette."

It's a few minutes before Jinot escorts a nice-looking woman into the living room and introduces her. "Cat, meet Lizette."

"Hello," I say as I look at this dark-haired, dark-eyed woman not much older than me. She's pretty in her print dress and heels. A matching purse is held in front of her waist. Her hair is pulled back in a neat little bun at the base of her neck.

I stand and move to shake her hand. *I didn't know Jinot had a sister.* "Lizette, it's nice to meet you."

"Likewise, Cat. I've heard so much about you," she responds, inspecting me closely.

I instinctively pull my sleeves up to my elbows and cross my arms in front of me. "I hope you've only heard the good stories," I say, looking at Jinot.

From the kitchen, Nadine calls, "Time for dinner!"

"What can I help with, Nadine?" I ask and move around Jinot and Lizette to help carry serving platters and bowls into the dining room. The round table is adorned with a vanilla-colored tablecloth and matching cloth napkins. "This looks lovely," I say. "Where should I sit?"

Jinot pulls a chair out for me. "How about sitting here."

"Thank you," I say as I watch him move around to the other side of the table. "Oh, you want to keep an eye on me. I get it."

Jinot smiles, "Like always."

We hold hands around the table as Mr. Rideau says a prayer. "Amen and let's eat," is followed by a clattering of dishes and serving-ware scraping bowls. The smell of fresh bread, warm from the oven, floats through the room. Butter melts over a warm slice on my plate.

Lizette is watching me. "How do you like being the only woman warden, Cat?"

Eyes around the table are looking at me. "Well, I really don't think about it that way," I say, trying to put words to my feelings. "Do I feel any different than a young man who's training to be a warden? I don't think so."

"Well, you're working with a bunch of men, doing a man's job," she presses.

There's an edge to her voice and a challenge to my career decision.

"I grew up around this work, Lizette, loving the outdoors and the environment. I don't consider warden work as 'a man's job.'" I watch for some indication from Jinot that he's siding with me. He glances up from his plate and winks but remains quiet.

"Well, you *are* out there, all night long... What do you talk about?" she asks.

I look at her, trying to figure what she's getting at. "We talk about warden stuff," I say.

Jinot lets out a small laugh, along with his parents. His laughter diffuses the tension in the room. "Cat fits in with the wardens, Lizette. She might do things differently than men, but it's effective."

Lizette is not convinced, I can tell.

I look to Nadine and compliment her on the tenderness of the venison. The whole meal is delicious. Jinot regales us with a few "Cat stories" that get the diners laughing. I can't help but laugh myself.

Hot apple pie with homemade ice cream is dessert. Although I'm busting-out full, I can't leave without a sample.

Jinot sits back in his chair. "I do want to make an announcement while you're here, Cat."

I look up from my pie, puzzled. Everyone is looking at Jinot, waiting for him to continue.

Lizette is leaning into him, and now he has his arm around her, pulling her closer. "Lizette and I are going to be married on New Year's." Jinot holds her hand up to show a small but pretty engagement ring on her finger.

"Ohhh," I say, stunned. Several thoughts all come together in my little pea brain. "That's wonderful," I manage, as disappointment shatters me. I look to the parents, but they are not surprised.

His face is happy. He turns to kiss Lizette and look into her eyes.

I watch from the other side of the table and want to scream, *No, you're making a mistake!* But my partner and good friend is happy. I look at them both and realize they fit together. I'm muddled and try to pull my feelings into cohesive thoughts. It's not working. I raise my wine glass, "To happiness."

"Thanks, Cat," Jinot says.

Clueless…

28

CHRISTMAS TREE THEFT

After the invitation and the dinner, my mood matches the dull gray skies and cold frigid temperature. Ida knows I'm in a funk and tries to distract me. "Cat, come on, you don't have anything you gotta do now. Come with me to check the landings in the Northwest Township. You need to get out and take a break from all those reports." She looks at me with a pouting face.

We know landings are notorious places for the public to take advantage of. These flat areas next to the water were used in log drives during the early 1900s. Logs were hauled onto the ice in winter and later floated downriver to sawmills. After the drives stopped, these landings were perfect spots to camp, picnic, and launch boats. A few people will monopolize the spot with their campers or leave refuse lying about. We've even found an abandoned school bus at one of them. Keeping the landings clean and available to others is important.

"I haven't finished my reports yet," I reply, but she knows I'm tempted.

"Look, you can scout the territory with me while I check on the landings and make sure they're clear."

Ida has been my sounding board. She shoots me a concerned look. "You haven't been out in the field in a week. Come on, you might find something...worth going after."

"OK, I'm in," I say a bit too quickly. "But I'm driving."

"Fine by me," Ida replies as we reach for our coats. We scoot out the door and head for her truck.

Punk Lutkins has also been in the office, follows us without speaking, and heads toward his truck. Punk's ego is as strong as a tree trunk, and he's hardheaded, as well. He comes to the office when he's required to be there or needs supplies, preferring to work alone, without supervision…or accountability.

"Where's that scheming suck-up heading all of a sudden?" Ida says, as I unlock the truck doors and lift a leg in.

"Nowhere good, I'm sure," I respond, as she climbs in the passenger side.

She adds, "I feel slimy just looking at him. I should give him my evil-eye look so he knows I'm watching him." With that, Ida gives Punk a grimaced stare while he wheels out of the parking lot, her big eyes small and squinty, her lips pursed and taut.

"Yeah, Ida, I'm sure you scared him," I say as we pull onto the road.

We head north on the west side of the lake. The water reflects the grayness of the day. Evergreens add color to the otherwise dull mocha woods that stand between us and the lake. We pull into the Misty Bay Road to check on a harvesting job just completed. We get to the landing and find that it's all cleaned out of equipment and logs that were heading to the turning mill.

"Looks good here," I comment.

"Yeah, from here it does," she replies. "Let's stop and walk it a bit."

Ida has her hands in her pockets as she walks into the cut. To me, it looks like a bombed site, void of lush green trees and other vegetation. Now only stumps and bark bleached by the sun dominate hopeful sprigs of green. "Look at these baby trees," she says crouching next to a tiny seedling. "This site had been cut so many times, I worried the place would just grow weeds. But look at the little spruce and balsam fir seedlings coming up. The cutters left the site in good shape, and in a few years, passersby will see the young trees coming back by the thousands."

"Critters will like it, too," I say. "Deer, moose, grouse, all love this young growth. We often see deer in these young cuts. They eat the browse and get away from bugs. As the trees get taller, it provides cover and protection. Let's head up to the northwest border."

We cross Three-Mile Bog a short time later and head east toward the lake. The road is winding through older cuts that were attacked by spruce budworm years ago. This state forest now has thickets of spruce and fir that are ten to twenty feet tall. We're fifteen miles off of blacktop in a remote area. Beautifully shaped, the conical trees remind us of Christmas to come. We continue around a bend and see mounds of these young trees lying next to the road. I slow the truck and note that the stems of the trees are freshly cut.

"Holy crap," Ida says in disbelief. "Keep going. Look at the stacks of trees ahead of us, too. There's no cutting allowed here!" She's on the edge of her seat and rolling down the window as if trying to get a better view of the illegally cut trees in this remote area.

"They look like they've been cut recently, waiting for a truck to haul 'em away," I reply, dumbfounded. We drive another quarter mile down the road and see hundreds of young trees that have been dragged to the road. They lie stacked with their trunks just feet off the road.

We come up on an old Chevy truck parked on the side of the road. No one is around it. We get out and look through the windshield to the dash and seat for clues. We listen for movement around us, but hear nothing.

"I've never seen this truck," Ida remarks. "Can you call it in to get the owner information?"

"Yep, good idea," I say. The truck information doesn't provide any clues, but Jinot radios that he's not far from where we are and will come see what's going on.

Ida and I find a hiding spot where we can park and watch the old Chevy and wait for its owner. We estimate 500 to 700 trees have been cut, each worth twenty bucks. We speculate that a self-loading truck will arrive, pick up the trees, and head straight for the city to sell them as Christmas trees.

Within the hour, we spot a warden vehicle coming down the road and assume it's Jinot. The vehicle stops and from the passenger seat jumps a man dressed in cutter pants and jacket. He grabs his brush saw from the back and signals a goodbye to the truck.

I tell Ida that I need to take this one myself. But her response is quick—"Like heck you will"—and she jumps in with me. We tear out of our spot and rush the government-issue truck, scaring the cutter into dropping his saw. We now see low-life Punk in the driver's seat. I stop so we're grill to grill with Punk's truck and get out. Punk is slow to move and not real surprised to see us.

"Well, look at Tweedledee and Tweedledum," he says, climbing out of his truck.

"Who you calling dumb, you little twit," Ida retorts. "We caught you red-handed, you slimy little tree stealer."

At that, the cutter speaks up with, "I cut these trees."

Ida and I turn to him in unison, not believing. We look to Punk, who grins and nods his head.

Jinot arrives in minutes and assesses the situation. We hear from the cutter that he has a permit to cut Christmas trees but somehow got turned around and found himself in the wrong area. Punk lets the guy talk while his satisfied smirk broadens and he nods an affirmation that the story is plausible.

"He's snaking his way out of this, Jinot," I say under my breath. "You know Punk hired him and is paying him to take the heat."

"Not much we can do about it today, Cat," Jinot replies. "Give the cutter a citation and we'll do the counting and picture-taking."

Punk says to the cutter, "You're in good hands, Reuben. I'm heading up the road to an appointment. Sorry Jinot, I can't stay and help." Punk gives Ida and me a self-satisfied look and slithers off to his truck.

The cutter quietly scuffs his feet, picks up his saw, and puts it in the back of his Chevy. He soon has his new citation and court date. Ida and I still believe Punk paid him off in some way, but we'll never know the truth.

29

AXEL

I'm halfway to the north end of my territory when the cold rain begins. Punk has been transferred to a post near the Canadian border. I'm not sure if Jinot turned him in or word got out that Punk's such a twit, but he deserves to be up north where he'll get lost. At least I don't have to worry about him being anywhere near me, and it's a relief.

I'm nearing the top of Eagle Lake on gravel backroads, lost in my thoughts with nothing to interrupt them. Camp owners come long distances to hunt here in deer season, but because the camps are so remote, it's easy to hunt after the season closes and not get caught. One main logging road weaves into the Northeast Township and crests the top of a hill. From this main artery, camp roads branch downhill toward the lake.

I'm snug in my old car, windshield wipers beating to the tune of "My Girl" on the radio. I'll lose the signal soon, with no station to replace it, so I'll only have the windshield wipers to keep me company amongst the hillsides. The day is gray and the woods are brown, but young white birch add contrast with their snow-white bark on slender stems—pretty even when leafless. And, of course, the dark-green of balsam fir is ever-present. The rain is transitioning to sleet, making the day even more dreary.

On my way along the remote road, I come upon a harvesting job. A huge yellow skidder sits on the side of the road. A large man has his head bent over the fittings of this massive machine that's at least twice the size of my car. Big mechanical arms on the machine are built to hold full-length trees as they're dragged from the landscape. The man looks up long enough for me to see dirty-blond hair peeking out from his orange hard hat. His beard is thick and the same color, but his eyes are clear-water blue. He nods a greeting without letting go of his wrench or the hydraulic hose he's working on.

Unthinking, I've slowed down, interested. I'm guessing he's about my age and ruggedly broad-shouldered. I return to my driving and speed up a bit. Sleet now builds on the sides of my windshield where the wipers pile it up. I turn up the defroster and the heat. Within minutes, I'm nearing the camps and take the landing road down to see if there are any residents. The lakeside camps may seem abandoned today, but these cottages have heard decades of laughter from families enjoying their vacation retreats, especially in warm months. In cold weather like today, you should smell wood smoke and coffee brewing if they're in use. But there are no cars or smoke, and nothing of interest, warden-wise.

The sleet is turning to a cold mist that looks like velvety fog through the woodland. My tires slip on the road as I travel back up the camp road. They currently grip, but driving conditions will only get worse as the mist continues coating the land and freezing on contact. I am asking for trouble by delaying my return to town. My thoughts turn to my tires' tread wear. *I've needed tires for a while,* I muse, *and I'd better get 'em before we get snow.* The icy glaze over the road is now shimmering and getting thicker. I slow on a corner and feel the car skate in slow motion to the road's edge, where the tires catch on tufts of weeds and humps of gravel, stopping me from sliding into the ditch.

I put the car in reverse and back away from my front-end nosedive. It begins sliding backward despite pumping the brake. I'm at the mercy of the ice and remind myself to get snow tires mounted *as soon* as I get back to civilization. Now facing a pretty steep hill, the car needs to climb it before I can drive back to the office. The side of the road has more loose gravel and tufts of grass along the shoulder that might help in traction. I gently step on the gas pedal, making the car creep up the hill and trying to dredge up momentum to overcome the slicker spots in the road. To no avail: halfway up, my wheels spin freely, and not only do I slow, but I cease moving forward and begin sliding backward again. *Shit.*

I pump my brakes repeatedly, then turn my wheel a little, trying to find traction. The car skates backward in slow motion, and I can do nothing but go along for the ride. My right rear wheel falls into the ditch and the car frame lands on the road with a thud. I find myself looking cockeyed up toward the treetops. *Shit.*

Well, I'm no longer moving backwards. But now what am I gonna do?

The door is heavy, and opening it means pushing up like the hatch on a submarine. But it's my tilted Toyota. I push hard and pull myself up limb by limb. My boots have little traction as they touch the ground. The door falls back, slamming into my shins. *Ouch and son-of-a-sea-biscuit!* It takes at least five minutes of trial and error before I get the right combination of door pushing, feet on the ground, and pulling my butt out of the seat before I'm clear of the car. The door slams fiercely shut, just with gravity.

My boots are like ice skates as I move around the car for support. I feel like a novice skater trying to maintain balance. Making my way to the passenger side, I observe what I already know: My rear wheel is dangling over the ditch while the frame rests on the road's edge, saving my sorry butt from sliding backward into the deep trench, which would be worse.

The car's back end is angled into the ditch and solidly rooted. But the front end is sticking out in the middle of the road, and these roads aren't wide. If a car should come up over the crest of the hill unexpectedly, we are both toast.

I could call for help on the radio... But then the whole county would know I've gotten myself into a predicament I can't get myself out of. Not happening—at least until I become desperate. I could try to jack the frame up and put stones and wood under the wheel... As I assess this option, I realize the ditch is too sharply angled and deep to make a firm base.

And freezing mist keeps caking on my head and shoulders. I pull an insulated raincoat from the backseat. It's nice and warm. The hood covers my head and ears, and I find gloves to keep my chilly fingers from turning to ice cubes. Walking up the hill is tricky as I try to find stable footing. My destination is the harvesting job.

Once I reach the crest of the hill, walking is much easier. I try to walk in the woods where footing is surer, but icy branches whip my face and I stumble on the uneven ground—right back to the road. Progress is slow, but at least I'm moving forward and can now see the skidder. *Where's the man and his truck? What do I do if he's already left?* I unconsciously slow while I weigh my options. *Well, crap.*

There's not much to do but move forward. I'm a few hundred yards away when I see the bearded wonder move out from around the skidder. As I get closer, I see his pickup has been hidden by the huge piece of equipment. He is still focusing on whatever he's doing and doesn't notice me approaching.

"Hi," I say from beneath my big jacket decorated in beautiful green and brown camouflage print.

His head perks up in surprise. "Hello!" he says, trying to figure out who and what I am. "You just out for a walk in the fresh air?" He's grabbing a rag and wiping the dark grease and fluid from his hands but otherwise is giving me his full attention. I notice his Carhartt jacket is wet with skims of ice on the shoulders. Water is dripping from his hard hat.

"Aren't your hands cold?" I have to ask.

"Not too bad," he says. "The hydraulic fluid is still warm." He looks at me quizzically. "You look like you're missing something, maybe, like, a car."

"Oh, you noticed," I say. "There's nothing like walking in a freezing rain."

"Let me guess, you belong to that little Toyota that passed by earlier, and you've abandoned it somewhere near the lake?"

"That's about it," I say. "You wouldn't have a chain in your truck that could pull me out of a ditch, would you?"

"Lady, I've got chains on tires, spare chains in the truck, and if you haven't noticed, the skidder has the mother of all chains on each wheel." He points to the tires wrapped in chains. "We just might be able to help ya."

I take a closer look at the huge wheels I'm standing next to. The tires on this behemoth are close to five feet high with chains encircling the entire perimeter of the deep treads. Each link is two inches long and made of heavy-gauge steel. This net of heavy metal crisscrosses the black tire surface with one-inch cleats that dig into ice and would crush anything underneath.

"Well, this is quite a machine," I say as I try to fathom the power it must have to drag big trees over stumps and rocks and bring them to the road. At this point, the skidder also has a shiny glaze of ice covering it.

"Yep, it is. Your timing is good," he says. "It's fixed and ready to rumble."

I look at the man and his machine. The man's skin is pale and ruddy from working outdoors. He reminds me of a Viking ready to shove off from shore: confident and ready for adventure.

"I suggest you sit on my lap in the driver's seat," he says, "where you won't slide off."

I look at the icy machine and the heavy tires, nervous. "I don't have much of a choice, do I?"

"Sure, you do," he replies. "You can walk back."

I watch him swing his long legs up to the bars that act as steps to the driver's seat. He sits down, pulls on some gloves, and starts the machine.

It roars and spits exhaust from a stack above the man's head. I wait for him to turn to me. With an extended arm, he says, "Well?"

I reach for the handle, pull myself up, and look at him. "Since I don't take rides from strangers, how about introductions?"

"Axel Anderson," he says over the rumble.

"Hi, Axel. I'm Cat," I say leaning toward his ear.

With that, I try gently turning to sit on his lap. He reaches around me for the levers. The machine grinds into gear and leaps, pulling me heavily into Axel's lap and chest. "Oh!" is all I can say as we lurch forward.

Axel's brown insulated jacket and pants are covered in a mixture of dark grease, dirt, and sawdust. His now gloved hands are expertly shifting gears and steering us down the road. I am intimately aware of his strong arms around me. The chains clank loosely around the tires as we move along. As the chains cut through the glaze of ice, the gravel underneath the machine grumbles and squeals.

Within minutes, we arrive at my poor little tilted Toyota. Axel suggests I get down and move away from the road. I hang onto the machine, carefully placing my boots on the ice, then sliding past my front bumper to the driver's side of the car. Axel turns the skidder around and backs up to the car. He climbs down onto the road, grabs a chain from the side toolbox, and lies under the front of the car to hook the chain onto something solid. *He's done this a few times.* The other end of the chain is wrapped around a sturdy part of the skidder. "Get into the car, put it in neutral, and steer it back onto the road," he says. "I'll pull you up over the hill."

I obey.

Axel urges the big yellow machine forward until the chain is taut. As I feel him pull the car toward him, the chassis scrapes the road until the right rear wheel finds the road surface and the car returns to level. I let the skidder's power and traction pull us over the hill so that we are both over the hump, so to speak. Axel stops the machine, and I inch a little closer to make the chain go slack, then put the car in park. Axel slides off the machine. While he removes the chain from his skidder, I show him I'm no sissy by lying under my car and unhooking the chain from the frame.

"Thank you, Axel," I say as I shake his big hand. "What do I owe you?"

"How about a drink on Friday night?" he says.

I hesitate. "I may be working Friday night."

"OK, how about Saturday night?"

"See, I never know when I'll be working. Here's what I can tell you: I like Pulasky's and will buy you a drink when we meet."

"OK... When will that be?"

"Maybe Friday, I can get off early," I say, afraid to share what I do for work. *Would he be turned off by the fact I'm a warden?* "Thank you for coming to my rescue. But I better go before my car freezes in place," I say, as I turn to get in the car. There's just enough room to pull around the big machine.

"Watch the ice, Cat."

"I will," I say, as I wave and slowly drive away.

As soon as I get a chance to call Ida, I do. "Do you know a logger by the name of Axel Anderson?" I ask. Then notice I'm holding my breath.

"Axel? Sure, he's a cutie," she starts. "But he's not really a logger... Well, maybe you could call him a logger..."

"Ida!" I blurt. "What about him?"

"I'm trying to tell you. And what's got you worked up into a lather, anyway? Geez."

"Please, just tell me," I say, settling down.

"Actually, he's a forester, kind of," she says. "He was in my class after coming out of the army. But something happened and he couldn't graduate with us. Missing a few credits, I think. Why?"

"I met him today. He pulled me out of a ditch so I owe him a drink."

"Axel's working up here?" she says, sounding surprised. "When you paying him back?"

"Depending on work, it could be this weekend," I say. "If I can get the night off, would you go with me?"

"You're asking me on your date?" she asks.

"No, we don't have a date," I say. "I didn't want to commit, so I told him I might or might not be there."

"What the heck you holding out for, girlfriend?" Ida asks. "Jinot's taken. Now there's Axel... Seems convenient to me."

After work on Friday, Ida comes to my house with a pizza for dinner and a beer. We chat, listen to music, and finish getting ready for Pulasky's. I want to look my best, so I put curl in my hair, apply a little mascara, and end with lip gloss.

"You know, this look didn't work so well on Jinot," Ida says.

"Jinot was taken and I was too dumb to realize it," I reply.

We arrive at Pulasky's a little before nine and find that my chief and his family band are providing the music tonight. *Cool!* The chief is up on the stage singing a Johnny Cash song, "I Walk the Line." Ms. Janelle looks lovely and has a beautiful voice that harmonizes well with Basil's. Their oldest son, Aaron, is on the drums. Billy, the second oldest, is on bass guitar. Both boys are underage for a bar, but they have obviously played enough to look comfortable in their surroundings.

I wave to the band as I walk past the dance floor to the other side of the bar. They smile and nod. Ida and I order beer and find a seat at the bar. It doesn't surprise me that I don't see Axel. It's early yet.

We sip our beers for a few minutes before deciding to head to the dance floor. The music is lively; Basil and his family do a great job of entertaining the growing crowd, and everyone seems to be having a good time. A few beers and dances later, the band takes a break. Basil comes over to talk with us.

"It's nice that you came out to support the band," he says. "I didn't expect you."

"We didn't know you were gonna be here, so this is a nice surprise," Ida blurts. "Cat's got a date!"

I can see the chief's expression change.

"I don't have a date, Ida…unless it's with you," I say, concerned with the chief's reaction.

"Oh, OK, you're just here to meet up with a cutie," she says.

I decide to take control of the conversation before it gets out of hand. "I owe this guy a beer for pulling me out of a ditch," I say to the chief with a shrug. "He may or may not show up."

"I see," Basil says. "Well, you look nice tonight, Cat. Not warden-ly, but nice." Basil reaches for a beer from Pop Pulasky and heads back to talk with his band.

"Wow, that was interesting," I say to Ida. "He didn't seem too pleased that I could be meeting up with someone. He didn't even comment on my kissing a ditch."

"Ah, he's probably got a lot on his mind, like what songs to sing next," Ida counters. "Besides, if I had two cute sons getting these girls all riled up, I'd be worried, too."

"Ida, they're underage," I remark.

"More reasons to be worried," she adds.

It's about eleven when Ida and I come off the dance floor, laughing at the moves Ida's been trying out. I spot Axel standing in the back of the crowd with a cold beer in hand.

"Hello," I say walking up to him. "I thought I was supposed to buy that for you."

"You looked busy," he says. "And I was thirsty."

"I wasn't sure you were coming," I add. He's cleaned up and in a nice collared shirt and jeans. The blue of his shirt matches his eyes.

"I wasn't either," he said. "I was at the university late. It took me a couple hours to get back, with the roads freezing up again."

Ida comes over with our beers. "Hi, Axel. I hear you helped Cat out of a jam."

"Nothing that a small machine with chains couldn't handle," Axel says.

"You still taking classes?" Ida asks.

"Yep. Tonight was dirt class," he says. "I never knew there was so much to learn about dirt."

Ida and I laugh with him because we all had to take Soils 101 before we graduated, but I can't imagine taking it on a Friday night. Axel has an easy way about him. I buy him his next beer while Ida and I drink seltzer. The three of us squeeze onto the dance floor for one dance under the piercing gaze of the lead singer, my boss.

As we leave the floor, a nice-looking blonde girl comes over to say hi to Axel, but she's clearly had too much to drink, trips, and spills her beer all over me before she's caught and held upright by Axel and Ida.

It's been a fun night and it's no time to get mad. "Well, that just tells me it's time to say good night," I say, looking down at my beer-stained clothes. Ida says she's ready to leave, too.

That leaves Axel to talk with his friend. He says he has to work in the morning and needs to leave shortly, as well.

Ida and I pack into her car so she can take me home.

"So, whaddaya think?" Ida asks seconds after closing her car door.

"He's nice," I reply.

"Well, that's the understatement of the year!" she retorts. "Plus, I gave him your phone number."

"You what?!" I scream.

"Sure did. Gave him your phone number when you weren't looking," Ida says, quite happy with herself. Then she giggles.

I look at her and have to smile, too. "So, you think he'll call?"

"Oh, yeah… I'd bet on it."

The next morning, I wake up with pleasant thoughts of Axel. The day is filled with mundane chores, but at least I can do them in a good mood. My phone rings around five that evening, and I answer in giddy anticipation. "Hello, this is Cat."

"You seemed to have a good time last night," the voice says.

I hesitate. "Yes, I did. Your band pulled in a lot of people, Chief. It was a fun night."

"Yup, that's what we do," he says solemnly. His serious and low tone is not normal. "I'm calling because I have a trapping complaint for you to work on."

"Now?" I ask, confused.

"Why? This isn't a good time for your social life?"

Oh, that's it. He's upset that I might not be available at his convenience... "No, sir, I'm on my way over...unless it's not convenient for you."

"I'll be waiting."

"Hello," Ida says, when I call her an hour later.

"Want to go out with me tonight?" I ask. "I need to let loose a little bit. You in?"

"'Course, I am!" she says. "Pulasky's? Basil's band should be playing there again tonight..."

"Nope, not Pulasky's. You mind going out of town, where people don't know us?"

"Heck, I like the sound of that," she replies. "I'll pick you up in an hour."

Ida drives to a tourist town in the next county. We like the idea of eating and drinking in a pub with a friendly atmosphere. Meanwhile, I fill Ida in on Basil's conversation with me. He told me I should focus on my job. That I've got a lot to learn and some man in my life is gonna ruin my opportunity to succeed. She lets me vent while we try a couple of the specialty drinks being offered.

I'm not sure what time it is when I find Axel behind me as Ida and I are laughing with the bartender. I'm inebriated enough to not care how he got there; I'm just glad to see him and offer to buy him a drink. He joins in the barroom banter. We're having such a good time, I lose track of my alcohol consumption, teetering as I stand. "Whoa, cowgirl," he says, holding me up straight.

"I'm not feeling so well," I say, trying to make my mouth work properly. I excuse myself and try to walk a straight line to the ladies' room.

Ida follows me in. "Axel's gonna take us home, Cat."

"Oh, isn't that nice," I say, polluted.

Axel waits patiently for us to gather ourselves. He escorts us out to his truck and deposits us in the passenger seat made for one. We giggle as we try to put the seat belt around us both. We're not paying much attention to him as he gets in the driver's side and puts the truck in gear. The next thing I know, we're at Ida's place and he's unbuckling our seat belt.

"First stop," he says, then walks beside Ida up to her door. "Where are your door keys, Ida?"

She has trouble finding them in her purse and seems to be stirring her hand in it like a witch with her cauldron. I laugh from the truck. Axel smiles, helps her find the keys, then unlocks her door and turns on a light for her before returning to the truck.

"So, how did you find us?" I ask, sobering up a little.

"Ida called," he said as he turns the truck toward my place. "And it's a good thing she did. Was there a reason you went to another county to get soused?"

"I'm feeling kind of sorry for myself," I say. "I'm a warden."

"I know."

I look at Axel, trying to read his face. "It doesn't bother you?"

"Nope. Why should it? It's not like I'm some poacher."

"Well, if you're not turned off by a woman who smells like a forest fire or deer guts," I say, "then maybe it would be because I work every night and can't have a life outside my work!" Quietly, tears start dripping down my face.

Axel reaches around to pull out a grease-smeared towel. "This is all I got," he says, looking helpless.

I take it and find an unstained corner in which I blow my nose without thinking. "Oh, I'm sorry!" I say, looking at him before we both let out a laugh and release the tension. We're now in my dooryard, and he gets out of the truck to come around and let me out. "Can I wash the towel for you?"

"Nah," he says with a chuckle and walks me to my door. "Do you need help with your keys?" he asks…maybe serious.

"No," I say looking up at him from my doorstep. "Do you want to come in?"

He looks into my eyes, hesitating. In the quiet moment, he leans into me slowly. His warm lips on mine are moist and luscious. His broad arms envelop me in comfort and safety. I melt into his body, wanting more. "I'd love to…but not tonight," he whispers. I pull away slightly, trying to gather my thoughts as I look into his face. His eyes are soft and understanding the moment. "Let's take this slow."

"But I don't want to take it slow!" I say, pulling back farther.

"You've had too much to drink and need to go to bed," he says in a big-brother tone. "Alone," he adds. "I have an idea…" he says, pointing at my patient Toyota sitting nearby. "I see you haven't bought your snow tires yet. I'll pick you up at ten tomorrow morning to go tire shopping. How's that for a first date?"

"That isn't quite what I had in mind," I answer, looking at him.

But that's what we do.

30

LYING IN WAIT

I'm finally in place after trudging a long distance to get to this stream. *Breathe. Get your heart rate down. Exhale…as slowly as possible. Inhale…again.* My body is responding, feeling the adrenaline seeping away. *Where does adrenaline go when you want to calm yourself, anyway?*

I'm perched on a ledge, hiding, with the brook bubbling below my feet. Its flow takes the melting snow downstream, washing the stones bare, too cold for moss to grow. The banks of the stream around me have islands of ice, but it's not yet cold enough to freeze over. Lingering warmth holds the winter's prison at bay.

The rocky clay banks of my perch are cold and wet. They smell of frost and mud and mold. *Breathe in. Exhale.* The fresh water has an acidic smell but is clear and cleansing. The deeper waters are cobalt and glacial blue. The shallows are transparent, with deepening ochre tones. Ripples dance in hues of creamy whites.

My target is within view. It needs my attention. Through the early-morning fog, it lies in wait. Its fur is light as air and teases the fog's misty droplets. They collect on its umber coat, lying still like a blanket, trying to keep the owner warm and dry. Small and vulnerable, once active and whimsical, it lies still. The envy of thousands, its coat is thick and warm and beautiful. The fur is soft and downy, light to the touch, just like its ancestors'. And so valuable.

The object of my thoughts doesn't need my pity. It's too late. It lies there while I watch and wait. The cold dampness is creeping through the back of my woolen clothes. The air is raw and gnaws at my fingertips. I wonder how and when my wait will end. *What will I say? What will I do?*

I don't know who will interrupt my solitude. My disgust for this sport will be evident, no doubt. But who am I more enraged at? The trappers who work hard to tend their traps every day and prepare the beautiful pelts? Or those who purchase and adorn themselves in God's creatures? What drives a person to slog their way through the wet and cold, take a life in a brutal manner, and prepare its hide for sale? As a warden, I ensure compliance with the laws that allow this. But my gut objects to this form of taking.

The noise of an approaching machine rudely interrupts the brook's trickling song. It stops within 100 feet of the mink. A man is dressed in brown bulky overalls and large insulated boots that look disproportionately large on his small frame. He is intent on his mission, expertly putting on his woven backpack and making his way to the trap. He has no idea that I am watching.

Smiling at his success, he bends over to disengage the harsh metal clamp from its lifeless prey. He looks briefly at the creature before placing it in a pouch he's carrying. With no ceremony, he pulls out a baggie of bait to reset the trap for another victim.

"Stop there, sir. Warden!" I bellow. Startled, he rises up and sees me, but stays silent. "Step away from the trap, sir." I jump across the brook and make my way toward him. He is still and standing up now. "You got a weapon on you?"

"No, ma'am, just a club for the critters." The voice of this young man is respectful and slightly shaky. He tries to get a better view of me as I come closer. "Ma'am, you scared the crap out of me. I didn't expect anyone out here."

"I need to see your trapping license, and while you're at it, why don't you tell me your name and where you live?" I say as I watch him. He's young, late teens maybe, gangly and spry. He's watching me with quick eyes and concern on his face.

"Wayne. Wayne Toole. I'm a wildlife student at the college. I live on campus there…here's my license."

"So, you're a wildlife student *and* a trapper? Have you read the trapping laws, Wayne?"

"Yes, ma'am. I trap to pay for my schooling. It takes a lot of pelts to pay for college."

"Regulations say you ask for permission before you cross private property, and you *must* put your name and address on your traps. Where's your name on the trap, Wayne? I don't see it, do you?"

Wayne bends over his trap and pushes the debris away from it. "No, ma'am. Boy, this isn't good. I'm pretty careful about following the law, Warden. I don't want a violation to get in the way of landing a job at graduation."

"Mark your traps, Wayne, and get permission from the landowners," I say as I begin to write a citation. "So, how's the trapping been this winter?"

"Good. I've done well, which means the population is in good shape."

"I gotta tell you, Wayne, I hate trapping. Seems like a cruel way of taking an animal."

"Yes, ma'am, but the population has to have some control or it affects the fish population, the farmer's chickens, eggs, and the like. I do think it's a sport like hunting. It's man against nature and certainly a part of this country's history. 'Sides, there's a big demand out there! If people were against it, they wouldn't be buying fur coats and capes, would they?"

"What are you, a college debater or something?"

"No, ma'am," he says with a cute grin. "I know better than to have traps without my name on them. This one might've slipped off or something."

"Nice try, Wayne. I'm issuing a citation for this trap and this instance. I need the mink you put in your pouch and will be taking this trap with me as evidence. You can check your other traps for compliance before I stumble onto them or get another complaint."

Wayne's grin disappears as he reaches into his pouch for the mink. As he extends it to me, he says, "How do you know *this* is the mink I pulled from this trap?" he says testily. "Don't you need to know that *this* is the same animal from *this trap*?"

"Hand over the mink, Wayne, and don't get wise." I take the small creature and look in its mouth. "Yep, this is the one." I hand the citation over. "Wayne, pay up the fine and get your other traps in order. If you have any questions about the chain of evidence or whether you can get out of the citation, look here." I hold out the mink pointing to the earring placed in its mouth. "That's mine." I pull away my hat to show the matching earring in my one ear. Wayne grins with a nod of acceptance.

"Got it, Warden. I'll go check my other traps," he says, extending his hand as if to say *You got me.*

Wayne walks over to his four-wheeler, mounts it, and waves goodbye.

I head in the other direction thinking about the industrious kid paying for his own education by trapping such beautiful creatures. *I wonder how many others do something like this to pay for their education in hopes of making a better living?*

31

CAROL

"Hey, stranger," Carol says in a friendly, welcoming way as I walk into her shop. "You look like you need a haircut, girlfriend."

"Yeah, you're right about that," I respond, shaking off the December chill. "It's been a long, busy fall, and I'm ready to get cleaned up again."

There is something charming about Carol's little hair salon. It's small and cozy with wood paneling and lots of plants tucked around the room. An older woman is sitting under the hood of a hair dryer, comfortably warm. She's gone back to her magazine now that she's scoped me out and lost interest.

Carol is a cute blonde. Her shoulder-length hair is tied up in a loose ponytail today. On me it would look messy, but Carol can pull it off, looking attractive, carefree, and sexy. Her pale pink sweater fits loosely over her young curves. Her jeans are worn in the right places and her old Frye boots complete the package. If she wasn't so nice, I could hate her.

I grab a tabloid with the latest pictures of actresses in their glamorous dresses and find a chair. Carol is finishing a little girl's haircut, taking great pride in the four-year-old's smile as she brushes the clipped bangs. The mom is sitting beside me watching Carol perform magic on her timid child. I can feel the pride in the mother's body language as Carol lifts the child from the chair.

"Thank you for being such a good girl," Carol says as she hands the youngster a lollipop.

"Thanks, Carol," the mother says, handing her a check. "We'll see you after the holidays."

"Sounds good, Monique. Enjoy your holidays, and don't forget the cookies for Santa!"

The door opens, providing a brief blast of cold air before Carol motions me over to the chair. "You probably won't need the booster seat," she says as she lifts it away.

"Not today, at least," I reply. "So how are you? It feels like I haven't seen you forever."

"That's because you've been working the whole fall, girlfriend. I've been around. Actually, I've been *around* more than usual. I broke up with Danny, finally."

"No kidding. Why?" I ask, anxious to catch up on her news.

"We've been dating for two years and it wasn't going anywhere. We never did anything but sit around watching sports or drinking beer with his buddies. I want to *do* things," she says.

I smile, understanding.

"My high school friend, Teresa, and I hooked up. We go dancing, head off to the shows, go shopping…. I've even had a couple of dates with some guys from out of town," she says, bubbling.

"Well, that sounds like fun."

"Yeah, it's a nice change. But I still have my eye on Jinot, Cat. What's it gonna take for him to take me out?"

"Good luck with that, Carol. He introduced me to his fiancée two weeks ago."

"No kidding… Well, another one bites the dust," Carol says, snipping here and clipping there. Before I know it, my hair looks healthy and thick again.

"You're wonderful, Carol. Thank you," I say as I hand her my payment. "I'm traveling for Christmas, but let's plan to get together after New Year's."

"Great, Cat. Let's do it. Maybe I'll have a new beau by then," Carol says with a wink.

December was both cold and snowy. With Christmas and New Year's now behind us, the landscape is white and icy with little to look forward to. Local establishments do their best to attract patrons by providing live music on the weekends. The parking lots fill with cars, trucks, and snowmobiles. It's mid-January and Axel is traveling. Ida and I walk into Pulasky's to see the chief's band play. The place is standing room only, but I spot Carol on the other side of the dance floor, walk over, and say hi.

"Meet Greg, Cat," Carol says. "He's from Buffalo County and works up here regularly."

"Hi, Greg. Nice to meet you," I reply, noticing his easiness. I warm up to him immediately.

Ida strolls up with a beer in each hand, one of them for me. We introduce her to Greg.

"What do you do?" Ida asks, taking the words right out of my mouth.

"I'm a sales rep for Ski-Doo snowmobiles."

"Oh, cool," I say, assessing him. *Nice-looking, personable, and has a good job. What's not to like?*

The band plays a few Johnny Cash tunes. Greg and Carol head to the dance floor to enjoy each other's company as Basil and Ms. Janelle sing "Daddy Sang Bass." When the music slows to "Remember Me," Greg and Carol come off the floor and take another sip of their beers.

"We're about ready to take off, Cat," Carol says. "Greg wants to take me out on the lake with this new snow machine. It has heated seats!"

"Be careful, Carol. Greg, do you know the lake well?"

"Oh, Cat, quit being such a…warden!" Carol says, half joking.

I look at them skeptically as they get up and go to the next room to put on their snowmobile suits.

At 6:30 the next morning, my phone rings. "Cat, there's been an accident on the lake," Jinot says.

"Snowmobiles?"

"Yep, I'll pick you up in fifteen minutes. Dress warm. It's not even up to zero yet."

"OK."

I layer up for the car ride with my snowmobile suit beside me. Boots, mittens, hat, and liner are also handy. I'm moving in slow motion, my body doing what's needed but my mind muddled with terrible questions that we'll need to answer once we get to the scene.

"What do we know so far, Jinot?" I ask as I settle into the passenger seat. Jinot hands me coffee and looks at me, concerned.

"Not much, Cat. A couple on the shore opened their curtains this morning to see an odd mess on the lake. They put binoculars on a debris field of snowmobile parts and what looks like a body… An officer is on the way up now to talk with them. He's going to direct us in."

"You know, Carol was heading out with her new friend last night," I say.

"There were a lot of people out last night, Cat. Let's see what we find before we worry about anyone in particular."

"Yep, I hear you. But let's get there fast, OK?"

Our flashing blue lights are pointless as we travel the empty roads this early in the morning. The roads are white from salt and frost. We learn from Dispatch where the closest entry point is. We pull Jinot's snowmobile off the trailer behind his cruiser and hook the rescue sled on the back. Then we gear up to be first responders.

As we approach the scene, a huge frost heave catches our attention. Several feet tall, it's easy to see in the daylight, but probably not obvious at night. A snow machine is toppled over beyond it and crunched on most sides from a violent rollover. Pieces of Ski-Doo metal and plastic dot the ice. Our focus is on a body lying on the other side of the frost heave. The body is big. Not small and ladylike. My guts wrench as I take a breath.

We stop and rush to the body to get a pulse. Deep-red blood stains are dark against the crystal-white snow, and the once warm blood is now frozen. And there are four legs—one body is on top of the other. There's no pulse on the man. As I look into the visor of the smaller victim, I feel for her pulse. I look at Jinot and shake my head, but he already knows. No pulse is found on her, either.

Tears well up suddenly and cloud my vision as Jinot radios Dispatch to call the coroner's office. We take pictures of the scene like we always do. But this time, we are quietly robotic and detached. We go through the motions as professionals, our emotions entombed within.

The machine had been traveling fast, given the distance from the frost heave to the shattered carcass of the machine. The impact had such force, it threw the passengers and rolled them several times before coming to a stop. We don't scream or shout or even clench our fists. We drag ourselves through our duties, for Carol and Greg. We save our rage, our anger, and our grief for later in the privacy of our own lives.

The details of her death swirl around me. I cannot let them rattle my head…or darken my heart. I've not had to deal with the death of a close friend or family member before now. I later avoid conversations when people speculate about the accident or blame either Carol or Greg for not knowing the lake has huge frozen banks of ice across its narrows. Drinking before driving. Traveling too fast. Greg versus Danny. *She just wanted to* do *things.*

I can't stop thinking about how I could've been more convincing that last night. *Stay! Let me have the keys! Please, don't go out tonight…*

I was powerless in influencing their decision. Now I'm relegated to investigating *and* mourning their deaths.

32

SNOWMOBILES

It's been weeks since Carol's death. Every time I hear snowmobiles racing around, I cringe. "I hate snowmobiles," I say to the chief. He just looks at me like he always does when he doesn't quite know what to do with me. "They're noisy and smell like gas. I don't know why people are so passionate about riding them."

"That's because they get you across the snow where no other *mobile* gets you," the chief replies, unsympathetically. "Now I need you to check on ice fishermen and hunters near the lake. Reports say they're hunting coyotes from their machines. The season for coyotes is open, but they may be carrying loaded weapons."

"Well, that doesn't sound very safe," I say.

"No, it isn't, but if they're in the heat of the chase they want their rifles ready."

"OK, I'm on it."

An old snowmobile is loaded on a trailer, and I head for the lake's park, which gives me access to the trail, the lake, and the hunting areas nearby. The lot has a couple of empty trucks parked and a crew that's just unloaded their machines. I can see that their new sleds are registered, so I don't bother them. My little Toyota and trailer don't give away my identity, so I take my time putting on my snowmobile suit, boots, and mittens. The temperature at the moment is hovering around twenty degrees, which isn't bad. But travel at twenty miles an hour and it becomes chilly right quick.

I take the cover off my machine and push it off the trailer. It's light, by snowmobile standards, but to pick up the skis and turn it in the direction I want to go makes me work up a sweat. *Damn, it'd be nice to have a reverse gear!* Once my helmet is on, I straddle the seat and start the engine. It chokes and coughs before it starts spewing smoke and carbon. *I hate snowmobiles.*

A well-traveled trail leads to the lake. Three groups of ice fishermen are near their small shacks. Because the wind is mild, they have their fish traps set up on the open ice. I watch for a while to see if anyone catches anything before bothering them. They don't, so I do...bother them. The first fisherman is an old man by himself. I identify myself before asking to see his license.

"How long you been out today, Mr. Weiss?"

"Came out about seven, I guess."

"Catch anything?"

"Not today, Warden...too nice."

"You talk to any of the other fishermen to see what they've caught?"

"Nah, but I can see they haven't pulled anything up. It's just a great day to be out."

"Then I won't bother you anymore. Have a nice day, sir."

I check the next two groups, all with valid licenses and registered machines. Clouds are rolling in and the air begins to feel damp, like snow's coming. I straddle the seat and head west off the lake toward the county snowmobile trail system and the hunting complaint. The trail is nicely groomed, so as I sled around a corner and see a fallen tree branch in my way, I steer away from it and find myself just off the trail, powdery snow flying around me before a buried log brings my machine to a sudden stop.

Shit.

Getting off the machine, I find myself in fluffy snow just about crotch deep. I stomp around, trying to compact the snow around the machine. Melting snow trickles down my visor and impairs my vision. My boots are bulky, made for warmth not agility. I trip over a buried limb and fall face first into wet snow crystals.

Shit.

It takes me a few seconds to feel something solid and push myself upright. I pull on the machine from behind, but it doesn't budge. I move in front and pick up the skis to toss the machine six inches closer to the trail. It takes several attempts before I hear a clank of metal under the hood. The cowling flips up easily but I can see the carburetor has fallen off the engine.

Shit!

While I'm studying the engine, a shot rings out in the distance, about a mile away. *Grrrrr!*

The machine is pretty much facing the trail. I hold the carburetor up and place it on the engine, the way I think it fits, pull my dog tag from around my neck, and tie it as tight as I can around the carburetor and whatever you call the gizmo beside it. With a prayer and a little talking to the machine, she starts. I gently push the throttle to get some traction. The belt grabs and moves the sled onto the trail, where I don't dare stop but head in the direction of the shot.

Shortly, the trail opens up to a field. I stop and listen for shots or machines. I can hear snowmobiles before I can see them. I drive up closer to get a better view. There's a person to my left about 200 yards away holding a rifle and looking toward a hillside where another person is positioned. I watch for a while and hear a snowmobile in the distance to my right. The closest man motions for me to meet up with him. The wind has picked up and the temperature is dropping.

"Hey, that's some machine you have there," he says as I turn it off. His bright-orange stocking cap is smudged with grease, and his dirty-blond hair escapes around the edges. His thin face is lined and weathered from years in the elements.

"Yep, and to think it actually runs most days is amazing," I respond. "What's going on, anyway?"

"Well, I saw you hanging back there and thought you'd like to come see up close. 'Course, I thought you was a guy."

"Nope, not a guy, but I heard a rifle. Was that you?"

"No, that's my uncle up on the hill there. See?" He points to the facing hillside. "My brother is on the snowmobile. He was driving a coyote with the machine, but my uncle missed. The coyote got away. Sheep got out of the barn and the coyotes are bold enough to come out in the daylight. They got a lamb this morning before we got here, so we knew they'd be back. The sheep are back in the barn but the coyotes want the rest of the kill."

"I'm sure they're hungry."

"No doubt, but there's no free lunch here, I'm telling ya. Those damn coyotes would eat ever' critter we own, if we don't shoot 'em first."

"Did your brother see any more?"

"Yeah, there were four of 'em when they broke apart. That's why we think if we stay quiet, they'll come back and we can shoot 'em. The blowing snow is making it harder to see, but the lamb is within view over there."

I look, but don't see much, which is A-OK with me. "I'll take your word for it. So, if you have four coyotes to shoot, does your brother carry a rifle with him as well?" I'm now moving around to keep my hands and feet warm while trying to get the information I need.

"Sure."

"Better keep it loaded while you're driving the coyotes, right?" I pry.

"Nah. Too dangerous. It's best he keeps the shells out of the chamber while he's bouncing around out there. He'll have plenty of time once those predators start feeding."

"Sounds right. Say, I didn't catch your name."

"Dewalt, Dewalt Collins."

"Cat. Nice to meet you, Dewalt. But I best limp home with my iron horse here. Looks like a storm's coming."

"Good luck with the horse, Cat. I'd follow you back, but I'd be leaving my post."

"No problem," I say, satisfied there are no loaded weapons on the snow machines and pleased that I didn't even have to tell Dewalt that I was a warden. I start the machine and take a wide turn to follow the trail back to the truck. Cold is seeping in as I take it slow. My hands are aching cold by the time I successfully load the snowmobile on the trailer and lock it on. My fingers barely have the power to open the car door. I don't bother to take off the snowmobile suit or boots while I start the car and try to get warm. It's not long before I'm back at headquarters to drop off the trailer. My fingers sting as though electricity is arcing through my veins. Blood is circulating finally. I back up the trailer and unhitch it.

"Cat, you look like you weigh three hundred pounds in that suit," says Basil, walking up behind me.

"Thank heaven there's enough bulk in my suit, because that's the only part of me that's warm!"

"Say, did the carburetor ever get fixed on that machine?"

The look on my face must've said it all…

"I'll make sure the mechanic takes a look at it tomorrow."

"Good. And ask him to return my tags if they're still attached."

On my ride home, I think of nothing but Axel, at home, cooking stew and homemade biscuits for tonight. But first, a hot shower.

33

THE ICE SHANTY

Late winter transitions to spring. Snow-melt from the hillside brook flows into the valley stream. Lake ice thins with each day's sun warming it slowly, then refreezing at night thinner and thinner. The daylight grows stronger with each dawn and mellows with each turn of dusk.

Longer days and warmer temperatures are welcomed by those who love the four seasons in the North Country. The weather pendulum swings from cold to moderate temperatures with sunny days warming the earth, and our souls, with the promise of spring.

"Fishing on a frozen lake in full sunshine is almost as good as being on a beach in July," I say to Jinot as we look over the lake before starting to cross. I turn my face to catch the warm rays. With my eyes closed, the warmth is welcome. Jinot is patient, knowledgeable, and handsome, and I appreciate all three attributes, even if he is spoken for.

"Really?" he says.

"Well, almost. Think about it: You're warm, the sun is shining bright on this sparkling snow, and you can see forever."

"In a couple weeks, you'll have a *real* beach showing up. With these warming temperatures, this ice won't last long. We need to tag these ice shacks with warning signs. If they don't pull them off the ice by the end March, they may find them in the bottom of the lake."

"That would be a surprise. You come out some morning to find a hole where your shack once sat!"

"Wait till the bill arrives for pulling the shack out of the lake... That's *another* big surprise."

Jinot gives the snowmobile gas, and we head out to the first of many stops. As he comes to a halt, I hop off and staple a warning sign to the door of the ice shack. Jinot draws a picture of the lake and adds owner names and addresses at each shack's location as we come up on it. If the shack is still in place after the deadline, we'll know who to cite, and where to send their citation.

The sun climbs bright through a bluebird sky. The air is fresh and calm. *This is the kind of day when I love my job*, I think to myself.

Around the bend, we see a shack off by itself near the inlet where a brook flows. Jinot hesitates for a second and turns to me. "That would be crazy ol' Roger Waters. Damn fool sets up near that inlet every year. Makes me nervous to see it, but he won't change his ways. I don't even want to get close with the two of us on this machine, I'm afraid we'll punch through."

"I don't mind walking, when you put it like that."

"I'll get us a little closer, Cat, but we'll walk the rest of the distance."

I nod agreement and we scoot to about 200 feet from the weathered little building with a twirling tail of smoke coming from its metal stack.

"Mr. Waters, you in there?"

"'Course I'm in here! Don't you see smoke? And who's dumb enough to ask, anyway?"

"Warden Rideau, Mr. Rogers. We're here to warn fishermen to get their shanties off the ice pretty soon." Jinot and I walk around to an open door facing the brook. I admire the view he has.

Mr. Waters is looking at us through the smoke of a cigarette dangling from his mouth. He takes a practiced drag on the butt before he lifts his rough, thick hand to pull it from his lips. Squinting through the haze, he takes us both in without moving from his stool. "Do I look like I'm worried, Warden?" he says in a slow, deep voice, husky from decades of smoke-filled lungs. "I've been fishing this lake longer than you've been alive, sonny."

"Yes, Mr. Waters, I believe you," Jinot says patiently. "And I worry about you enough for the both of us…"

"Well, Warden, that's mighty nice of you to worry about me, but think I can take care of myself."

I watch him slowly lift the cigarette to his lips again, then flick the ash with a practiced finger as if he's done it a million times—which he probably has.

"So, when does the law say we need to be off the lake?"

"March thirty-first, sir...officially. But given this location, Mr. Waters, I think you'd be a lot better off if you pulled off in the next week or so. Temperatures are barely freezing at night to build ice under you."

A cynical smile spreads beneath the squinting eyes before he chuckles, "Nice of you to worry, Warden, but I'll be careful."

"Yes, sir." Jinot nods for me to hand Mr. Waters the warning before we turn to go. Mr. Waters barely turns as he opens the door to the woodstove and throws the warning into the flames. We walk back to our snowmobile through snow that is the consistency of mashed potatoes. The snow is softening quickly. "Damned ol' fool.... Let's make sure we have his address, Cat. We may need it someday."

Seven days later, my phone rings at ten at night. "I need your help at the Waters ice shack, Cat. Get ready."

"What's going on?" I say, looking at Axel and realizing that he'll have to leave to keep our secret.

"Mrs. Waters called. Her husband never made it home tonight," Jinot says. "I've called the sheriff's department and the fire department to be on standby."

We arrive on shore near where the shanty should be, but there's only open water where the shack once stood. We holler for Mr. Waters and scour the shoreline. Jinot and I borrow a nearby aluminum boat and push it out to the open water, but there's no sign of Mr. Waters, his shack, or his snowmobile.

Looking down into nothing but blackness, Jinot says with concern, "It's about fifty feet deep here. But look at the film of oil and gas floating on the surface. I'll bet the snowmobile is down there along with Walter and his shack. We'll have a recovery planned first thing in the morning."

Jinot turns the boat to shore and shares the information with the emergency crews standing by. "If Walter's not on shore, he's at the bottom of the lake. We'll meet here with divers tomorrow morning."

Riding home in the dark, Jinot is quiet.

"You tried to convince him, Jinot. Damned ol' fool wouldn't listen."

34

MUD SEASON BLUES

It's early spring, according to the calendar. Snowmobilers have put their machines away for the year. Woods workers are bringing their equipment in for annual maintenance. Mud-caked excavators, bulldozers, harvesters, skidders, and cranes parade through Eagle Lake Shores on the way to their annual checkups. The massive metal hulks, hauled on low trailers, barrel past us. Heaven help anything that stands in their way. Caterpillar yellow and John Deere green barely peek through a rough year of dirt and grime. Each scratch and dent on their metallic skins tells a story of a big boulder moved or a stately tree cut from its stand, and there are a lot of stories.

If their exteriors are any indication of what their motors and hydraulics look like, the maintenance folks will have their hands full. Other than the mechanics, the town is in an idle mode with little to do until the ice flows out, road postings are down, fishing season opens, and the tourists return.

It's bleak and raw most days with snow flurries changing to cold rain and sleet, making us wonder if the sun will ever show again. Mud coats everything. Frost heaves shake cars apart as they try to navigate the roads with the fewest bumps. The communal mood is almost as bleak. Men congregate at the diner and women bring their yarn and quilting projects to the senior center for some social time. Both groups are hungry for a change in the season and in their days.

Axel encouraged Ida and me to join Pulasky's horseshoe-throwing team for something to do. We're the only women on any of the teams we play, so we're meeting a *lot* of men. Unfortunately, most of them are nearing sixty and not Ida's type. Axel's friend Jeb is the only one our age *and single*. They call us the "Horseshoe-Throwing Hustlers." Especially when we beat 'em.

Ida and I are talking about last night's competition while she pores over her aerial photographs for her spring tree-planting projects. I'm finishing my quarterly warden report to give to the chief: How many "pinches" did I make with snowmobilers and ice fishermen? (Not enough.) How many sportsmen were stopped? (Lots.) How many miles did I travel? (Too many.) How many hours of formal training did I receive? (What's formal?)

The outside door to the office opens bringing in a fresh blast of cold air and a jovial "Hey, how ya doing?" in a loud male voice. "I need a fishing license for the year."

"Sure, Wayne. I can help you with that," says Heidi. "What's new?" she asks as she gets the paperwork ready.

"Funniest thing; the old girls at the senior center have hired themselves some dancers."

"Dancers? What kind of dancers?" Heidi says, somewhat distracted.

"Not just any dancers," Wayne says, chuckling to himself. "They're coming from the casino down south. You know, Clydesdales or something."

"Chippendales?" Heidi asks, now very focused.

Ida and I push away from our desks and head for Wayne. "Did we hear that right?" I ask. "How do you know this?"

"My mother told me about the ol' hussies at the center," Wayne explains. "They're trying to come up with fundraising ideas—bake sales, craft fairs—you know, the usual. Then ol' Bessie throws out the male dancer idea and all the old ladies got excited! Ma said there was no bringing them to their senses after that."

"So, when they coming?" Ida starts getting all wound up. "Who gets to go? It's not only for seniors, is it?"

"Heck if I know. Ma was so embarrassed, I didn't dare ask any more questions."

"Well, Bessie's my neighbor," I say. "We'll get the details from her."

A few hours later, Ida and I are knocking on Bessie's door with a bottle of wine between us. Bessie answers her door, sees the wine, and greets us like family, "Well, girls, I like visitors who bring refreshments. Come on in!" Bessie's dressed in jeans and a nice cozy sweater that's hand-knit. She has a grandmotherly grin and a warm charm about her, as always.

We follow her inside as she digs into her kitchen drawer for a corkscrew. I uncork the bottle while she reaches for three glasses.

"To what do I owe the visit, ladies?" she asks.

I pour the wine and hand Bessie and Ida each a glass. "Well, rumor has it you've got a fundraiser coming up," I say.

"We sure do!" she says as we clink our glasses together. "Best idea we've had in years! We've got Chippendale dancers coming to town, and I can use your help. We only have three weeks to sell tickets and ask for donations to help the town's senior center."

"Well, we'll do *anything* to help the senior center, as long as we're first in line to buy two tickets," Ida says.

"Good, I was hoping you two would help," Bessie replies. "The only place big enough to handle the crowd is the center's party room. It doesn't have a stage, but the school janitor says he's got some staging he can loan us. The ol' girls are making baked goods for the evening, and Vessie's Market will get a couple kegs of beer at cost. We need to sell a hundred and fifty tickets, which you girls can help with."

We brainstorm until the wine bottle is dry about how to canvass the area for ticket sales. Full of ideas and excitement, we leave with our assignments lined up.

Ticket sales don't elicit the same excitement everywhere. The local Baptist minister writes his opinion in the Eagle Lake Echo under the headline, "Loose Ladies Lack Moral Leashes." His parishioners do their best to discourage friends from buying tickets, but speculation about the fun, the excitement, and good old curiosity do more to encourage sales than to dissuade them.

Ida and I are told to sell tickets on our own time, so we do. We take tickets to horseshoe nights and Pulasky's, encouraging men to buy tickets for their brides. We have no trouble selling out. "I need one for my wife," says Clyde, a log truck driver. "And for her sister."

"That would be my wife," says Ernie, Clyde's partner. "She's so excited, they're shopping for the event."

The following week, Bessie appears on the front page with this quote: "Beat the Mud Season Blues and help Eagle Shores' Senior Center at the same time with a little fun and entertainment!" Pastor Dud is quoted as saying, "We don't need that kind of entertainment to rile up the fair ladies of Eagle Shores. We have Bible Bingo, New Testament Tale-telling, and Saturday singalongs to entertain the idle."

Ticket sales soar.

On the day of the event, the senior center is buzzing with preparations. Glitzy decorations are brought in bags by slow-moving seniors. Something resembling a disco ball is hanging from the ceiling. Anticipation of the night is buzzing through the town like a hot wire around a horse corral.

Ida says she'll meet me there, encouraging me to show up at least a half hour early. What does one wear to a male dance review being held in a senior center during mud season? I opt for a skirt, a colorful sweater, leggings, and knee-high boots. My *go-to* outfit for *going out.*

The parking lot is jammed with cars, overflowing into the church's lot. Even finding a spot on the street a block down is hard. Music blares from the center like it's a nightclub. Gaggles of women are walking toward the building all a-twitter. Julie, from the diner, is checking coats at the door for a buck each. "Hey, Cat!" she says, "isn't this a hoot?"

"Hi, Julie. Yeah, this is great!" I say. "You're gonna be able to see the show, right?"

"Of course; I get to escort the dancers from their dressing room when it's time! Ida and I helped Bessie earlier so we could get good seats!"

"Smart girls. Where's Ida now?"

"She's guarding their door so none of the patrons try to sneak a peek. I've never seen so much excitement!"

"Anything to help a good cause," I say. "I'm gonna work my way in, Julie. See you later."

Through the doors to the main room, beer glasses are full and ladies are jiving with the music. A group of middle-aged women are up on the makeshift stage dancing as if they've practiced their moves together. Young enough to be able to move, but old enough to have lost their shyness, they are entertaining the room of early onlookers.

Long tables surround the stage with chairs perched side by side and gray-haired ladies occupying each one, shoulder to shoulder. Behind these front-row seats are gals of all ages, anticipating a fun-filled night, smiling at one another, laughing and swinging with the music. A couple of men are hanging back with Cliff, the senior center's audio man. I walk back to greet them.

"Cliff, you got everything under control?" I ask. Cliff has a table in front of him with switches for power, lights, and each of the speakers in the back of the room. A tape deck marked "Chippendales" sits off to his side. It's playing now.

"So far, so good," he says. "Merle and Mort volunteered to come protect me in case these women get out of control."

"I thought I recognized you guys," I say. "You look different without your deputy uniforms on."

"You look kind of different out of uniform, as well," Merle replies, taking my extended hand, bringing it to his lips, and kissing it.

I blush.

From this vantage point, I see the disco ball is made of sequins glued to a large Styrofoam ball. Lights from below project different colors onto the ball through a rotating multicolored lens. "Hey, my parents lit their Christmas tree with something like that."

"Yep, mine too," says Cliff. "Thank heaven we still had it."

"Well, the old place looks pretty good, Cliff," I say.

"Yep, I've never seen it this lively before. Thank our friend Bessie, the organizer."

With that, the music dies down and Bessie takes the stage. "Is everyone having a good time?" she asks through the amplifiers. The crowd claps, whistles, and cheers. "Thank you for coming, and for helping us raise money for the Senior Center of Eagle Shores!" More cheers. "It takes a community to make this happen, and you know who you are, so let's not waste any more time patting ourselves on the back. Let's get to the reason we're here! Please welcome Chip and Dale!"

From the shadows of the men's room come two bulky hunks dressed like Paul Bunyan look-a-likes in red flannel shirts and tight-fitting Kevlar logger pants. The music throbs to "Let's Party," and the crowd goes crazy. The ol' girls in the front are bouncing, clapping, and twittering at one another. The rest of the crowd is whistling and swaying. Canes tap and arthritic joints crack to the music.

"They're dressed just like my husband!" one hollers.

"No, Christine, they're clean and smell good," her friend hollers back.

The opening song blends into the next. No one seems to mind that it's only one Chip, only one Dale. Chip is blond and very friendly. Dale is dark-haired and mysterious-looking. Each has a bronzed, exotic tan and no one cares where they got it. It just looks... well, *fab-u-lous.*

Each dance number gets the crowd more energized and engaged with these handsome young men. Within a couple of songs, the dancers have taken a layer off to show six-packs that don't have pop-tops and biceps that only belong to men who work out—a lot. At intermission, a couple of cute size-two locals are talking with the boys while the rest of us grab another beer.

"I think that was just a warmup!" I holler to Ida, who is in the beer line.

A middle-aged lady next to me says, "Good, because I *am* warmed up!"

The lights blink on and off, quieting the lines and encouraging everyone to find their spot again. Before you know it, Cliff plays "Crazy Train," and the crowd responds in a lather. Chip and Dale do not disappoint. They shimmy into a hard-charging dance that delights the patrons as if they were all teenagers. The ladies are giddy with excitement and energy. Bessie stands on her seat hollering, "Come to *my* train, baby!" I can't help but laugh at her and clap. I hope I have as much fun as Bessie when I'm her age.

The next set shows the genius of the tunes. It quiets into a gyrating rhythm that lures lots of dollar bills from coin purses into the tight shorts and suspenders of each dancer. The ol' girls in the front row pull ones and fives from their pockets to keep Mr. Dance in front of them. When they run out of money, the girls behind them come to the rescue with bills of their own.

By the time the last dance is over, everyone has spent their money and their energy. For that night, they've laughed and danced, forgetting their mud season blues. They bubble out of the center feeling absolutely lighthearted, unable to contain their laughter.

The event is the topic of conversation for months after. The senior center had the best fundraiser ever, and the husbands and boyfriends, who welcomed their happy, hot, and bothered women home, think it ought to be an annual show, and the dancers leave asking to be invited back anytime. The afterglow of the evening brightens the rest of mud season.

Clyde says, "Those boys should be invited back every year! My wife hasn't stopped smiling since they danced here."

For our own reasons, Ida and I agree.

35

THE BOY

Opening day of fishing season is a much-anticipated event. Ardent fishermen watch the ice slowly melt from their favorite spots in the weeks prior, local shop owners eagerly ring up the sales of new fishing poles and baits sure to lure the catch of the day. Wardens plan their routes and coverage of the region's fishing hotspots. The winter has been cold, the spring wet, and the mud season—well, muddy. Opening day promises to be warm and sunny with slight breezes comfortably cooling the air.

Conservationists, concerned with overfishing and declining fish populations, target the most popular fishing waters. Hatcheries built in the 1930s during Conservation Corps days raise thousands of fry for release in the wild. Large tank trucks lumbering from the hatcheries are easy to spot along the roads pumping small fish into waterways. Unfamiliar with their new environment, young fish are easy prey for the baited hooks of even the most inexperienced fishermen.

The southern part of the county is rich with brooks and trout streams meandering through woodlands. Farm fields are greening up in the spring's warmth. Trees are budding out and the air is fresh. The morning dew gives the land a glistening coat. The sun rises as a yellow-kissed glow, encouraging winter-weary fishing novices out to enjoy the day.

I'm at a small pond fed by a trout stream that's not too far from town. It's been stocked by the fish hatchery. Walking its edge is easy, making it a popular spot. It's Saturday, so families mingle with young people teaching their friends how to fish. Most are chatty as they cast their lines in the brook beneath the bridge. One child is rewarded with a tug on his line. In seconds, he reels in a small brook trout to be admired by his father. He smiles and lets it flop back into the stream.

I'm watching the fishermen before I even get out of my car, looking for anyone who may keep fish or who holds a pole before I start checking licenses. Some may hide their poles and deny fishing when they see me approach. Most are law-abiding and tolerate my brief interruption. Some are eager to hear of other hotspots or gossip of the biggest catch so far. They are out to enjoy the day and like talking. I watch for a while, then move on to the next spot.

I park my little Toyota a short distance from my next stop, Stoney Brook. Watching through binoculars, I take note of the anglers, their movements and catches. People of all sizes and shapes are standing up and down the brook with poles in their hands hoping for easy catches. Families with kids and grandparents are hovering over this little body of water with bobbers within feet of touching one another. Children squeal with joy as another unlucky fish is snagged from its home. I watch and smile as a family breaks out their camera to capture a beaming child holding his flapping quarry.

My attention turns to watch the anglers on the bridge, where the action is subdued. One little boy seems to be by himself. I guess him to be about six years old. His closely cropped hair is dirty-blond, and his face has the gray pallor of one not active or used to being outdoors. Although the day has turned warm, he's wearing an ill-fitting jacket and baggy pants that hang on his tiny frame. He is concentrating on his line in the water, ignoring or unaware of the jovial mood of the others. He seems out of place there by himself. I move the car near the bridge, get out, and start introducing myself and checking licenses, keeping an eye on the boy.

While meeting the families and congratulating the successful anglers along the bank, I keep watching the little guy. I'm near the bridge when he moves quickly to pull his fishing pole over the bridge rail and drops it on the road haphazardly. He pulls himself up to the rail and looks down in horror. Climbing the embankment to his side, I ask if he's all right. The boy shakes his head with a slight guttural sound and points to the stream beneath us. Lying in the shallows not far from the bank is an old reel still connected to the line on his pole. The boy is beginning to panic as he shakes his arms and paces, unable to contain himself. I tell him not to worry and lower myself down from the bridge abutment to the stream's bank. Kneeling down, I reach for the old reel and rescue it for the panic-stricken little boy.

His relief is almost immediate as I make my way up the bank to the bridge. His tear-streaked face watches me intently as I reach for his pole and attach the reel to it once again. I find out his name is Tommy and gently explain how I am adjusting his equipment for him. His sobs are quieting as he chokes out a weak "Thank you."

We are crouched on the bridge, hovering over his pole and reel as a shadow falls over our work. Startled, we both look up to see a larger-sized version of the little boy. I notice the boy's reaction when his father asks what we're doing. The boy looks up in fear, then quickly looks down again. I get to my feet and notice the man isn't much taller than me. He, too, is thin and pale. The way he holds himself is slightly off balance, and he sees that I'm sizing him up. I explain the reel falling into the water and the boy's concern.

"Damn kid," the father says with a sour tone.

The boy is fading into the background as I focus my attention on the father and make light of the situation. The father introduces himself as Ralph and goes on to share that he has multiple sclerosis, which hinders his ability to get around much. He tells me he brought the boy out, but not because he wanted to. This information registers some sympathy but not enough to justify his treatment of Tommy.

Ralph tells his son to put his stuff in the car because he's caused enough trouble. The boy quickly obeys without a sound as I mildly protest. It is such a beautiful day, it seems too early to quit. Ralph ignores me and heads toward the car. He slowly opens the door and lowers himself behind the wheel. The boy opens the back door and sits behind his dad in the backseat. As they pass me, I wave to the small boy, who frowns and slouches down in the seat. His small hand waves meekly in return. His father at the wheel looks straight ahead.

It's early afternoon and the sun is high. Fluffy white clouds billow against the cornflower-blue sky, a wonderful diversion.

I hear the happy sounds of families. "Look what I caught, Dad!"

"Wow, son, good catch!"

It's a beautiful day for most of us, but I continue to think of the sadness on Tommy's face, which dims the beauty of the afternoon.

I meet all kinds of people in my work. Some, I cite because they break the law. Some, I enjoy meeting and learning from them. Then there are people like Tommy, who I hope survives his current situation with a warm memory of a warden who helped him and seemed to care.

36

SPRING FORWARD

May is a gift to the northern climates for withstanding long cold winters. Blizzards, ice, and mud season are forgotten when the sun is high and temperatures warm to sixty degrees. Trees burst with red buds sprouting tiny leaves that shine in lemon-lime colors to greens that glow in the sunlight. Nights are still cool enough to keep the bugs at bay. "Yeah, I'm not sure if they just don't hatch," Ida says as we head out toward Fox Pond, "or if the brave ones that do come out are zapped by the cold."

"I love this time of year," I remark as we drink in the sun's rays streaming through the windshield. "You can almost see the leaves being born from each twig. Birds are returning and making new nests. Grasses are greening up and you can smell spring coming alive."

"I like the freshness of the air," Ida replies. "It's light, with smells of fresh mud and clean water. You can feel the warmth of the sun reflecting off the dark earth. It's like the earth is coming alive, roots growing and sucking in moisture so trees are reborn after a long hibernation. Heck, I feel like *I'm* coming out of hibernation, shedding long johns and wool coats."

I smile, also feeling the lightness in freedom from my heavy jackets. We roll down the windows to enjoy the morning air blowing through the cab of the truck. "Wow, it'll take a while to blow the winter sand and grit out of this truck," I say as we both roll our windows up halfway.

We turn off East Lake Road onto Fox Pond Road and take a tote road to the north. Ida has tree sampling to do in some parcels that were harvested a few years ago. "Spruce and balsam fir were harvested for lumber and paper products. I need to see what we're getting for seedlings now. While you check out Fox Pond for fishermen, I'll be roaming around down here doing my sample plots. Pick me up when you're done."

"OK. I've got my radio and citation book with me. You got everything you need?" I ask.

"Yep," Ida says as she reaches over the truck bed for her stake and line to sample and count tree regeneration.

Ida and I walk up a trail that traverses the plots she'll be sampling. It's a steep hill, but as we climb and turn around, the scenery across the valley transforms from individual trees in a forest to a sea of light-green colors against the dark evergreens of pine, spruce, and fir.

"One good thing about a harvested site, you can look across the landscape and appreciate the beauty of forests down in the valleys and on the hillsides," I say, more to myself than to Ida, who's having trouble breathing after hiking up the trail. As we near the top of the harvested site, Ida turns left to start her first sample. I still have some distance to trek to the pond.

"I'll find you in an hour or so," I say heading up the hill again.

The ridge is almost all stone and boulders with very little soil to support vegetation, let alone trees. Lichen and moss cover the boulders in patches, giving them a mottled greenish-gray splashed haphazardly over the surface. Where soil has landed in rock crevices, a fern or stunted tree is eking out a living. Rounding the top of the ridge, I see a large depression that has collected wind-blown sediment over the decades, providing enough soil to grow a grove of black spruce. In the center of the depression is a beautiful little pond that allows fly-fishing only.

Some generous soul has carried a canoe up and left it there for fishermen to use rather than waste their time fishing from the shoreline. From the edge of the pond, I spot two people in the canoe. The lone canoe on the clear pond, with early-sprouting trees in the background is picture-ready. Both the man and the woman have apparently fly-fished before. They are pretty good at casting their lines out and enticing a bite.

I watch for about twenty minutes and decide to call them in and check their licenses. They haven't caught anything, but who knows how long I'd have to wait before they tire of their activity. I whistle to get their attention, then holler, "Game Warden! Paddle in so I can check your licenses." Then I wave them in and hold up my badge just in case they hadn't heard me.

I have startled their tranquility, and they are slow to put their fly rods down in the canoe as they talk. They finally pull a paddle from the bottom of the boat and stroke toward me at the speed of a sloth.

"Good morning," I say. "Sorry to take you away from your fishing, but I'll need to see fishing licenses, please, and then I'll let you get back to your day."

The young lady is quick to pull her license out and hand it to me. "Jessica" smiles and starts chattering on about the beautiful day. They hadn't expected to find anyone up on the pond, let alone a warden. She has brought her friend up to show him the remote mountain pond, as he is only visiting for a short while.

"Oh, where are you visiting from, sir?" I ask.

"I'm in the Peace Corps stationed in West Africa, Warden," the young man says.

"How long you been there, out of curiosity?"

"Five years."

"Wow, that's quite a commitment.... Do you have a license, sir?"

He pauses before admitting, "No, Warden, I don't."

"It's my fault, Warden," Jessica says. "I talked him into it. He's only here for a couple days and didn't want to buy a license for one day. I told him I knew a place, way out of the way..."

"Yes, it could be your fault, Jessica. He's got to have a license just like everyone else," I say.

"Do you have any identification on you, perhaps a Peace Corp badge or paper?"

"Yes, ma'am, I do." He pulls his driver's license and Peace Corp identification from his wallet and hands them to me.

"Bob Dunfy, I'm pleased to see you're telling me the truth. I'm impressed that you've volunteered, and I'd feel like a schmuck if I issued you a citation today. It's important you enjoy your time off. So here's what I'm gonna do. I'm taking your information down. Stop by the department headquarters in Eagle Shores today and buy your fishing license there. When I check their records tomorrow morning, I throw away your contact information and not issue a citation."

"Warden, I appreciate it. That'll work just fine," Bob says as he smiles at me, then at Jessica.

"That's great, Warden. Thanks," Jessica says.

"Go ahead and enjoy the rest of your day..."

After stuffing the information in my pocket, I turn and walk away from the pond. The trail is cool under the black spruce, but after I leave its canopy, the sun is especially warm. I take a diagonal walk in the direction of where I think I'll find Ida doing her plots. I walk around a huge boulder to find a mother black bear and two cubs breaking open a rotten log. Momma spots me about the same time I spot her. I yelp, turn, and hustle away. I didn't look back but can hear her growl and rustle in the other direction. I don't want to run, but a momma bear is not to be disturbed with her cubs around.

"Holy crap!" I hear Ida scream, hustling and clumping all through the brush to my right. I'm hoping the bears are heading in a different direction than Ida is. I try to intercept my friend, but she's moving faster than I ever thought she could.

"Ida! It's me… You're OK!" I find her heaving, breathless and bent over like she's about to have the big one. I notice that she's missing her shirt and has only her bra holding those double D's in check and a light sunburn on her shoulders. "What're you doing?"

"I'm soaking in the sun while doing these damn plots," she replies. "No one's around, so why not? Then that damn bear nearly scares me to death!" She leans back to suck in another lungful of air.

I'm laughing out loud. "Did you get a good look at the momma and her cubs?"

"Hell no! All I saw was a big ball of black fur, heard a growl, and I was off in another direction."

Grinning, I say, "Well she appeared to be as scared of you as you were of her!"

Ida collects herself and gets her heart rate down as I finish laughing.

We only have three more plots to do, and we make as much noise as possible to warn the bears that we're around.

By noon, Ida and I both have our shirts off as we lie on the hood of her truck sunning ourselves in our bras. Lunch is eaten and lying back to enjoy the rays seems like a treat.

"You got to hand it to those people who siesta every day," Ida says. "They know how to lie back and smell the roses. How come we don't do this in America?"

"Good question…"

"This is gonna help me digest my food better, too. We gotta elect people who believe in siestas, Cat."

I couldn't argue her point. It feels delightful.

37

SPRING FISHING

"Have you ever fished in a stream, Cat?" Jinot asks as he drives us from headquarters.

"Not that I remember."

"Where *have* you fished?"

"On a dock with a cane pole and a bobber. And I remember one time fishing from a small boat on a lake. My dad threw the lure hard, showing me how it was done. It snagged in his earlobe and had to be cut out."

"You're joking, right?"

"Nope, I'm not," I say. "And boy, was he embarrassed! He walked right into his buddy's house with a Rapala dangling like an earring. I didn't have enough strength to cut the hook. I was laughing, he was mad. We never fished from a boat again."

"Well, today you're gonna learn about brook trout and fishing in a stream," Jinot says, letting me know the agenda. "I'm taking you to one of my favorite spots. It takes a while to get there. The farther you are from the road, the better the fishing. So we're taking the ATV in to save on walking."

"Sounds good. You seem more relaxed today, Jinot. What's going on?"

"Rain's coming in, the fish will be biting, and there's not going to be the usual public out with the threat of rain, so it'll be quiet. We can fish without getting calls. You did bring rain gear, didn't you?"

"Yes, I have my rain gear," I say, a little annoyed. "You don't have to keep checking up on me."

"Well, did you bring your waders, then?"

I have to pause before admitting, "Crap..."

Jinot smiles. "I brought an extra pair, just in case we could fish. They're my mom's old pair and will probably fit you all right. I doubt Lizette will ever wear 'em." He looks at me and shrugs.

Interesting.

We drop the ATV from the bed of the truck and gather our gear. I climb up behind Jinot, holding onto him with one hand and the ultra-light rods with the other. We're following a narrow trail next to the stream that's shadowed by tall pine and underbrush. As I look ahead, the trail seems to disappear behind a curtain of branches. The path leads us to an open area where the woods seem reluctant to enter a meadow. After about thirty minutes of riding deeper into the woodland trail, Jinot turns the vehicle perpendicular to the stream to cross it. He takes it slowly and urges it onto the opposite bank when the front wheels slip and we get hung up. Jinot tries to back up, but the mud provides no traction for the supposedly all-terrain vehicle.

"Shit. Cat, dismount and let's look at this." Jinot climbs off the machine and stands back. The stream's current is strong, and the back of the machine is forced downstream, wedging it into the two banks.

"We gotta get some wood and rocks to put under the wheels."

"OK, I'll look for wood," I say as I drop my backpack and the rods nearby.

Finding wood is not a problem. Finding the *right* wood takes time. I gather the heaviest pieces I can carry back to the stream. "How're you coming on the rocks?" I see he's made good progress under the front tires. The clouds are now thick and dark, making the morning seem like dusk. "We can use these, can't we?"

"Yeah, that'll build up the base," Jinot says. The clouds open up to drop a steady sheet of pouring rain. The dark day now has a wash of silver from the cool spring showers. We fight the stream's current to place the wood on its bed and have it stay in place. We work for another hour gathering, moving, and wedging more wood under the machine. The stream rises up to my waist and the current is building strength, swirling around us. I'm now chilled through my layers of rain gear, waders, and clothes.

"The ATV is acting as a dam," I say to Jinot. He looks like he's been swimming and just came up for air. "Look, the current is fighting everything we're trying to do. I don't think the two of us will budge this today." His clothes and hair are soaked and plastered to his skin. Water is running off his face like a shampoo commercial, but he's not smiling as he stands back and assesses the situation.

"Damn it… You're probably right. And I hate to admit it."

"We can walk back, let the rain stop, and bring back reinforcements with equipment," I say as we stare at the vehicle while the current wedges it ever more solidly into the high banks. Neither of us wants to leave the ATV where it is. More importantly, we don't want the chief to know we left it where it is.

"DAMN IT!" Jinot bellows with fists clenched. Then he climbs out of the stream. "All right, let's go."

I climb out and bend to pick up the fishing rods. Water spills from the top of my waders. Jinot is watching and looks quizzically at me. "What?" I ask.

"Cat, you're gonna have to take those waders off and drain 'em before we start back."

"Why?"

"You're supposed to have the rain jacket *over* the waders so rain doesn't flow into your boots like a funnel."

I look down at my raincoat nicely tucked into the bib of the chest waders. "No kidding…" As I move, I realize I slosh. I unbuckle the waders and peel them to the ground. Every inch of exposure lets more water flow from the boots. It would be difficult enough to walk back with the waders on, but filled with water adds at least another twenty-five pounds. Now every inch of my clothing is stuck to my skin like a spring roll in a rice wrapper.

The walk back to the truck is long. We drive back to headquarters listening to the beat of windshield wipers with the backdrop of the fan blowing warm air around us. We're still wet, but now a warmer wet that doesn't suck the heat from our skin.

The chief is cool. "Well, you know what you have to do tomorrow," he says, looking at our dripping carcasses standing before him. "You realize you've left public property unattended in the field?"

"Yes, sir," we say in unison.

"But you're gonna retrieve it tomorrow, before we have to fill out a dozen reports about damaged or stolen equipment?"

"Yes, sir," we repeat.

"Then get out of here," he says, shaking his head.

After leaving Basil to stew, I have to laugh looking at Jinot. We are a sorry pair, but a pair and partners. It feels good to have Jinot as my partner in a blunder. Momentarily. We agree to meet the next morning, after the rain stops, and return with reinforcements.

I'm disappointed that we didn't fish the river, but boy, the hot shower felt good. With a few sticks of wood in the woodstove and dry clothes on, I am comfortable as the rain continues into the afternoon.

38

THE FISHERMAN

Each new spring day brings changes to the landscape with colors transforming from dull browns to glorious greens. The tree canopies emerge shyly, but at the base of the trees, early spring flowers are already full and vibrant against last year's brown leaves on the forest floor. Gentle warmth and sunlight allow woodland flowers to thrive before they are too shaded and the summer heat becomes too much for continued growth.

This time of year refreshes me. The slow rebirth of spring, seeing the earth awaken from a long hibernation, makes me marvel at the wonders of nature as I travel. And this is my work life. How lucky am I? Fresh air, free of exhaust fumes, rushes into the car as I roll down the windows.

I drink it all in as I travel the Tomorrow River Road. I'm also looking for fishermen. But I can enjoy the ride just the same while trying to focus on my task.

Usually, vehicles parked near bridges signal the presence of fishermen. Waders on and poles in hand, folks walk upstream against the current, trying to catch big fish—in this case, trout. I haven't seen much during the week, but this morning, a small old pickup is parked in a field on the river side of the road, and it could belong to an angler who has walked to a more remote stretch of water. I pull in, park behind the truck, and start snooping about. I watch the field and adjacent woodland for any sign of the owner. No one. I walk past the bed of the truck and marvel at the number of empty beer cans it holds. Hundreds of silver cans fill the bed of the truck. *Wow, that's some collection.*

No one is in sight as I walk up to the truck cab. It's messy, but no beer cans are inside the truck. *Good; you don't want them inside.* There's no indication that this person is mushroom hunting, fishing, or out for a nice walk. I return to my car, back it onto the road so as not to block a law-abiding landowner and call in the truck's license plate. I want to check on the owner of the vehicle, still suspecting that he, and maybe a partner, are fishing. It's important for Dispatch to record the vehicle's make and license in case there's a problem later—like I go missing...or something. I tell Dispatch I'm on foot and head for the woodland.

The sun is warm and bright, but the air is a cool sixty degrees. The woodland floor is soft and moist. I have my backpack of gear. I see recent footprints and follow them for a while. White and pale-pink trillium are blooming. I have to take a picture of the delicate blossoms. The river is *shushing* over rocks and around bends, providing a pleasant background noise. Marsh marigolds grow on the riverbank. I crouch down on one knee to get a close-up of these glossy yellow flowers. The contrast between the sun-colored blossoms and the lush dark-green foliage is picture-perfect. Up close, I adjust my focus on the plant...and spot movement out of the corner of my eye.

I pull away from the camera just in time to face a thick gray snake who's lapping his forked tongue at me. Its head is bobbing and the hood, extended cobra-like, looks ready to strike. My heart skips a beat as I suck air involuntarily. I'm off my knee as quickly as I can retreat. The snake bobs its head and spits its tongue at me, but I'm now at least six feet away and calm enough to get a good look at it. Normal snakes give me the creeps, let alone one that looks like a cobra. This reptile is only about eighteen inches long, but it's at least an inch and a half thick. It's short and thick for a snake. I had no idea we had snakes like this in the North Woods.

I don't get a picture of the marigolds, but I take one of the snake from a safe distance to identify it later. Then I head for the river. I see the current is swift from snowmelt and April rains. The rushing water seems a blessing after last fall's drought. I see there have been a few people coming to the banks from this direction. They've trampled the edge to get into the water or to throw a lure in from shore. I choose to walk alongside, heading upstream in the direction fishermen would fish.

Fishermen in their waders will walk into the current to toss their lure ahead of them. The sediment they disturb from the river bottom floats away from them. Upstream, fish are unsuspecting. (Jinot had to teach me that.) I am cautious about making too much noise as I walk around bushes and downed trees. I don't want to spook someone into dropping their evidence. The moss and ground vegetation are soft green. I'm admiring the beauty of tender shoots bursting out of hibernation when another movement catches my eye just as I'm about to step over a log.

Below my approaching boot are the ears and eyes of a tiny fawn looking up at me from its curled-up position beside a downed tree. It is perfectly still, big black eyes unblinking, as my boot hovers within a foot of coming down on it. Its fur is wet, just hours old. Its body is thin, without developed muscle. Momma is probably watching me and wondering what I'll do to her precious baby. I am so taken with this tiny spotted creature that I have to spend a minute admiring its size and ability to lie by itself without flinching. I look around for its mother but see nothing. She's there somewhere. I know.

Detouring around the fawn, I continue following the river's edge as it weaves through this wooded nursery. Not too much farther on, I hear humming coming from the river. I walk toward the low voice that's singing a slow, sweet song, an unfamiliar tune. I can see the source as he casts his ultralight fishing rod, sending its silver line and lure into the current.

From this spot, I lean against a tree and get comfortable to watch and assess the situation. The man is in his late forties, with dark hair curling under his cap and over his shirt collar. His dark beard is trimmed and salt-and-pepper in color. He looks vaguely familiar, and it's not because he's five ten and one hundred and ninety pounds. It's his ruddy complexion and small but bulbous nose.

Professor Clements was my college chemistry teacher, a jolly individual who made chemistry fun and interesting. Registration for his classes always filled fast. You felt lucky to get into his lectures and *very* lucky to get into the small three-hour labs where you put your knowledge into action. My actions were more trying for him than for me, I'm afraid.

I'm smiling, thinking back on our conversations, when I hear splashing at the river. It looks like he's caught a small brook trout. He carefully takes the hook from its mouth and releases it, delicately, back into the river. This is a good time for me to approach him.

"Professor Clements, before you proceed..." I start. "Let me check your fishing license." He squints in my direction as I make my way toward him and into the open.

He seems annoyed at first, and then he recognizes me. "Catherine?"

"Yes, sir, and local game warden," I reply with a smile.

"Well, well," he says, making his way to the river's edge where I'm standing. "You didn't pursue chemistry, I take it."

Smiling at him, I say, "No, sir," and shake his hand. "I don't think chemistry was my strongest subject."

His eyes are dancing with amusement. "You never could follow lab instructions the way they were written. Had to do it your way."

"You remember," I say, embarrassed.

"How could I forget your almost blowing up my chemistry lab," he says, only somewhat joking. "I'll bet you still don't follow recipes when you cook."

"Who actually follows recipes?" I respond. "I had to find a career using other skills."

"I see that. Now, about that license," he says while digging into his chest waders to pull out his wallet and license. "Here it is."

"Thank you." I look at his license and notice that his first name is Ted. "Do you get up this way much?"

"I have a cabin not too far from here," he says. "This is my solitude. I can drive to the university from here if I want to."

"That's nice," I say. "Is that your truck in the field?"

"Probably," he says. "It's the small black Ford."

"Yes, that would be it. Let's check your creel, and then I can let you get back to your solitude."

The professor turns his wet wicker basket around so he can show me what's inside. He opens the lid to display, glistening and wet, two unopened silver beer cans. "Not the kind of catch you're interested in, I'm afraid."

"Better than too many fish or ones too small, Professor," I respond. "Enjoy your solitude, sir. It's good to see you."

"Likewise, Catherine. Be careful."

"Yes, sir, and you as well," I say, remembering how many early-morning classes he missed, the redness and puffiness of his face when he lectured.

I turn and begin the walk back to my car, avoiding the areas of fawns and snakes, and moving on to other spring fishermen.

39

THE WOODCHUCK

Wardens work when people play, which is a lot—especially weekends and holidays. But during the summer, our night hours aren't normally scheduled, compared to working deer shiners in the fall season. It seems less frenetic, anyway. I'm home this morning when Bessie knocks on my door.

"Cat, you home?" she hollers.

It's a reasonable five after seven, looking at my bedroom clock. "Yep, Bessie, I'll be right there." I've been up since six, had four cups of coffee, and decided I needed to run, so I'm in my running gear. Unlocking the door and seeing Bessie on the other side, I ask, "What's up?"

"Cat, I need your help. I got a woodchuck burrowing under the barn and coming out to eat my vegetables. I don't mind sharing, but he's already eaten all my herbs. Have you got a live trap we can use to get him before I lose all my plants?" Bessie's look is pleading with me to provide any help I can.

"You don't want to shoot it?" I say without thinking.

She looks shocked. "Oh, no, dear. I just want it out of my backyard."

"I'm sure I've seen a live trap at the office, Bessie," I say giving her my full attention. "Let me bring it back here today, and we'll see if we can catch the critter and take him off the premises."

"Thank you so much, Cat," she says. "I tried hanging smelly soap and human hair near the garden, but nothing is scaring it away. He doesn't take a hint that I'm frustrated and desperate," she says with her fists clenched. "If this doesn't work, we'll move on to more drastic measures."

"I gotta get my run in anyway, so I'll jog to the office and make sure the trap's there," I say.

"Thanks, Cat," she says with relief.

The tree canopy provides a cool shaded place to run along the lakeshore. Sunshine reflects off the water, brightening my day. I see a couple of older men motoring out with fishing poles sticking up from their aluminum boat like antennas. As a warden, I'm finding I'm always suspicious and thinking the worst of people. *Have they got a license? Have they got their PFDs?* I was never a negative thinker before this job.

Swallows flit from tree branches out over the water, doing aerobatics while chasing bugs for their breakfasts. They swoop over the lake, catching the sun's rays on their iridescent wings.

Nine months ago, a jog to the office had me huffing. Now I'm just warmed up as I reach for my key to the office door. Heidi won't show up till around eight a.m. I walk back to the garage and look over the shelves to find the trap. It takes me a few minutes to locate it. I'll sign it out when I return with my car.

I'm locking the door when Gus drives in. "Is that the summer warden uniform?" he asks.

"Yeah, you like it?" I reply. "Wait till Punk finds out *he's* gotta wear it." Gus laughs. "Hey, I was just here to find a trap I could use for a couple days. Bessie has a woodchuck. I'm gonna come back and get it if that's OK."

"Sure, no problem," Gus responds. "Bessie has her problems with critters, doesn't she?"

"Yeah, but at least this one doesn't take four people and a truck to haul away," I say. "See you later, Gus." With a wave, I jog back to my place and take a swim to cool off before I start my duties.

Once I shower and get dressed, I head for the office to get the trap, sign it out, and leave. Bessie sees me near her barn and brings out carrots and lettuce to use as bait. "I've got my own version of bait, Bessie," I say, holding out a jar of peanut butter. "Carrots and lettuce may work, but peanut butter is enticing and foolproof."

"Well, whatever works," she says as she watches me put a tablespoon of the chunky style on the trigger of the trap. She throws in a couple of carrot pieces for good measure. I place the trap opening by the hole next to her barn. The door is open, the trap is set and ready for its victim.

"We'll see what we get overnight," I say. "Meanwhile, I gotta get to work."

"Well, let's hope we get our little scofflaw the first night," she says as we part company for the rest of the day.

The next morning, I hear banging on the door before my eyes are open. "Cat, Cat, come look at what we've caught!" Bessie chirps. I lie in my bed for a minute, thinking about how comfortable I am.

"Does it have to be now?" I say, hoping for at least another half hour of leisure and laziness. But Bessie knows my addiction.

"I have your coffee right here with me," she sweet-talks.

"Those are the right words," I say in anticipation. I pull on my shorts, grab a T-shirt and head for my door. I open the latch and reach for the coffee with one eye open. "What do we have?" I ask.

"Oh, you'll have to come and look," she says with a gleam in her eye.

I don't bother with shoes. The green grass and mud are soft underfoot. As we near the barn, I can see the trap. I try to focus on what's inside the wired walls. It's moving around, but the tall weeds mask it enough that I can't identify it from here. Each step gives me another clue. Bessie is unusually quiet.

Oh, I see black. Drawing closer, oh, I see a tail. Oh, crap…! I see white. "Bessie, you said it was a woodchuck!" I exclaim as I stop to look at her. "That's no woodchuck!"

A huge, indignant skunk dares us to approach.

"Oops," she says with a sheepish grin, knowing that she can stand back and watch how I'm going to handle this.

We step a little closer to get a better view of our prisoner. "He's huge," I say. "I didn't know they got that big."

"Me neither," she confesses.

I drink my caffeine and try to think how I'll approach the problem. *Do I call for reinforcements, like Gus? Or can I handle this by myself?*

"Gus," I say as he picks up his phone, "have you got time to help me with a skunk today?"

"Sorry, Cat," he says, "I'm working up north with another biologist."

"I understand," I say, deflated. "Any idea how to approach it in a trap?"

"Carefully," he says and laughs.

I cringe with an audible groan.

"No, seriously, Cat," he continues, "carefully. Put a blanket over the cage and let it sit for a bit, maybe fifteen minutes," he says. "That's to make it relax and not see you coming. Do I need to say, don't put it in your car?"

"OK, that makes sense," I say. "Anything else?"

"Yeah, don't wear anything you wanna wear later, and have plenty of soap sitting outside your house," he says with a chuckle.

"Thanks for the advice," I say before hanging up.

"Well, Bessie, I gotta make some preparations." After I tell her the plan, she volunteers an old blanket and a pair of jeans she's outgrown. I gladly accept the donations and walk back to my cabin to change. "And I gotta have more coffee," I say over my shoulder. "I'll meet you back here in fifteen minutes."

I find an old T-shirt and a bandana. But I'm not sure if I'll wear the bandana over my hair or my nose. The jeans are falling off my hips, so I cinch them with a piece of rope and make my way out to do battle with Mr. Skunk.

Bessie sees me, grins, and comments, "You look like a hick cousin I have." She hands me the coffee and I drink it to rebuild my courage.

"As long as I don't get fumigated during this exercise," I say. I get in my car and back it in toward the barn. As I get closer, I slow down so I don't piss off the prisoner. I get out and gently close my car door. "No sudden noise or movement, Bessie. We'll be cautious and slow."

I pick up the blanket and unfold it to its full twin size. Holding it in front of me as a shield, I creep up to the cage. Mr. Skunk is watching me, turns…and I retreat. "I don't like to see that end pointing at me," I say to Bessie, who's watching from a safe distance.

"I don't blame you," she laughs. "Do you think he's just aiming, without the intention of shooting?" she asks.

"Only the shooter knows, I'm afraid. But I'm going in." I walk slowly toward the cage with the blanket held outstretched in front of me. I hum a low, slow lullaby, hoping to calm the skunk like some baby.

"What're ya singing to it for?" Bessie asks.

"It's supposed to be relaxing."

"Well, Cat, no offense, but that ain't a relaxing tune."

"It may be relaxing to a skunk," I say softly as I concentrate on my target.

The skunk turns and exposes his back end to me again. I stop but don't retreat. *Does a skunk exhaust itself if it sprays? Is it reluctant to spray? Hmm…*

I begin talking low and soothingly, proceeding at the pace of an unwilling bride coming down the aisle. I am tempted to throw the blanket over the cage and run away. But I don't. Patience, forward movement, s-l-o-w-n-e-s-s, is key. No quick movements. We don't want to startle our guest. I stand next to the cage with the blanket covering one side and gently drape the rest of it to cover the top and other sides. Once it's covered, I escape to the safety of Bessie's side as if I've just lit a firecracker.

"Yahoo, Cat, nice job," she says as she gives me a high-five. "Now what?"

"We wait," I say. "You got a watch on? According to Gus, we need to wait fifteen minutes. Time for another cuppa Joe."

When Bessie gives me the sign that time's up, I make sure the rope's extending from my trunk and ready to tether the cage. The cage is quiet.

I reach for the wire handle and try to carefully pick it up. The cage is wide and the contents are heavy. I can pick up one end, but not the other. I don't want to drop it. "Bessie? I need your help," I say. "I gotta have you pick up one end of the cage."

"Really?" she says. "And this was going so smoothly before now."

"Yeah, come up here and give me a slow smooth hand up."

She helps me lift the cloak-covered cage up onto my car and I tether it to the trunk. "Well, that was easy," she says.

"I need you to come with me," I say as I look at the question mark on her face. "I can't lift it off the car without your help."

She reluctantly shrugs and moves toward the passenger seat. I have to clean off my gear and last night's coffee cups before making room for her legs as she gets in the car. "Where are we going?" she asks.

I really hadn't given it much thought, but I'm thinking I need to find a place that's relatively close by, but on property that we don't care about.

"I have a great idea," I say. "There's a farm that will love a skunk—Pitts' Farm," I say, smiling at the thought. I'm still mad that Grandpa Pitts snookered me into believing his poaching lies. Bessie agrees his farm is a perfect home for an "additional" skunk.

The Pitts farm is within view beyond a woodland. We lift the skunk carefully off the car and uncloak the trap's door. Before we unveil it completely, I pull open the trap door. So far, no spray. We unveil the trap so Mr. Skunk can study the new surroundings. We have the exit pointed toward a woodland ditch and water.

"I thought the skunk would want to leave the trap quickly," I say. It doesn't. I walk up to the back of the trap and gently say, "Shoo." It turns its backside to me and I step backward in a hurry. "Maybe it thinks we're gonna feed it again."

I look at Bessie, who shrugs her shoulders. "What are we gonna do, Cat? I'm hosting the bridge group in an hour at the senior center."

"Let's try scaring it out of the cage," I respond.

We get a couple of sticks and bang them together, hitting the road and walking closer to our friend, but still keeping our distance. Its backside is turned to us, but it moves slowly from the cage and onto the road. We want a little bit more clearance before we pick up the trap. A few minutes later, the skunk has ambled into the woods, the trap is re-tethered to my trunk, and I'm back in the driver's seat.

"We did well," Bessie says. "And I've got quite a story to tell the girls at the senior center. Do you mind if I give them your name in case they have critter trouble?" she asks innocently.

"No problem," I say as I turn around on the road and head back toward home. "Give 'em my name," I smile at her, "as long as you'll trap and ride shotgun with me."

40

JULY 4TH

The morning shows promise of bright sunshine warming the day to temperatures that call for bathing suits and boating. There is not a cloud in the sky. Eagle Lake reflects the sunlight as if the water itself is sparkling. Easy laughter and joyful sounds emanate from the screened porches of simple cabins lining the shores. Summer is now in full swing during this Fourth of July weekend.

Independence Day celebrations last several relaxing days, with beer and barbeque being staples and in great supply. Fresh pine scent flows from all directions along with friendly chatter and bantering between family members and friends. For them, it's no work and all play. For us, it's not only a long workday but a long weekend of holiday patrolling.

The lakes will be teeming with activity. Summer cottages have been opened and show signs of life with boats docked outside, freshly painted chairs on the decks, and brightly colored towels hanging neatly over the rails. It'll be near eighty degrees today with a slight breeze making it a perfect holiday.

Smells of bacon frying and wood smoke from morning campfires welcome neighbors and visitors alike. "Hmm, that bacon smells good," Jinot says as we assess the lake. "I can almost taste it from here."

"Yeah, puts my morning cereal to shame," I reply. "I think my *stomach* can even smell it cooking."

We are standing on the shoreline of Eagle Lake looking through our binoculars at the various boats on the water. Jinot gets permission to use this lot to launch our boat so we aren't spotted at the public landing. Nothing ruins our opportunity for catching lawbreakers more than being spotted before we can spot them.

Orange and yellow kayaks are peacefully paddling along the shoreline. The paddles are almost synchronized in their strokes, allowing the boats to glide across the shallows. They also have life jackets on. Our attention turns to motor boats farther out on the water.

"Take notes as I read off the descriptions, Cat."

"OK," I reply, "I'm ready."

"Blue-and-silver Lund, registration number WI 5505. Man and woman are both fishing at ten oh five," Jinot says as he looks at his watch. With his binoculars, he continues to scan the water. "Blue-and-white Princecraft, registration number IL 10-8395. Three adult males, all fishing. And it's ten oh seven. We'll put the boat in and check the guys first."

Our boat is standard-issue aluminum in unbecoming duck-drab-brown. We put the boat in with ease, Jinot at the helm. "Keep an eye on the couple in the Lund while we check the men. My guess is when they see us, they'll head for shore."

Jinot turns our boat sideways into the Princecraft so we can talk side-to-side. "Morning, gentlemen," I say. "How's the fishing?"

"Just started after breakfast," a guy with a dark-brown mullet says. "Hardly have our lines wet, Warden."

"OK, let's check for life jackets and fishing licenses."

All three reach for their licenses, which is a good sign. Of the three, the one with the biggest gut and thick back hair has his shirt off, of course. "Here's my license, Warden," he says with a wink as he reaches across and hands it to me.

"Charlie Osgood from Chicago, Illinois. Thank you for your license," I say and return it to him with a smile. *You make friends when you can.* I see he is sitting on his life preserver, which is OK in the eyes of the law.

Jinot is checking the second and third licenses when I look over to the couple in the Lund. They've started to head for shore. With a nod in that direction, Jinot hands the licenses back to Charlie's two buddies. "Thanks for your time, gentlemen. Have a great day."

Putting the boat in gear, we speed over to catch the Lund before it hits shore. We meet up with them just as a middle-aged woman is hoisting herself out of the boat. The man is still in the stern. "Hello, Warden," he says with a nervous smile. Both Jinot and I turn to him.

"Good day, sir. Yes, we are game wardens. Can we check your licenses, please?"

Midlife Momma keeps walking up the shore, ignoring the conversation. "Ma'am, that means you, too," I say, as I step out of the boat and pull it onto the sand. "Ma'am?"

Momma turns around indignantly and says, "But I wasn't fishing."

"Excuse me, ma'am, but we know differently. We were watching you from shore at ten oh five. Please produce a license if you have one."

"I've got my license here," says her partner from behind.

Jinot reaches for the man's license and looks at the name and address. Darrell Dumsfield lives in Arcadia. "Thank you, Darrell. Is your fishing friend related to you?"

"Yes, Warden, this is my wife, Marilyn. Marilyn's a good woman. She just came out to keep me company, see."

Jinot steps out of the boat and walks toward Marilyn as I hang onto the bow to stabilize it.

"Marilyn, you don't have a fishing license, do you?" Jinot asks politely.

Marilyn looks at Jinot as if he has a match and she is TNT. But she does not respond.

"Marilyn, by evading me and failing to surrender your fishing license, not only will you get a citation for fishing without a license, but I'll also cite you for obstruction. If you don't have a license, please provide some other form of identification."

The fuse has run down and Marilyn explodes, "I can't believe you both are harassing me on the birthday of our nation! I come out here for peace and quiet with my husband to honor our independence and you are treading on my rights!"

Jinot backs up out of arm's reach and lets her spew…

"This is a family weekend! I finally get a day off, and we just want a little peace and quiet. You all just come bouncing out to bother us law-abiding citizens. You ought to be ashamed of yourselves! *And*, I want you to know, I am a *taxpayer*!" she bellows, energy level still rising.

As she talks, I witness the intensity well up from her core and continue to erupt. I'm glad I can witness it from fifty feet away.

"Are you done?" Jinot asks politely.

"No, I'm not done! You are both harassing me, for no good reason!"

"Marilyn, we can do it the easy way or hard way. Either show us some identification, or we'll have to take you in to the courthouse and process you there."

I look at Darrell, who is showing no sign of getting involved. Head down and shaking it from side to side, Darrell holds his tongue.

"Darrell," I say, looking for some reasonable response, "do you have Marilyn's identification somewhere handy? Would you mind getting it for us, and we'll leave you both alone?"

"Marilyn! They've had enough. If you don't want to give them your driver's license, I will."

Marilyn shoots Darrell a look that would kill a lesser soul. She huffs and begrudgingly trudges to the boat to pick through her purse. In a moment, Jinot has her license and writes a citation to Marilyn. Once the citation is written, Jinot gives her a copy and wishes her a good rest of the weekend.

Cursing under her breath, Marilyn keeps ranting while Darrell sits in the back of his boat, ready to leave Marilyn on shore alone.

Jinot walks to our boat, signals to get in with a head wave, and we back out onto the pond and away to safety. Out of earshot, I say, "Holy crap… I'm glad I'm not Darrell!"

"Poor fella… We ought to just shoot him and put him out of his misery," Jinot says.

It takes us a few minutes to plan our next moves and shake off the tension Marilyn caused. It's not long before numerous boats are touring the lake pulling skiers or blow-up toys in circles as screams of joy and terror echo across the waves. We sidle up to a blue bowrider as one skier is coming out of the water and another is taking the skis. Four girls, preteens, all legs and braces, giggle and smile as they spot Jinot. He talks to the driver and commends him on the safety of his boat and riders. Each girl is wearing a life jacket of pinks or purples. "Yep, gotta take care of my little angels," he says. "They certainly don't think about it themselves."

More giggling from the bow. "Oh, dad," comes a high-pitched little voice. "Can we go now?"

The driver looks to the heavens for patience. "Yes, darlin', in a moment." He smiles weakly and says, "I'm on duty, Warden. Need anything else?"

"No, we're good," Jinot replies. "Have fun, girls, and be safe."

We wave and hear them twittering away while the next water skier drops into the lake.

"You've got some young admirers," I say, turning toward the open water. Jinot just smiles.

It takes us a few minutes to catch up to two Jet Skis careening across the open water. Both boys are in their late teens, obviously enjoying their time on the water. These young men are comfortable talking with us, pointing in the direction of their camp and telling us about their Jet Skis. They've been coming to the lake for years and know it well. They tell us of boats on the other side of Rock Island that we may want to watch. "Partying and littering," says the tanner of the two young men. "Makes it bad for the rest of us, ya know."

"Yep, we know," I chime in. "That's why we're here."

"We appreciate the tip, fellas," Jinot says. "Be safe and enjoy yourselves."

Jinot turns the boat to Rock Island. "I think I know where we can safely wait and observe," he says above the motor. "Rock Island has a tip of land that juts out to the south side. We'll pull the boat in on this side and walk over the island to get a view of the party on its north side."

"Rock Island seems to live up to its name," I say as I climb out of the boat and try to wedge the boat's bow between two boulders buried in the bed of the lake. I tie the rope around a tree that stretches out over the water. Its roots are exposed where soil has eroded away with the lapping of waves over the years. More rocks are exposed.

"Hand me my binoculars and thermos, if you don't mind," I say as Jinot makes his way to the bow. I hold the boat steady as he climbs out onto the rocks and jumps over to land. We cross over the point and get a view of several boats anchored in Rock Island cove. Young people, probably in their early twenties, are laughing above the music we hear. Three bikini-clad girls are in a 17 foot red-and-white Bayliner.

"Cute," Jinot says matter-of-factly.

Three young men are in a similar-size Wellcraft. They're leaning over to the girls' boat. Music is blaring from the Wellcraft. The young men have nothing but bathing suits on, showing tanned and athletic bodies.

"This looks like a good viewing point," I say as I find a comfortable spot, sit, and open my thermos. "We might have to stay here a while."

"Yeah, too bad the view's so poor," Jinot says with a grin. "This *will* be a good spot. See the drinks being passed back and forth between boats? How much you want to bet the trash doesn't go with them? They've probably borrowed the boat from Daddy and can't take a load of empties home."

The sun beats down on the boats. They all jump into the water to cool off. The girls gently scream as they hit the cool water. The boys laugh in low baritone voices. All swim a bit and eventually climb back into their respective boats. Fresh bottles and cans are opened. We can see the girls are drinking Coke from cans. In the Wellcraft, Cutie #1 is in black swim trunks drinking Budweiser from a bottle, Cutie #2 is in white trunks with blue print and is drinking Coke from a can, and Cutie #3 is macho in camo-colored trunks drinking another bottle of Bud. Within the hour, Macho Man starts leaning over the boat and filling empty cans and bottles with lake water. Unfortunately, he lets them sink to the bottom. The time, 12:35, is noted. Macho Man then takes a pee off the port side, also noted.

"Well, I think we've seen enough," Jinot says. We rise, dust ourselves off, and head for our boat.

"It's too bad they couldn't surprise us," I say, shoving the boat back as I pull myself into its bow. Jinot starts the motor. I wind the line and lay it in the bow as we make our way around Rock Island Point and toward the two boats. I watch the boaters and drinkers watch us coming toward them as little Ms. Pink Bikini rudely points at us. Jinot angles us alongside the Wellcraft and the men.

"Good afternoon, gentlemen…and ladies," I say as I stand and hold us in place. "We're game wardens and need to make sure you have the necessary life jackets on board." I spot a six-pack of Bud with two unopened bottles in the bottom of the boat, tucked underneath the console as three life jackets are raised to be counted. "How's everyone doing on this fine Fourth of July?" I ask. Jinot is looking over the side of our boat toward the shallow bottom.

"Good," says almost everyone. Most eyes are looking down, but a few are anxious to see where we take the conversation.

"Ladies, please hold up your PFDs for me," I say. Ms. Pink Bikini reluctantly stands and grabs the same jacket that her girlfriend grabs, argues and releases it. I watch her as she lifts several boat seats and finally pulls out a faded old jacket that looks like it might fit Babe Ruth—late in life.

"May I see that jacket, ma'am?" I ask holding my hand out to receive it. She complies, with hesitation. The jacket is old, but the fabric is still holding together. I return it to her. "Thank you, but I do recommend you get a life jacket that might fit you. This one looks like it could float away without you, not offering much protection."

"OK," she says without giving any further thought to what I've said.

No one's committing to a conversation.

Jinot has a fishing net taken from our boat's side straps and is scraping the lakebed.

"Guess what he's doing?" I ask the group. "Sir in the camo trunks, what's your name?"

"Nick."

"Nick, did your parents give you a last name?" I ask. "And while we're at it, do you have an ID on you?"

"Yeah," Macho Man says to both questions as he reaches in his trunks and hauls out a driver's license. "Vitrolli. Nicholas Vitrolli."

"Thank you, Mr. Vitrolli. I'll look at the license, and perhaps you can tell me what my partner is going after." I watch Nick shake his head in denial. "Mr. Vitrolli, I see you are twenty-one years old. That's good."

I watch Jinot pick up three bottles with the net and place them in the bottom of our boat. The labels on the bottles are Budweiser. "Nick, do you know where these bottles came from?" Nick is still shaking his head back and forth without making eye contact. Jinot reaches in to retrieve another bottle and several cans.

"Don't know," he said meekly. The other five bystanders have found the farthest point on the boats to escape to and are urgently monitoring their feet.

"Well, you see, Nick, my partner and I have been watching you for the last forty-five minutes. But guess what we saw in the last fifteen minutes? Yep, you guessed it. We watched you and marked down each time you filled a bottle or can with water and sank it to the bottom. Gentleman in the black trunks, what's your name?"

"Tony. Tony Marsden," says Mr. Black Trunks.

"Mr. Marsden, please show me an ID." I watch Tony open a boat compartment to retrieve his license. "Thank you," I say, looking at his ID. "You are twenty-one as well. Good. Who is the operator of this Wellcraft?"

"I am," says Mr. White Trunks. "It's my dad's boat."

"Please identify yourself and show me the boat registration." After looking at the registration for one Barry Pease, I compliment Young Pease on not drinking alcohol while operating the boat, saving himself from a field sobriety test.

Jinot has collected all the bottles and cans he can see and is writing a citation. Our attention is now on Mr. Vitrolli.

"Nick, as you can now see, we've witnessed and have evidence of littering, for which you are being charged," I say. "This citation is being issued, and you can either come to court or pay your fine. Do you have any questions, Nick?"

"No, ma'am," Nick says, still inspecting his toes.

After handing Nick the citation, Jinot and I start the motor and head away from their boats. Both boats come alive with comments and shrieks, including, "Oh, my God, I can't believe they saw that! How much is that gonna cost?"

Jinot and I head toward the shore. Word has spread that the wardens are here and offenders will find other methods of entertainment and be on their best behavior. We head for other bodies of water to patrol into the early evening. By the time I'm home, I can feel the sun- and windburn on my face and arms. I pull a beer from the fridge, take a swig, and head for the shower. Tomorrow might be a shorter day, as most vacationers will be off the lakes and headed for home by late afternoon.

I can only hope...

41

AUGUST

Cars whiz past my car, feet from my door. I turn on my little Toyota's flashers, which is parked off on the breakdown shoulder of this four-lane highway. A tractor-trailer passes, rocking me in place. Ten yards into the ditch, I see the dead doe that was reportedly hit a few nights ago. She is big and bloated from the August heat. There's no way I'll be able to lift her onto my trunk and haul her to the animal graveyard.

I retrieve my trusty shovel from the car and place my handheld radio near the doe. The ground is sunbaked and hard. I jump on the shovel head to break the soil's crust. I adjust the shovel and jump a dozen times to dig a hole big enough to bury the animal. It's hot and I'm digging. It's humid and I smell the sourness of rotting flesh.

As I work my way deeper and wider, I hear Dispatch call a county deputy: "We have a report of some hippie burying a body along Highway Twenty-Five, southbound." It takes me a minute to climb out of my still-too-shallow grave and reply.

"Three twenty-two to Dispatch."

"Go ahead, Three twenty-two."

"You have a report of a hippie on Highway Twenty-Five, southbound?"

"Ten-four."

"Is the location around mile-marker sixty-four?"

"Location is south of exit sixty-eight."

"Ten-four, Dispatch. I'm your hippie with a shovel."

"Ten-four, Three twenty-two. Copy that, Deputy?"

"Ten-four, Dispatch," he responds and rolls to a stop behind my car.

He turns his rotating blues on for effect and through the loudspeaker barks, "Hands up, hippie!"

I throw down the shovel and raise my hands above my head. Who knows what people think as they drive by.

Merle gets out of his cruiser with his hands on his holster as he walks between his car and mine with a big grin on his face. "Hey, Rookie! What kind of body you burying, anyway?"

"Glad you're here," I reply. "I could use some muscle." Merle reaches out to shake my hand. I wipe mine on my pants before taking his.

It's been a while since I've seen Merle. We catch up on local news and what he's been up to.

"You've had quite a year," Merle says. "I've been keeping track of your stops. You've made progress since I first met you—what? almost a year now. Didn't know if you'd make it, kiddo."

I laugh. "That goes for both of us."

"Wardening is a tough line of business. At least as a deputy, I'm usually on a schedule," he says. "You've had bear complaints in the middle of the night and seem to work every night in the fall."

"That's why I like it, Merle, something new all the time."

"Well, I'm proud of you. Now, give me that shovel and let's get this doe buried."

"I won't turn down an offer like that." We finish the highway burial and wave goodbye.

The next day, the chief tells me Vern Ledoux has called for me to join him at the university. He wants me to talk to the new law enforcement class about the work we've done over the past year. "It sounds like fun," I respond.

"We've got a Hunter Safety Course coming up next week, as well," Basil continues. "I'm gonna have you teach a couple sections and sit in on the rest. You may have to teach it yourself someday."

Young, fresh faces greet us at the Hunter Safety class. Many are dressed in some form of camo-colored clothing. Sitting in the back are a couple of dads wanting to share the class with their youngsters, and off to one side is a man I recognize from deer season. "Mr. Ditts, good to see you!"

He smiles, showing that he still needs braces and a good dental hygienist. "Good to see you, too, Warden. Thought I'd finally get my class in before this season starts."

I teach the section on wildlife habitat, the importance of food, water, and cover. The chief teaches hunting laws, heavy on the *Thou shalt not... or else!* A local gun shop owner has volunteered to teach firearm safety. The kids are attentive, some dads fall asleep, and Mr. Ditts sits in the back, listening carefully. I'm impressed when he actively engages in the conversations with good questions.

One freckle-faced boy with a lisp asks Basil, "But what if my mom has my orange clothes in the wash and I want to go hunting?"

Basil's answer: "Either wash your clothes and wait for them to dry or put them on dirty. You gotta have orange on."

The Hunter Safety Course is fun and ends with the kids thinking we're good guys. If you follow the rules, game wardens can be cool people. This class is a great way to start a career as a hunter, and it's invaluable that the students have friendly first experiences with wardens. Know the rules, play by the rules, and enjoy the sport. I enjoy the openness of the students, who are generally hungry to learn about wildlife and how hunting can help keep the number of animals in check.

But I focus on the gun shop owner, Mal, after meeting him in the class. I join him at his shop a few days later. He shares the benefits of a used .38-caliber handgun he has for sale. With a six-inch barrel, it will be more accurate than a four- or two-inch snub-nose of the same caliber. If I buy it, he'll throw in two boxes of shells and an hour's lesson. I spend more time shooting in the next few weeks than during my whole first year working. Vernell Ledoux, the training officer, is holding a qualifying session at the end of the month and I want to be ready. It means I can better protect myself and others who might be in harm's way. I've been lucky in the first year by meeting up with reasonable people. But I don't want to go into hunting season unarmed again.

Mal is a good teacher, offering pointers and showing me how to clean my weapon after each shoot. He's patient, knowledgeable, and actually wants me to be successful in the qualification. "You are gonna do fine," he tells me. "Don't get nervous. You've got this."

I see sincerity in his face, which adds to my confidence.

There are about twenty individuals at this afternoon's qualification. Some are state troopers. Serious, cocky, and off by themselves. They are trim, with close-shaved haircuts—former military, I'm guessing. Some are county deputies—less chiseled, gregarious and joking. Then there are a few park rangers and wardens that came from different parts of the state. Most are requalifying, but a couple of us haven't been here before.

Vern is focused on the seriousness of firearm safety. He reviews the rules of the gun range with absolute detail. There will be no messing around, or dismissal from the range is certain with a follow-up to the superiors. The tension rises, and I can feel the heat of anxiety creeping in. I look at the group of men around me, jaws tight, arms crossed at the chest, and sunglasses hiding their eyes. Testosterone is pumping, no doubt. I'm outnumbered nineteen to one.

Vern calls the first five names to the line. These officers are veterans, practiced and confident. A timekeeper is on Vern's right side. Another man with binoculars is on the other. Vern reviews the shooting drills and expectations by reading from his sheet. Any mistakes will not be *his* fault.

"Step to the line!" The participants methodically walk up to the line, shaking their arms to relax them. Black holsters carry not only their firearms, but several magazines of ammunition.

"Load and make ready!" Each officer draws his weapon from its holster, loads it with ammunition, and reholsters it. They stand with their hands out to their sides, direct and confident.

"Shooters ready?" Vern asks.

All say, "Yes."

"Stand by..." and, finally...

"Fire!"

Milliseconds later, we hear a barrage of gunshots sounding like a war zone. Their legs are bent; arms are at shoulder height and outstretched toward the silhouette targets in front of each shooter. Then the shooting peters out quickly.

"Cease fire!" Vern commands. "Holster your weapons!" Most have their guns reholstered already.

The shooters then prepare to shoot with their non-dominant hands; from a kneeling position; from around barricades; and from the prone position. At the end of the test, they walk to their targets, check their scores, and make sure they are requalified. They are released and walk back, more relaxed, toward those of us waiting our turn. Each of them has qualified, and they are now acting like it's no big deal.

I'm impressed. They make it look so easy.

I'm in the last group to qualify, affording plenty of time to worry about my shooting and build the tension. My nerves are electric; I need to move around. The shooters waiting with me exchange nervous looks and grim faces. Their jobs may be on the line. If I don't shoot well, I'll have another opportunity someday. I've worked without a gun all this time, but my goal is to prove to everyone, including myself, that I can do this.

The only good thing about being last is that a number of the best shooters have left and won't be watching me. I'm called up to the line with the others who are here for the first time. It's been a long afternoon. Vern takes a drink from his water bottle and watches us approach.

There is no familiarity for me in his eyes. Strictly professional. I walk past him as he studies his clipboard. I remain focused on the range, the commands, and what I've trained to do. I shake my hands out as I've seen the experienced shooters do and jump in place a few times to work the kinks out of my feet.

"Rookie! You here to shoot or jump rope?" Vern says. I hear the others snicker at me.

"Ready to shoot, sir," I say, heat rising to my face.

"Shooters, step up to the line!"

The rest of the commands for the first drill are burned into my brain, and my body reacts like a robot. I'm focused. I take deep breaths to relax. I'm comfortable with my grip and squeeze each shot off as Mal taught me. My shots are placed properly on target through the different challenges. As I reholster my revolver from the final test, I know I've done well.

Vern follows me down range to my target. "You did well, Rookie. Congratulations." I look at Vern and feel his warmth return. We look at the grouping of my shots. "Not bad, Cat. Looks like you're finally qualified." He smiles broadly and shakes my hand, then folds me into a warm embrace.

Not everyone is as successful, with several asking if I could give lessons. I can't stop smiling now that it's over and I've passed the test. Swept up in the moment, I jump up and down with my arms raised like Rocky Balboa, excited and pleased.

We clean up the range before Vern offers to buy the first round at Pulasky's for the three of us wardens who have qualified. We meet at the bar, relieved and ready to celebrate on Vern's dime. We toast each other for a job well done just as Basil and Jinot walk through the door. "Hey, did you hear? I passed!" I say, raising my glass.

"Of course we heard! That's why we're here!" Basil answers, coming through the small crowd to give me a hug.

"Now you can cover my ass when I need it," Jinot says, smiling, as I get a hug from him as well.

Vern interrupts the laughter and says to Basil, "Don't you have something to say?"

We look to Basil as he turns to me and says, "Congratulations on your first qualification, Cat. But we're here to also celebrate your first anniversary as a warden." The group chimes in with various hoots, accolades, claps, and comments.

"A year ago tomorrow, this young lady comes walking in my door not knowing a thing about wardening," he carries on. "Falling on her face, getting up, and dusting herself off...she's become a part of our team. Congratulations, Cat."

With pats on the back, smiles from the group, I can't help but feel happy and a sense of belonging. It's been a full year of hunting, snowmobiling, spring fishing, and summer boating. It's been a year of firsts, working in all forms of weather, meeting all kinds of people...and learning to live and work within an old establishment, trying to navigate a way to make my contribution.

"And you had your doubts, Chief," I say.

"Yes, I did, Cat. But you proved me wrong. And as we all know, that's a first for me..."

Laughter bursts from the group. After all, it has been a good year for *first times*.

At that, I see Ida burst through the door to give me her big ol' bear hug. "You did it, girlfriend!"

I look beyond her shoulder and see Jeb, our horseshoe partner. I pull away and look closely at her, questioning their arrival together. All she does is shrug and smile a big smile. I punch her in the arm. "Good for you, Ida! I'm happy for you."

"I hope we're all happy now," I hear a familiar voice behind me. The crowd quiets. Turning, I see Axel coming across the floor. He grins and I can't help but smile back.

"Yes, we're all happy now," I say as he sweeps me up in a warm embrace and doesn't hesitate to kiss me in front of Basil, Jinot, Vern, and the others. What do you know—*another first...*

ACKNOWLEDGMENTS

I've had these stories in my mind for decades. Bringing them forward took the unending patience and support of writing friends and editors: Denney Morton, Dave Norman, John Leggett, Joan Kotz, Nancy Bills, Rose Ducey, Jane A. McNeish, Larry Dyhrberg, Fernando De Leon, Lindy Hough, Francine Knight, Tana Leonhart, Sidney Lincoln, Barbara Kautz, and Ruth Story. They taught me how to write. Early readings from Chris DeSantis encouraged me to continue. And to Genie Dailey, who put the finishing touches to this story.

Thank you all.

Kim Camery serves as conservation warden

A native of Harlan is serving as one of the first women in the state of Wisconsin to serve as a conservation warden. Kim Camery, 20, of Sun Prairie, Wis., is the daughter of former Harlanites, Mr and Mrs Miles Camery of Albuquerque, N. M. Her father is with the U. S. Fish and Wildlife Service.

Miss Camery is the granddaughter of Mrs Elsie Hansen and Mrs Joe Camery, both of Harlan.

She is studying for her natural resources degree from the University of Wisconsin-Stevens Point. As an intern in environmental law enforcement, she has served the past six months as a Portage County warden.

In 1976, Kim Camery Millick was hired as one of the first women ever to be a game warden. Working nights, holidays, and weekends as a conservation warden in the outdoors of central Wisconsin, she was introduced to elements of the harshest cold, the darkest nights, and the sweetest spring days. Every contact with the public could mean conflict. Armed and sometimes drunk citizens added more than an element of danger, especially when one was not armed oneself. Events in the author's career as a warden and later as a forester in the great North Woods of Maine come to life in this fictionalized novel, the rookie's first year.